THE RELUCTANT PARTING

THE RELUCTANT PARTING

How the New Testament's Jewish Writers Created a Christian Book

JULIE GALAMBUSH

HarperSanFrancisco
A Division of HarperCollinsPublishers

FIRST HARPERCOLLINS PAPERBACK EDITION PUBLISHED IN 2006

Library of Congress Cataloging-in-Publication Data is available.

ISBN 13: 978–0–06–087201–4

ISBN 10: 0–06–087201–2

06 07 08 09 10 RRD(H) 10 9 8 7 6 5 4 3 2 1

For Rob and Aaron

CONTENTS

FOREWORD

When I was a child, my favorite part of the comics page was the cartoon puzzle featuring a drawing of an ordinary scene—say, a family on a picnic. The challenge consisted in the directive to, say, "Find the hidden man." Turning the page this way and that, one examined the picnic scene—Mom unpacking the wicker basket, Dick and Jane playing ball, Dad at the cookout grill, Spot nipping at the ball, clouds in the sky, the spreading leaves of a tree. Suddenly, snap! All at once, a tree branch appeared as an eyebrow, the thicket of clouds as a head of hair, Dad with his spatula had become the line of a delicate nose. With an unwilled shift in focus, the picnic scene was gone, replaced in its entirety by the face of a friendly-looking man.

Julie Galambush accomplishes a shift in perspective like that with this book. She takes the most familiar literature in the Christian world—therefore, perhaps, in Western civilization—and by turning it this way and that, enables a wholly new picture to emerge from the well-known lines. The hidden man who snaps into unprecedented focus through the readings of "New Testament" texts offered here is Jesus—but Jesus as rarely seen by either Christians or Jews, Jesus as a Jew, a figure who preached nothing but the God of Israel until (or even after) the day he died.

The book's central concern is less with Jesus, however, than with the communities of his first followers, and there, too, Galambush accomplishes a breathtaking shift in focus, providing a far more complex—and far richer—view of early Christian impulses than is ordinarily available. In addition to a hidden man, there is a hidden communal reality—not a "church" yet, perhaps no longer a "synagogue," but not a single reality in any case. Part church, part synagogue, part Jewish sect, part Gentile association—all unfolding in a period of massive cultural and religious mutation. The multiplicity of responses to the evangelion of Jesus by first-century Jews and Gentiles, ranging from radical apocalyptic fervor to enraged rejection, and everything in between, is itself a forgotten wonder of the Christian story, much as the varieties of Jewish self-understanding in the era, dramatized by twentieth-century discoveries at Qumran, are also only now being understood.

Some of Jesus' early followers were fully and permanently Jewish—conservative Palestinian Jews, but also worldly, hellenized Jews of the diaspora. Such Jews recognized Jesus as messiah and understood him within the context of expressly Jewish expectation. Some of these Jewish Christians were radical opponents of the Roman empire at a time of increasing military pressure against resisting Jews, and some were resigned to the Roman sway, if not friendly to it. Some early followers were Gentiles, including religiously inclined pagans (so-called God-fearers) who brought to the Jesus sect a prior interest in—even reverence for—Judaism. There were regional differences and class differences, all leading to differences in emphasis and interpretation as the Jesus tradition began to jell around certain stories, sayings, memories, philosophical categories, and midrashic inventions. A sense of such lively distinctions among the varieties of responses to Jesus was mainly lost across the decades and centuries, as texts were canonized and as orthodoxy was defined and enforced.

One of this book's accomplishments is the way in which Julie Galambush, in a marvel of close and original reading, identifies and explicates these various paradoxical, if not contradictory, themes within the New Testament texts themselves. She reads with a concern to enter wherever possible into the point of view of those who wrote these texts and first read them. That alone marks her project off from the more traditional method of reading texts in the light of later "orthodox" interpretations.

The gospels and epistles, together with Acts and Revelation, represent multiple visions of the significance of Jesus, some of which are in stark tension, even conflict, with one another. The great shift in focus occurs—and here I write as a Christian—when the reader is enabled to perceive that tension as part of the internal dynamic of the early Christian reality itself—tension, that is, within the broad circle of those who accepted the messiahship of Jesus, instead of tension, as it is usually recalled, between those who followed Jesus and those who rejected him. This is the crucial insight.

The modern crime of racial anti-Semitism was prepared for by the Christian anti-Judaism that spanned two millennia, beginning with the "church's" early understanding of itself as the bipolar opposite of "Judaism." It is commonly noted now, even outside scholarly circles, that the conflict between Jesus and "the Jews" that marks so much of the New Testament narrative reflects a conflict not of Jesus' time but of the subsequent period, a generation or more later, when those who followed Jesus were in conflict with those who rejected him. The argument is fierce (and the language is polemical) because, just as the gospels, derived from oral traditions, began to be written down, the entire world of Judaism was thrown into crisis by the Roman destruction of the temple in 70 C.E. What was it to be a Jew without the temple? Some Jews answered by saying that Jesus was the New Temple, and others by saying that to be a Jew was to be centered on the imagined Temple of Oral Torah. In this more sophisticated reading, the gospels and other New Testament texts are understood as embodying one side of an argument between Christ-affirming Jews (and their Gentile communicants) and Christ-rejecting Jews.

But in Galambush's reading, we see through to a deeper and richer level of complexity. What if the argument reflected in the "Jesus-versus-the-Jews" dynamic of the texts is not only—or even mainly—between Christ-affirming Jews and Christ-rejecting Jews, but between one group of Christ-affirming Jews and another? What if the much maligned group "the Jews," who are made explicitly responsible for the blood of Jesus in Matthew, or who are literally demonized in John, includes Jews who honor Jesus as messiah but disagree over what, precisely, his messiahship means? To take the most obvious example of such tension, the dispute over whether Gentile converts to the Jesus movement had to be circumcised—had, that is, to become Jews in order to become Christians—has been relegated in Christian memory to the status of a fairly minor argument that was more or less efficiently resolved by Saint Paul (who died before the gospels were written), but what if that argument was definitive and long-standing, wrenching Christ-following communities across decades, and territory. What if "the Jews" who wanted to attack Paul in Jerusalem, early in the New Testament period, were Christian Jews who objected to his apparent denigrations of Torah? What if "the Jews" who cast Johannine Christians out of the synagogue, late in the New Testament period, were Christ-following Jews who took offense at John's application of Logos imagery to Jesus—or at John's apparent readiness to call this Jesus-Logos "God"? What if the New Testament, in sum, is less concerned with judging—or condemning—that large majority of Jews who had nothing to do with Jesus or his followers, than with refuting those within the nascent "church" who wanted only to continue regarding it as the "synagogue"? What we would have here, in such a case, is less the church against the synagogue than the church against itself.

Why does this matter? As long as the New Testament is read as an essential Christian condemnation of Jews and Judaism for the rejection of Christ as, first, the Jewish messiah and, then, the Word of God who was "with" God and who "was" God, Jews and Judaism will be at risk. The misremembering of Christian origins has been lethal, and if it continues, it will be lethal again. The momentous achievements of post-Holocaust Jewish-Christian dialogue, in which contempt and suspicion were replaced by civility and respect, are not enough. The source of Christian contempt for Jews must be uprooted. A subtle but transforming shift in focus must occur in the way Christians perceive their foundational texts. That can in no way be accomplished by a rewriting of the texts, an expunging of the foul anti-Jewish polemic, nor can it be accomplished by pretending the anti-Jewish slanders are not there.

Julie Galambush's great achievement with this book is to show that just such a shift in focus can be accomplished by a deeper reading of the texts themselves. A proper grasp of the multifaceted, progressively more complex texts reveals a multifaceted, progressively more complex text-producing community that defies reduction to the good-versus-evil polarity that is the ground of Christian anti-Judaism. With erudition and eloquence, Galambush gives us a moving example of a new biblical literacy that has momentous relevance for the future. Drawing on the enormous body of scholarship that has transformed New Testament studies over the last generation, and distilling it with wit and feeling, she provides the kind of breakthrough in understanding that will be possible to Christians only when they learn to read the profoundly "anti-Jewish" texts as if they themselves are Jewish. But Galambush also shows that, to do that, a reader must enter more fully into the complexities of the communities that produced the texts in the first place.

Overwhelmingly, those communities were Jewish. In that simple but nearly forgotten fact—forgotten by Jews and Christians alike—lies the key. The argument over what it is to be the "true Israel" is a profoundly Jewish argument—one that goes on within Judaism to this day. And as the Jewish scholar Jonathan Levinson points out, thinking of the biblical tradition in which siblings are always attempting to supplant one another, in nothing more than in its supersessionism does the Christian habit of mind reveal its Jewishness. In forgetting the Jewish character of its origins—a forgetting that began to happen when Gentiles more and more dominated the Jesus sects after the Roman destruction of the center of Jewish Christianity in Jerusalem—the church even forgot the permanently Jewish character of its Lord. If it had not done so, the histories of Jews and Christians would be very different.

Jesus remains the hidden man of Christian faith. He is the hidden man of Jewish memory, too. The polemical use to which he has been put precisely against the Jewish people made it impossible for Jews to see in him anything but an antagonist—the antagonist that appears in the traditional reading of the New Testament. But Julie Galambush suggests that this hidden Jesus, coming into new and unprecedented focus through the texts themselves (not through the "historical" push behind the texts), can have a fresh set of meanings to Christians and Jews alike. Christians can recover Jesus as their Jewish Lord who preached nothing but the God of Israel. Jews, while affirming the shema with permanent independence from Jesus and those who follow him, can nonetheless recognize in him an embodiment—as this Christian sees it, at least—of the longing for God's reign that remains central to Jewish hope.

—*James Carroll*

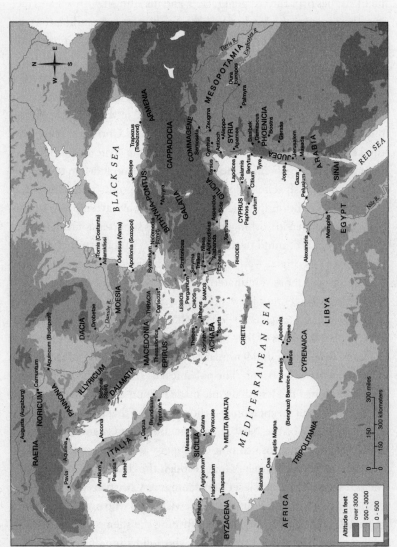

The Eastern Roman Empire in the First Century C.E.

INTRODUCTION

> [The New Testament] is a Jewish book. . . . A Jewish spirit and none other lives in it; . . . Jewish faith and Jewish hope, Jewish suffering and Jewish distress, Jewish knowledge and Jewish expectations. Judaism may not pass it by, nor mistake it, nor wish to give up all claims here. Here, too, Judaism should comprehend and take note of what is its own.
>
> - Leo Baeck, *Judaism and Christianity*

> Throughout the centuries leading up to our own it was customary, in fact commendable, for Jews to shun the New Testament.
>
> - Samuel Sandmel, *A Jewish Understanding of the New Testament*

IF, AS BAECK CLAIMS, the New Testament can justly be considered a Jewish book, it must be ranked as one of the strangest Jewish books ever written. This is a "Jewish book" that holds the Jews responsible for murdering the beloved son of God. It vilifies the rabbis as hypocrites and liars, and has served as the pretext for centuries of abuse and persecution of the Jewish people. It is a book most Jews neither own nor read. What can it possibly mean to call the Christian scripture a Jewish book? *The Reluctant Parting* seeks, in part, to answer that question: to take the New Testament authors' Jewish identities seriously, and so uncover the meaning of the New Testament as, at least in its beginnings, a Jewish book. The result is a surprising, and surprisingly painful, story—the story of pious, first-century Jews who sought to renew their Jewish identity, and instead created a new religion.

The Reluctant Parting began as an experiment at Temple Bet Aviv in Columbia, Maryland. Bet Aviv had hired me to teach a class on Genesis

1–3; over the course of our studies, however, the class repeatedly brought me questions about how *Christians* read the Bible. The questions came as no surprise; my students knew that I had been raised a Christian, had been ordained, and had served as an American Baptist minister before my conversion to Judaism. A Jewish professor of Hebrew Bible with prior experience as a Christian minister, I had become accustomed to answering Christian questions about Jews and Jewish questions about Christians. In fact, my ability to serve as a bridge between the two communities had been an unexpected side benefit of my conversion. As my course at Bet Aviv drew to a close, some participants asked whether I would be willing to teach another class the following semester. I suggested that, given their interest in how Christians use the Bible, we might consider reading some New Testament texts together. Only in retrospect do I realize my presumption in making such an offer—inviting synagogue members to study New Testament in *shul* with a former Baptist minister. The response was not an immediate yes. After a few awkward moments, the members concluded that they would need to consult the education committee before deciding whether it would be appropriate for the temple to sponsor study of the New Testament.

Ultimately, Bet Aviv decided they could trust me to conduct a genuinely *Jewish* study of Christian texts. I remain deeply grateful for their decision. Over the course of the next few semesters we read through Romans, Luke-Acts, and Matthew. What we found there surprised us all: a deep sympathy for the early Christians' religious quest; humor, especially over hot-button issues facing the apostle Paul ("So, would he have allowed the non-Jewish spouse onto the *bema** or not?"); and an unexpected opportunity to think through contemporary questions about what it means to be Jewish. Exploring the New Testament as, in Baeck's phrase, "a Jewish book," we found ourselves exploring the meaning—and the boundaries—of our own identity as Jews. By the end of our work together my class had convinced me to undertake what they cheerfully dubbed, *The New Testament for Jewish Dummies*, my as-

---

*The platform from which the Torah scroll is read.

signment, to answer the question, "How did nice Jewish boys come to write the Christians' book?" Five years later, I present them with my response.

The Reluctant Parting is written with Jewish readers especially in mind. Its goal is to represent the New Testament authors as credible Jews, and so provide a sense of "what happened" to make Christianity so different from anything modern Jews recognize as Jewish. The need to understand the New Testament's Jewish authors *as Jews*, however, stretches far beyond the Jewish community. Rereading Christian texts in their Jewish context can profoundly affect the way Christians understand their own faith and heritage as well. To rethink the Jewish origins of the New Testament is, to a certain extent, to rethink the meaning of both traditions.

For Jews, the New Testament is uncharted territory. This means that, apart from understanding the Jewish intentions of its authors, understanding the New Testament itself has value as a matter of cultural literacy. Western art and literature are shot through with Christian allusions; contemporary politicians espouse "family values" based on a specific kind of Christian belief. School and work calendars continue to be organized around holidays Jews don't celebrate. Knowing the basics of Christianity is, simply put, useful for living a Jewish life.

For American Jews, understanding Christianity has become increasingly important, as a means not only of knowing our culture, but of knowing and relating to our own families. With intermarriage rates hovering around the fifty percent mark, most American Jews either do include or soon will include Christians as family members. And the rising intermarriage rate brings more than trees to the living room; it brings Christians into the synagogue and Jews into church. Intermarriage will continue to raise difficult questions about the boundary between Judaism and Christianity.

My own son, for example, as the Jewish child of a converted mother, has both Christian and Jewish grandparents and cousins. Every year, as we help his maternal grandparents celebrate Christmas, we are invited to sing, "O come, O come, Emmanuel, and ransom captive Israel, that mourns in lowly exile here." It is my responsibility to help make sense of such experiences for our son. Do Grandma and Grandpa think *we* are mourning in lowly exile? Why do they think Israelis are captives? Every year we rehearse the origin of Christian images of Jews and Christian claims to be "Israel": "Well, Jesus was a Jewish teacher, and his first followers were all Jews . . ." By explaining Christianity competently in Jewish terms I give my son knowledge that I hope will help him survive as a minority. I want him to be comfortable with Christianity, but I also want him to have a firm knowledge of the differences between Judaism and Christianity. A clear understanding of Christianity's origins is an essential tool as we seek to come to terms with intermarried American Judaism.

The period in which the New Testament was written was a period of remarkable diversity within the Jewish community. The neo-Platonist writings of Philo, the apocalyptic instructions of the Dead Sea Scrolls, the teachings of Rabbi Hillel, and the historical narratives of Josephus provide some sense of the wide range of Jewish culture and religious practice in the first century. The followers of Jesus were simply one more sect in an era of Jewish sects. As such, their writings provide a fascinating look at the ongoing debate that was early Judaism. From a Jewish perspective, the story of Christian origins is not a tale of heavenly triumph; in Jewish terms, the Jesus movement was a failure: more Gentiles than Jews signed on, and eventually the group was denied any place within the larger Jewish community. In this regard the New Testament writings comprise a sort of case study, a sampler of the thoughts and arguments of Jewish sectarians struggling to redefine their Jewish identity. The New Testament authors fought, ultimately in vain, to maintain their legitimacy as Jews. Read as a Jewish book, the New Testament becomes the story of a reluctant parting—the closing arguments, the last hopes—before Christians ceased, sometimes angrily, sometimes sadly, to be a part of the Jewish people.

For Jews, the New Testament can help explain not only what modern Christians believe, but also the way in which Judaism and Christianity are simultaneously joined and separated at the root. For Christians, a Jewish reading of the New Testament offers very different rewards. First and most obviously, if Christians fail to appreciate not only the Jewish context in which the New Testament was written, but also the Jewish *goals* of its authors, they are missing much of what those authors tried to say. Understanding the New Testament authors' identity as Jews—Jews committed to remaining Jews—dramatically changes what one sees in the New Testament. Most Christians, for example, find it difficult to understand why so many early (Jewish) Christians were horrified at the idea of admitting non-Jews who had not undergone full conversion—that is, not conversion to "Christianity," but to *Judaism*. Why would one need to convert to Judaism in order to be a Christian? Such a perspective is almost inconceivable to modern Christians. Similarly, Paul's discussion of dietary laws in Romans 14 brilliantly captures the dynamics of mistrust between more- and less-observant Jews. The issues involved are obvious (even contemporary) to Jewish readers, but obscure to Christians. Reading the New Testament through Jewish eyes allows Christians to grasp meanings that would otherwise pass them by. Ironically, a Jewish reading of the New Testament provides Christians with an "insider" reading of their own texts.

In addition to giving Christians insight into overlooked—and sometimes crucial—aspects of the New Testament's original message, a Jewish reading can provide a much-needed awareness of the anti-Jewish aspects of Christian scripture. In arguing for their belief in Jesus as messiah, the New Testament authors frequently engaged in polemic against those who disagreed with them. Because the sect of Jesus' followers was a Jewish sect, these arguments are necessarily directed against other Jews. Frequently, they are even directed against other Jewish members of the Jesus sect. Over the centuries the original context of such debates was lost; consequently, Christians have inherited a legacy of texts that often appear simply to condemn Jews as Jews. Understanding such polemic as part of an inter-Jewish, or even an inter-Christian argument can provide a welcome corrective to centuries of Christian disparagement of the Jews.

A Jewish reading of the New Testament can also allow both Christians and Jews to identify more subtly negative images of Jews that have unconsciously become the daily bread of perfectly well-meaning

Christians. Take, for example, Luke's parable of the tax collector and the Pharisee. Both enter the temple to pray, but the tax collector seeks God's forgiveness while the Pharisee indulges in self-congratulation. As a child, I quickly learned that I was supposed to act like the tax collector and not like the Pharisee. For me, however, this lesson included an unconscious assumption that the tax collector, who modeled the correct relationship toward God, was a *Christian*; only the smug old Pharisee was a Jew. Sometimes reading with Jewish eyes means *opening* one's eyes to layers of anti-Judaism within the Christian tradition. As such, a Jewish reading opens the door to a new stage of Jewish and Christian understanding.

The Reluctant Parting seeks to reconstruct the ways in which the early Christians saw themselves and their movement in relation to the rest of the Jewish world. It is an attempt to enter the imaginative world of Jesus' followers who not only lived, thought, and worshiped as Jews, but took it for granted that their movement had a Jewish future. Can we understand Matthew, the scribe who painstakingly depicted Jesus as a true teacher of Torah, and then turned to portray the entire Jewish people calling for Jesus' blood on themselves and their children? If we miss the tragedy of this pious Jew, who unwittingly gave warrant to the slaughter of his own people, we have not yet encountered the painfully ambiguous truth of the New Testament as a Jewish book. Yes, the New Testament expresses, as Leo Baeck observed, Jewish hopes and expectations, but it also expresses a deep-seated rancor, born in the anguished parting between one Jewish group and another. To understand the "Jewish expectations" of the New Testament's Jewish authors requires a radical act of reimagination, stripping away centuries of assumptions about who Jews and Christians are—and are not. To read the New Testament in all its strangeness as a Jewish book, one must step back, if only for a moment, behind the reluctant parting.

The core of *The Reluctant Parting* consists of a book-by-book discussion of the New Testament and its authors. Each of these sections provides an overview of the individual New Testament book, highlighting the way in which each author balances his claims about Jesus as messiah and risen Lord with his commitment to nurturing the *Jewish* identity of the community for which he writes. Thus, Paul, for example, struggles fiercely to explain *on the basis of Torah*, how Jesus can be the messiah despite having been crucified. Luke seeks to prove, also on the basis of Torah, that non-Jews should be allowed into the sect without undergoing circumcision. Each author pushes the boundaries of his Jewish identity; none consciously abandons it.

In addition to the central discussion of the New Testament texts themselves, sidebars provide explanations for some of the more confusing aspects of contemporary Christian belief—issues like the origin of Original Sin. Because many readers (Christian as well as Jewish) are unacquainted with the historical circumstances in which the New Testament was written, Part One provides an overview of the history of the late post-exilic period, and introduces the contents and arrangement of the New Testament, including a brief discussion of early Christian writings that were not included in the Christian canon. Readers whose only interest is in the specific books of the New Testament should feel free to skip directly to Part Two.

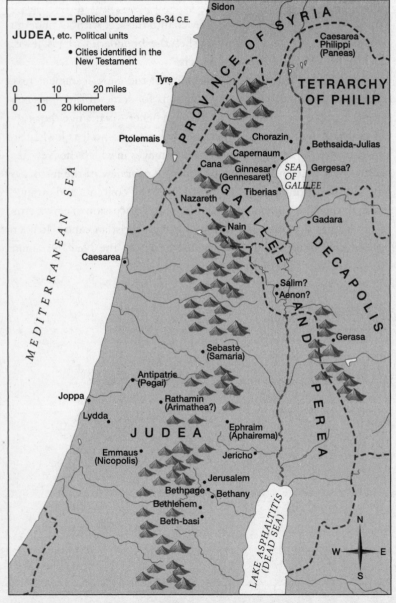

Roman Palestine in the First Century C.E.

BEGINNINGS:
FROM JEWISH SECT
TO GENTILE RELIGION

THE JEWISH WORLD IN
THE FIRST CENTURY C.E.

J UDAISM AS WE KNOW IT TODAY did not exist in Jesus' lifetime. In the first century C.E. the Jews were not the one people and one religion portrayed by the Hebrew Bible and later, by the rabbis, but a socially and geographically diverse group with a broad range of norms and beliefs. Certainly, first-century Jews understood themselves as the continuation of biblical Israel, but exactly how that continuity should be expressed was a question with many answers. The fact that Jesus and his followers who wrote the New Testament were first-century Jews, then, produces as many questions as it does answers concerning their experiences, beliefs, and practices.

Two interrelated factors are essential to understanding the Jewish experience in the Roman period: diaspora and empire. Diaspora—the phenomenon of Jews permanently settled outside the land called Israel (or, as the Romans called it, Palestine)—had been a fact of Jewish life at least since the relocation of northern Israelites (the so-called lost tribes) throughout the Assyrian empire in 722 B.C.E. While almost nothing is known of these earliest diaspora communities, with the Babylonian exile of 586 we begin to have documentation of Jewish life in Babylonia and in Egypt. Over the centuries these diaspora communities were to became major centers of Jewish life, with temples in (at least) Elephantine and Leontopolis in Egypt, and the great study center in Mesopotamia that would eventually produce the Babylonian Talmud. The members of these far-flung communities, while fully engaged in the cultures of which they now formed a part, nonetheless remained "Judeans" or, as the word has evolved in English, "Jews." By the first century C.E., many "Judeans" would never have set foot in Judah; in fact, the majority of Jews resided in the diaspora.

Living as minorities across the Mediterranean and Near Eastern world, diaspora Jews developed various strategies for maintaining their cultural and religious identity. Most still revered Israel as the land promised to Abraham, the Torah (the first five books of the Hebrew scriptures) as the word of God, and the Jerusalem temple as God's chosen sanctuary. Many held at least the ideal of making a pilgrimage to the holy city of Jerusalem. All faced daily decisions about how to "act Jewish" (and how "Jewish" to act) in a non-Jewish world. No authoritative Talmud or Mishnah existed to provide the rules. Who was to say how a "good Jew" decided what groceries to buy or how much to socialize with Gentiles (non-Jews)? The pressures and opportunities facing diaspora Jewish communities made for a wide range of Jewish practice and belief, from the Neoplatonist thinker Philo to the rabbinic sage Hillel. In the first century, one Jew's version of piety might be another's definition of apostasy.

The experience of diaspora cannot be separated from the phenomenon that had, to a large extent, created the diaspora: empire. Following Israel's early subjugation to Assyria, Babylonia, and Persia, in more recent centuries the Macedonian (Greek) and Roman empires had brought about profound transformations in the ancient world. When Alexander of Macedon set out to conquer the world, he took with him a remarkable ideal: to bring the blessings of Greek civilization to all peoples, creating a universal community. To facilitate this goal Alexander took with him architects, engineers, and philosophers, established cities throughout his realm, and encouraged intermarriage between his troops and local women. What Alexander created, of course, was a culture unlike either those he encountered or the one he had hoped to reproduce. The Hellenistic or "Greekified" world was a new cultural system in its own right. The Greek language became the common tongue for public discourse and commerce, and would remain so for most of the centuries of first Greek and then Roman rule. Greek institutions such as the gymnasium—an educational as well as athletic center—were established in every region.

In addition to such intentional changes, the new empire brought new taxes, more contact with foreign merchants and mercenaries, and often, a division between an elite who were eager to cooperate with the overlords in hopes of gaining status in the new world order, and a less-privileged majority who were less eager to part with traditional ways. For Judea (roughly the southeastern Mediterranean seaboard, including the ancient territories of Judah and Samaria), the ambiguous legacy of Alexander was further complicated by his early death and the subsequent competition between two of his generals, Ptolemy in Egypt and Seleucus in Syria, for control of the eastern Mediterranean seaboard. From 326 to 200 B.C.E. Palestine was controlled by Ptolemy and his descendants, who took little interest in the Jews' internal affairs. Between 200 and 196, however, the political landscape of Judea changed dramatically. First, in 200 B.C.E. the Macedonian (Seleucid) rulers of Syria gained control of Palestine from the Ptolemies. Then in 196 Rome, whose forces had been steadily expanding eastward, issued a proclamation to the effect that it was now the "protector" of the Greek-speaking peoples of Europe and Asia. The combined claims of the Syrians and the Romans meant that the Judeans were now the vassals of Syria but under the vaguely defined "protection" of Rome. The period of Syrian, Jewish, and Roman competition for control of the Jewish homeland, roughly the second century B.C.E., would produce wide-ranging changes in the Jewish community. Many of these changes, from popular disaffection with the Jerusalem priesthood to an expectation of God's immanent and decisive intervention in history, paved the way for the sect that was to become Christianity.

In 200 B.C.E. many Jews, especially in the upper classes, had greeted Syrian (Seleucid) overlordship enthusiastically. Not all the population was pro-Seleucid, however, even in the early years, and factions soon grew among families seeking control of the temple and its financial assets. In 175 B.C.E. Antiochus IV "Epiphanes" took the Syrian throne in Antioch. He sold the office of Jewish high priest to a priest named Jason, who promptly transformed Jerusalem into a Greek-Syrian city, complete with gymnasium, and with Antiochene (Syrian-Greek) citizenship for its prominent residents. Jason's actions "put Jerusalem on the map" as part of the Hellenistic world, but they also marginalized traditional YHWH-worshipers of all social classes. Jason, however, was soon outbid for the priesthood by a rival, Menalaus, with no priestly credentials beyond his pocketbook. Chaos ensued, and a prolonged period of fighting among various Jerusalemite factions. Eventually, in 168 Antiochus sent troops to end the civil unrest. According to 2 Maccabees 5, he slaughtered or enslaved thousands in Jerusalem and departed with wealth looted from the temple treasury. According to 1 and 2 Maccabees, Antiochus outlawed all Jewish religious observance, rededicated the temple to Zeus, and erected a new altar in the temple for pagan sacrifices. The claim is probably exaggerated; Antiochus did, after all, continue to sponsor Menelaus as high priest. Clearly, however, Jewish observance was sufficiently suppressed that in 167 rebellion broke out in the name of traditional Judaism. The rural family of Mattathias, also known as the Hasmoneans, led a popular revolt against those—both Jews and Seleucids—in control of Jerusalem. In 164 Antiochus agreed to restore the Judeans' right to "enjoy their own food and laws" (2 Macc. 11:31), that is, he ended religious persecution. By 142 B.C.E. the Jews had been granted limited independence from Syria under a Hasmonean high priest and ruler.

The struggles of the Seleucid period marked the Judean community in the homeland indelibly. By the beginning of Hasmonean rulership in 142 society had become fragmented by years of conflict. In particular, cynicism over a religious leadership that could be bought and sold had fostered the growth of Jewish separatist movements—movements that rejected the authority of the Hasmonean leadership and claimed that they alone embodied the true Israel. These separatist movements were shaped in part by their response to a new and previously unknown experience: religious persecution—oppression based solely on worship practices. People had long grappled with the question of why God allowed the righteous to suffer *despite* their righteousness. Now they had seen the righteous suffer and die *because* of their righteousness. The experience of religious persecution proved to be the catalyst for a developing belief that those who had died for their faith in this world would be rewarded in *another* world—life after death through resurrection. Jewish thought had already become infused (probably through Zoroastrian influence) with the idea of a cosmic dualism, of good and evil powers at war with each other. The persecutions of the second century B.C.E. seemed the very embodiment of such a struggle—truly the work of the Evil One. Belief in a cosmic struggle, however, brought with it the conviction that good would ultimately triumph over evil.

An important agent in the triumph of good over evil was to be an "anointed one," or messiah (from the Hebrew *mashiah,* anointed). In 2 Samuel, God had promised that an anointed son of David would rule over Israel forever. The obvious lack of a Davidic ruler, together with experiences of oppression under Greek and Roman rulership, had fueled speculation that a final anointed one, *the* messiah, would one day be sent by God to free the Jewish people. Scribes began to search the scriptures for hints about how and when God might send this messiah and rescue Israel. By Jesus' day, developing new "knowledge" about the messiah had become a sort of cottage industry among those skilled in interpreting biblical texts. Taken together, the new beliefs that were forming in the centuries prior to Jesus' birth—in a cosmic struggle between good and evil, in the expectation of good's final triumph and of life and judgment after death—would shape Western religious thought for millennia.

This anticipation of God's final and decisive victory over evil was expressed in a distinctive worldview: apocalyptic. The apocalyptic outlook sees the rapid approach of the end of time, the moment of God's triumph and his judgment of the world. In Jewish thought, ancient longings for a new anointed king, or "messiah," became transmuted into a longing for *the* messiah, God's appointed savior, who would appear in the last days to lead the faithful in their triumph. Those who suffered death rather than abandon their religious practice became, not wretches forgotten by God, but martyrs, religious heroes whom God would reward for their faithfulness unto death. The martyrs, of course, could only receive their reward *after* death, by means of resurrection. Messianic expectations, cosmic dualism, martyrdom, and resurrection—an entire constellation of beliefs absent from ancient Israelite religion—suddenly took center stage. In some respects Jewish life continued as it had done for centuries: the rituals in the Jerusalem temple followed forms set down in Leviticus, and the rhythm of sabbath and the festivals went on as always. But in the final centuries before the Common Era, Jewish popular imagination had come to occupy a far more colorful religious landscape, one in which history was fast approaching its end.

The Hasmonean era (from 142 to 63 B.C.E.) proved not to be a golden age of Jewish independence, but a period of ceaseless turmoil. The Syrians continued to claim hegemony over the Judean state, and invaded whenever opportunity arose. When the Syrians were not attacking, the Judean leaders themselves, as the historian Josephus tartly remarked, enjoyed "leisure to exploit Judea undisturbed" (*Ant.* 13.273). The Hasmoneans proved brutal and fractious: Alexander Jannaeus is reported to have killed more than fifty thousand of his own people. They were also given to murdering one another, and to settling claims to the throne through civil war. In 64 B.C.E., when the Roman general Pompey arrived in Syria to extend Roman control over the area, two warring Hasmonean factions each sent delegates imploring him to intervene on their behalf. Pompey came to Jerusalem only to find one claimant to the throne already barricaded in the temple complex. The Roman general laid siege to, captured, and entered the temple, and awarded the throne to the other claimant. Ultimately, the Hasmoneans paid dearly for Rome's support. With Pompey's intervention, Judea officially became a "client kingdom," exercising limited home rule, but now owing both taxes and obedience to Rome.

Roman rule of Judea was an uneasy affair from the start. After an initial twenty years in which Judea was overseen by inept and greedy Roman governors, in 40 B.C.E. Rome appointed Herod, a native of Idumea (now southern Jordan), as a client king. In order to claim his new country Herod first had to wage war against it, following up his victory with a series of brutal reprisals. Herod's reign was long, grand, and tempestuous. Best known for his spectacular reconstruction of the Jerusalem temple, he was equally happy to sponsor temples to Roman gods. Factional fighting continued throughout Herod's reign, exacerbated by his slaughter of his Hasmonean wife, children, and in-laws. (The emperor Augustus quipped that he would rather be Herod's pig [*hus*] than his son [*huios*]. The remark suggests that despite his flagrant disregard for human life, Herod may have kept Jewish dietary laws, thus sparing the pigs.)

The precise nature and extent of factional divisions in Hasmonean and Roman Judea are difficult to discern. In histories written around 90 C.E., Josephus mentions three groups that had been active since Hasmonean times, and a fourth that joined them in the Roman period: Sadducees, Pharisees, Essenes, and later, Zealots. Sadducees (perhaps named after Zadok, the priest of David) were Judea's aristocrats, either descended from high priestly families or more recently connected with the temple hierarchy through their wealth. The Sanhedrin, the council of elders in Jerusalem, was controlled by Sadducees, and headed by the high priest. Members of the wealthy upper class, the Sadducees tended to support Roman rule. They were religiously conservative, accepting no beliefs (in particular, the belief in a resurrection) that did not appear in the Torah.

The Pharisees seem to have been drawn from merchant and landholding classes. They held seats on the Sanhedrin and exercised varying degrees of political power in different periods. The Pharisees, whose name is based on the Hebrew *parash,* or "separate," were more punctilious in observing religious law than most Jews, a fact that "separated" them from the generally less stringent populace. The law followed by the Pharisees was, however, biblical law as filtered through the interpretations of "the elders," a tradition of Pharisaic teachings known as the Oral Torah. The Oral Torah, which was believed, like the written Torah, to have been given to Moses on Sinai, includes a number of tenets such as belief in the resurrection that are not clearly present in the Hebrew Bible. The Pharisees considered their application of the law to be more rigorous than and therefore superior to that of either the average Jew or the Sadducees. Eventually the Pharisees, whose Oral Torah came to be written down in the Mishnah and Talmud, gave birth to the rabbinic Judaism that is the direct ancestor of modern forms of the tradition.

The Essenes were even more separate than the Pharisaic "separate ones." Rejecting the legitimacy of the Jerusalem cult and temple as defiled, scorning those (including the Pharisees) who followed "smooth ways," they created isolated communities in which to lead lives of extreme ritual purity. The Qumran or "Dead Sea Scrolls" group comes close to matching Josephus's descriptions of an Essene community. If the Qumran group was typical, these Jewish "puritans" shared (and furthered) the messianic and apocalyptic expectations of the period. They practiced immersion in the *mikvah* (ritual pool) as a form both of purification and of initiation into a new mode of life. John the Baptist's followers were probably an Essene or Essene-like community. Their separation from society at large formed part of their preparation for the upcoming climax in the struggle between good and evil. Such groups saw themselves—separated, purified, and prepared to live or die with the coming messiah—as the only "true" Israel, the lonely remnant who stood firm while others were corrupted by wickedness.

In addition to the Essenes, who envisioned both a heavenly and an earthly, military struggle against the forces of darkness, there were the Zealots, revolutionaries who sought to bring about a new Israel through the overthrow of the Romans and their Jewish supporters. Some of these revolutionaries were heralded as "messiahs," God's anointed agents who would bring about his rule on earth. Although it is not always clear who was to be counted as a Zealot, rioting, rebellion, and politically motivated brigandage occurred regularly enough for us to assume that groups attempting to foment violent revolution were a factor throughout the period of Roman domination.

The vast majority of Judeans would have belonged to none of these distinct parties. In Judea as in the diaspora, Jews seem by and large to have continued to revere the Jerusalem temple and to pay an annual tax to support temple sacrifices. Reverence for temple and tradition, however, like a love of flag and country, does not preclude resentment or anger against those in charge of traditional institutions. Corruption in high priestly circles was widely known, and generations of abuses by Roman governors as well as Judean kings had taken a toll on public morale. The tax burden under the Romans was high—as much as 25 percent of a farmer's produce might be owed directly to Rome (plus whatever was collected by client kings). And the system known as tax farming, in which individuals bought the right to collect taxes due to Rome, meant that in every region someone made his living from whatever he could collect *in addition* to the official taxes. Tax farmers were ordinarily drawn from the local citizenry, in this case Jews, thus furthering division and resentment within the community. While most people were far too preoccupied with survival to embrace one of the dominant parties of the day, sympathy for one or another of them—admiration for the Pharisees' learning or for the Zealots' patriotism (or both)—must have been widespread. The Romans and their client kings ruled over a people who gave them no particular loyalty. Torah, temple, and land still commanded respect. Rulers were a different matter.

JESUS

IN PERHAPS 4 B.C.E., the year of Herod's death, Jesus of Nazareth was born into the unstable world of Roman Palestine. About thirty years later, he died by crucifixion. Judging from the little that we know of either Roman Palestine or the events of Jesus' life, his story does not seem all that unusual. Crucifixion was the standard Roman punishment for insurrection; thus, whatever else he was, in Rome's eyes Jesus was one in a seemingly endless stream of Jewish rebels. Early narratives about Jesus describe him as a teacher, one whom crowds willingly followed. He is also described as a traveling miracle worker, specifically, a healer. Diseases in antiquity were frequently considered the work of demons, and a traveling healer, as someone who could chase out demons, carried a certain amount of religious authority. Galilee (north of Judea), Jesus' home, was known for both its rebels and its miracle workers; Jesus' calling as a teacher, healer, and sometime rabble-rouser would have been unusual, but not unheard of in Roman Galilee.

Jesus' own understanding of his identity is virtually impossible to reconstruct. He referred to himself by the epithet *Son of Man* (Greek, *huios tou anthropou*), an expression that first appears in the book of Ezekiel meaning, roughly, "mortal." The phrase was used by another Galilean miracle worker of the first century C.E., Honi "the circle drawer," apparently as an expression of self-abnegation. The term has a complex history, however, and in the biblical book of Daniel as well as the apocalyptic 1 Enoch, the "Son of Man" appears as a heavenly, possibly angelic figure who ushers in the era of God's triumph. Jesus seems to have used the phrase in both ways, now saying that "foxes have holes, and birds of the air have nests; but the Son of Man [this mere mortal] has nowhere to lay his head" (Matt. 8:20) and later, quoting Daniel, "They will see the 'Son of Man coming on the clouds of heaven'" (Matt. 24:30). Almost without a doubt, Jesus either identified himself or was identified by his followers during his lifetime as the messiah, God's agent for the overthrow of the evil powers of the age. The gospels suggest that he embraced this role. During Passover he rode into Jerusalem on a donkey, implicitly fulfilling Zechariah's prophecy that the king would come, "lowly, and seated on an ass" (9:9). Passover was a time when tens of thousands of Jews packed into Jerusalem to celebrate God's liberation of Israel; it was frequently also an occasion for anti-Roman rioting. Any charismatic figure acclaimed as messiah during this festival of national liberation was likely to provoke Roman reprisals. Certainly, it would have come as no surprise for such a figure to be crucified as part of a more or less routine attempt to keep the peace.

Jesus' death was the predictable fate of messiahs in Roman Palestine. Other messiahs, people like Theudas in 45 C.E. and Bar Kochba almost a hundred years later, gathered their followers, prepared for the liberation of the Jewish people, and instead were killed by Rome. But if Jesus' death was unremarkable, what followed was unprecedented. As Josephus put it, "Those who had in the first place come to love him did not give up their affection for him" (*Ant.* 18.63). That is, Jesus' followers did not give up their belief in Jesus as messiah, even after his death. Such loyalty would have been utterly inexplicable in terms of Jewish messianic expectations. The messiah was, by definition, someone who would triumph as part of God's cosmic triumph over evil. The exact content of messianic expectations varied from group to group, but a messiah who died without establishing *something* like peace and justice was simply not the messiah. If Jesus' painful and humiliating death proved anything, it was that he had not been the messiah. Why, then, as

Josephus noted, did his followers continue to follow? The answer is a matter of speculation or, for a Christian, of faith.

Shortly after his death, Jesus' followers came to believe that, far from marking the end of their messianic hopes, Jesus' death had marked the beginning of God's promised kingdom. At least some of those who had followed Jesus began to experience him as present and performing great acts of power in their midst. Their experience convinced them that Jesus had been resurrected. And if in Jesus the resurrection of the dead had begun, then in fact God's final triumph over evil was at hand. Seemingly overcome by the powers of this world, Jesus had instead overcome the power of death itself. Their "failed" messiah had been vindicated as the Chosen One of God. Jesus' followers soon regrouped and began to spread their apocalyptic message among an already restless Jewish population. The end was at hand, and Jesus, God's now-exalted servant, was God's agent, offering the hope of resurrection to all who followed his way. Within a few years of Jesus' death, a group of Jesus' followers had coalesced into a new sect within the turbulent mix that was first-century sectarian Judaism.

PARTING OF THE WAYS:
JUDAISM AND CHRISTIANITY

THE BAND OF JESUS' FOLLOWERS who proclaimed his resurrection did not see themselves as members of a new religion. On the contrary, in light of Jesus' resurrection they had become more convinced than ever of their belief that God would intervene to redeem the Jewish people and defeat not only Rome but death itself. A change of religions would have been the last thing on their minds. Within only a few generations, however, this marginal sect of a provincial people had been transformed into a largely gentile religion whose adherents spanned the Mediterranean world.

The nature, causes, and timing of the so-called parting of the ways between Judaism and Christianity are hotly debated. A few things, however, are universally agreed upon: although Jesus' first followers were Jews, mostly from Galilee, by 100 C.E. most members of the Jesus sect were Gentiles of the diaspora; by the fifth century "Christianity" had become a fully separate religion from "Judaism" (though even at that late date some groups resisted the split). Within those very broad parameters, the question of when the Jesus movement ceased to be a Jewish phenomenon is nearly impossible to answer. Even in antiquity different people would have given different answers. Members of the sect whose ancestors were Jewish, for example, probably continued to see themselves as Jews far longer than Gentiles whose parents or grandparents had joined the sect when it was still a largely Jewish community.

Ultimately, the answer to when the Jesus sect ceased to be Jewish depends on how one defines "Jew" or, more to the point, how people in Roman antiquity decided who was a Jew. Informed Gentiles would have known that Jews (as a rule) circumcised male babies, observed the sabbath, ate kosher food, and worshiped only the God whose temple was in Jerusalem. But what if someone who was ethnically Jewish were to do only a few of these things, or none of them? Was he or she still a Jew? In most contexts, the answer would have been yes, since being a Jew (or "Judean") was a matter of one's family of origin, not a matter of religious practice. But what if a non-Jew were to begin "living as a Jew"? At what point, if any, did such a person "become" a Jew?

A New Testament example illustrates the problem. In Acts 16 Luke describes Paul's assistant Timothy, whose mother was "a Jewish woman who was a believer" (in Jesus) but whose father was "a Greek." Timothy is an uncircumcised member of the Jesus sect, of mixed parentage. Is he a Jew or not? As nearly as we can tell, the rabbinic dictum that a Jew is the child of a Jewish mother was not yet widely recognized, so that can't help us. Luke, however, says that Paul had Timothy circumcised "because of the Jews" in the diaspora communities where he was working. Why? "Because they all knew that his father was a Greek," that is, they were aware that he had not been circumcised. Timothy was perceived by at least some diaspora Jews as a Jew, albeit a nonkosher one because he was not circumcised. More significantly, it was not his belief in Jesus as messiah that other Jews found problematic, but his being uncircumcised. Did Timothy consider himself a Jew? His gentile father surely did not. Legally and socially, Timothy had been a member of his father's household. If Timothy's father had wanted him to be a Jew, he would have had him circumcised. Now, however, in order to gain acceptance within the diaspora Jewish community, Timothy chooses to become circumcised. Before his circumcision, Timothy seems to have occupied a religious no-man's land—a Gentile to Gentiles, an assimilated Jew to Jews. Only when he joins a Jewish sect (the Jesus movement) does he undergo circumcision, thus making him fully Jewish in the eyes of both Gentiles and Jews. For Timothy, becoming a Christian meant becoming *more* Jewish rather than less.

Timothy's case is instructive: if we cannot be certain whether a single, known member of the Jesus sect was or was not considered a Jew (and by whom), the question of when *all* Christians stopped being considered Jews in all regions by everyone will not be easily answered. The split was never as absolute as one might assume. In antiquity, ethnically Jewish groups such as the Ebionites continued to observe Jewish law while affirming Jesus as messiah as late as the fifth century C.E. But long before that time most Jews, most Christians, and most pagans (devotees of the Roman gods) had begun to distinguish between "Jew" and "Christian." While it is impossible to isolate a single date and place at which Jesus-followers stopped being Jewish and became "other," it is relatively easy to trace the changing makeup of the Jesus movement from Jewish to gentile, and to elucidate the tensions that caused Jew and Gentile alike eventually to consider the Christians, as an early Christian writer called them, a "third race."

After Jesus' death his followers, believing that Jesus' resurrection represented the beginning of God's cataclysmic judgment, reorganized in order to spread their beliefs. Such a group would have seemed unremarkable in first-century Judea, where new versions of Judaism, many of them heralding the apocalyptic end times, emerged regularly, either to flourish or to vanish. The new group would have been about as noteworthy as a new storefront church in modern America. Certainly, most Jews did not consider a now-deceased Galilean preacher named Jesus to have been the messiah. But neither would they have been offended by someone claiming that he was. The Jesus sect simply offered a variation on the popular theme of messianic expectations. While insignificant to most Jews, however, the sect would have been eyed with suspicion by temple authorities. The sect, after all, venerated a criminal executed for rebellion against Rome. The high priests were the Jewish community's liaisons with Rome, and as such, responsible for keeping the peace. To the extent that they might have been aware of the group, they could hardly have been pleased. But whether the Jesus-followers were regarded as a commonplace sect or a potentially problematic cell, no one would have doubted that the group was Jewish.

The movement's change from Jewish sect to gentile religion can, at one level, be explained quite simply: while most Jews took no interest in the group's claims, many Gentiles did. Jesus' followers had consisted primarily of Galilean Jews, at least some of them living in Jerusalem. After his death they continued to observe Jewish law, including temple worship and sacrifice. We do not know when or why Jesus' followers first moved beyond Judea, except that they were eager to reach as many Jews as possible before the end time. Unlike the Qumran group, who withdrew from society in order to prepare for the final struggle, the Jesus group engaged in an ardent quest to spread the word, so that all might be prepared to meet God's judgment. The book of Acts (and see also Matt. 28:15) is almost certainly correct that the movement initially sought only to reach other Jews. As it turned out, within a decade or so after Jesus' death non-Jews from Asia Minor (modern-day Turkey) had shown sufficient interest that the core group in Jerusalem was called upon to decide the basis for including Gentiles as members. Some refused to admit them unless they underwent full conversion to Judaism, including circumcision for men; others argued for their unqualified acceptance and allowed missionaries to grant Gentiles full membership without formal conversion.

The decision by some members of the movement not to circumcise converts seems inexplicable from a modern Jewish perspective. How could observant Jews so easily abandon the rite that had for centuries been a universal prerequisite for males' conversion? The answer lies in the group's apocalyptic expectations. Biblical prophecies of the last days regularly included visions of the Gentiles ("the nations") joining Israel: "Many nations shall come and say, 'Come, let us go up to the mountain of the Lord, to the house of the God of Jacob; that he may teach us his ways and that we may walk in his paths' " (Isa. 2:3). Jesus' followers believed the last days had come. What better confirmation than the arrival of Gentiles on their doorstep? The ancient prophecies, however, though predicting the Gentiles' arrival, gave no directions for what to *do* with them when they showed up. Did they need to become

Jews, or only to join in worshiping Israel's God? Members of the sect reached different answers on this issue, but as the movement spread across the Mediterranean those who insisted on full gentile conversion quickly became a minority.

The attraction of the Jesus movement for non-Jews living in the diaspora can be attributed, at least initially, to the presence of Gentiles already loosely affiliated with diaspora synagogues. Jews, who formed between 5 and 10 percent of the population of the Roman empire (compared, for example, with 2 percent of the population of the twenty-first-century United States), often associated with Gentiles in social and civic arenas. While some non-Jewish observers found Judaism's distinctive practices either bizarre or objectionable, others were deeply impressed by the antiquity of the religion and the dignity of Jewish beliefs. Many Gentiles, called in Acts "God-fearers," frequented synagogues, sometimes serving as financial patrons and observing some Jewish customs. Most did not convert. The greatest single barrier facing potential converts to Judaism was undoubtedly circumcision. In a world without antisepsis, circumcision was not only painful but dangerous. Socially, it was considered both barbaric and shameful. Whatever interest gentile males might have had in affiliating themselves with the local Jewish community, that interest would have been considerably diminished by the prospect of circumcision. The Jesus sect's offer of circumcision-free membership would have appealed to many whose interest in Judaism stopped at the initiation ritual. As semi-converts to Judaism, God-fearers seem to have welcomed the opportunity to become full members of this new and less restrictive Jewish group.

As the sect spread across the Roman world, it also attracted gentile pagans (worshipers of the Greek and Roman gods) not already associated with synagogues. For these as for other Gentiles, the Jesus movement had a certain cachet: it was both exotic and, as part of an ancient tradition, venerable. But the Jesus sect offered two things other forms of Judaism did not: one was a specific savior-figure through whom one could attain both spiritual transformation and personal immortality; the other was, so to speak, membership on reasonable terms. Many first-century Jews believed in a resurrection of the dead in which all would be raised and judged, as the book of Daniel puts it, "some to everlasting life, and some to shame and everlasting contempt" (12:2). Jesus' followers added two distinctive claims: that this resurrection had already begun in the person of Jesus; and that having himself been raised from the dead, he was now available as a source of spiritual transformation, and to assist them in attaining a favorable outcome at the last judgment. In the language of Greco-Roman society and religion, Jesus was a heavenly patron. These three elements—personal immortality, spiritual transformation, and a heavenly patron to assist in both—were already known in the ancient world from other "exotic" religious groups, generally referred to as mystery religions. Cults like that of Isis carried the allure of offering their members spiritual transformation as well as the security of an afterlife, something not generally available in Greek or Roman popular religion. The Jesus sect thus provided both the attractions of a mystery religion and the dignity of an ancient and respected tradition. And it didn't require circumcision.

Despite the attractions of the Jesus sect for many Gentiles, it also entailed one serious drawback: the social costs of monotheism. The Greco-Roman world was a polytheistic world. The existence of the gods—many gods—was a fact of daily life. Some were traditional for one's family or trade. Others literally came with the territory, as patrons of lands and cities. Still others ensured the fertility of crops and animals or healed illnesses. In such a culture the belief in and worship of only one god seemed to demonstrate an uncommon lack of sense. Why deprive oneself of the benefits of the gods? Moreover, why invite their anger? God-fearers would have found the notion of a single, invisible god philosophically appealing, but that appeal did not necessarily translate into a willingness to abandon worship of the gods. After all, even if one concluded that the gods weren't real, one's neighbors most definitely were, and offending the neighbors could bring almost as much trouble as offending the gods. Most community functions included ceremonies honoring the appropriate deities; dinner parties often took place in special sections of pagan temples. To neglect the worship of the gods was to exclude oneself from the social network. And worse, neglecting the gods invited their retribution against the community as a whole. Abandoning traditional religion was often seen, not as a "personal" choice but as a gesture of disregard for the community's norms and safety. While Jews had a recognized duty to honor their ancestral god (a god who was known to be unreasonably jealous of other deities), Gentiles who abandoned the gods set themselves up to be perceived and treated as enemies of the people. Unlike God-fearers, who might participate in some aspects of Jewish life while continuing to honor the gods, those who actually joined the Jesus sect were making an absolute commitment to monotheism. God-fearers and other gentile pagans who chose to join the sect often generated resentment and reprisals from family and neighbors.

Gentiles who joined the Jesus sect sometimes encountered resentment from another quarter as well: diaspora Jews. Jewish communities had existed throughout the eastern Mediterranean for centuries. Jews wrote and spoke Greek and participated in local civic life. Some rights, such as paying an annual tax to the Jerusalem temple rather than to the gods of Rome, were protected, at least in principle, by the emperor. But the Jews were also vulnerable. Public resentment of Jewish privileges, their neglect of local gods, and, perhaps especially, their refusal to blend into the imperial melting pot, had been known to erupt in violence. At least twice, in 19 and 49 C.E., Jews were expelled from the city of Rome in response to public unrest. Just as Jews in the homeland needed to be mindful of the Roman authorities, diaspora Jews needed to respect public opinion. In this regard the Jesus sect was a problem. Their founder had been executed for sedition against Rome; they encouraged belief in "the kingdom of God" (rather than that of Rome); they conspicuously drew Gentiles away from their responsibilities to family and state. And they were Jews. They were, in short, a liability for the Jewish people. At the same time that they attracted many gentile converts, the Christ-following communities of the first-century diaspora also faced animosity from both Jewish and gentile sources. As this inconvenient sect came to be composed increasingly of Gentiles—and began to draw reprisals from local pagan communities—it became both simple and prudent for the larger Jewish community to disavow it altogether.

Writing during the tumultuous decades of the sect's change from Jewish to gentile sect, the New Testament authors seem not to have conceived of "Christianity" as a religion distinct from Judaism. Paul writes of the Jews as "them" (sometimes disparagingly), but does so only when writing to *gentile* congregations. Moreover, his polemic against "Jews" is directed against only Jewish members of the Jesus sect (usually those who advocate circumcision for gentile converts). Paul's "Jews" are not Jews in general, but what we would call Jewish-Christian opponents. When, as in Romans, he writes to a mixed Jewish-gentile community, he emphasizes the community's identity as a "branch" growing from and dependent upon the trunk that is Israel. That branch has not been severed from its trunk. Later New Testament documents show communities with various relationships to other Jews. Almost without exception, these documents reflect Christ-following communities' struggles to renegotiate the meaning of Jewishness in light of Jesus' messiahship. Like other Jewish authors of the period, the authors of the New Testament reached differing conclusions as to the shape and boundaries of Jewish identity. On the basis of the New Testament, however, one cannot conclude that a new religion called Christianity existed at the turn of the second century C.E.

Where, then, if not in the pages of the New Testament, can we find the great divide, the benchmark demonstrating that two separate traditions have come into existence? The conventional starting place has long been the *birkat ha-minim*, the "blessing" (euphemistic for "cursing") of the heretics, supposedly added to the eighteen blessings of the daily Jewish liturgy in about 90 C.E. Scholars have often considered this nineteenth "benediction" a means for flushing Christians out of the synagogue, as it involved cursing either Christ or themselves. The gospel of John's prophecy that "the Jews" would put Jesus' followers "out of their synagogues" (*aposynagogos;* 9:22) looked like a direct reference to the *birkhat ha-minim* and a forced parting of the ways. In recent decades, however, almost every aspect of the *birkat ha-minim* hypothesis has been brought into question. First, scholars have realized that rabbinic authority was far more limited in the first centuries C.E. than rabbinic texts would have us believe.

Thus, even if first-century rabbis had cursed Christians, it is unlikely that most Jews would have known or cared. Second, the *birkat ha-minim* curses neither Christ nor Christians, but "sectarians" or heretics. All of them. *Any* Jew who is not a rabbinic Jew is cursed. And finally, while the rabbinic texts claim that the blessing was added in 90 C.E., no text earlier than the third century mentions it. Thus, the story of the *birkat ha-minim* may simply represent what later rabbis thought *should* have happened at a much earlier date. In short, the blessing against the heretics tells us nothing about "Jewish-Christian relations" in the first century C.E.

It is probably most reasonable to understand the two traditions, Christianity and rabbinic Judaism, as refining their respective self-definitions over the course of the second century C.E. The Mishnah, for example, a body of rabbinic law codified about 200 C.E., attempts to draw firm boundaries as to what constitutes "real" Judaism. According to tractate *Sanhedrin,* only those Jews who affirm the resurrection of the dead and the Mosaic origin of the Oral Law (rabbinic legal tradition) have a place in the world to come (10.1). That is, the rabbis excluded most Jews from their definition of a "good Jew." During the period that early rabbinic Judaism was attempting to establish itself as authoritative, the Jesus sect was becoming more difficult to defend as "Jewish" by any definition.

Religion did not exist as an isolated category in the ancient world; nationality and religion were intertwined. After the first century, the Christ-followers were no longer predominantly "Jews" in the ethnic sense. Nor did they follow the recognized Jewish customs, most notably circumcising their sons. To most Gentiles, the sect of Jesus-followers would not have seemed like a Jewish sect. Neither "good Jews" nor good worshipers of the pagan gods, by the end of the first century the Christians had, at least in some regions, distinguished themselves sufficiently from the Jews to be regarded as social and religious misfits. In Asia Minor, home to a thriving Jewish community as well as to early forms of the imperial cult, Christians began to face sporadic local persecution. Eventually the Romans, needing both to keep the peace and to defend the honor of Rome, intervened.

The beginning and extent of Roman persecution of Christians is debated, but letters between Pliny, governor of Pontus and Bythinia in what is now northern Turkey, and the emperor Trajan in about 112 C.E. illustrate the issues involved. Pliny writes to the emperor for advice on how to deal with the "pernicious superstition" of the Christians. Pliny evidently finds the group harmless, noting that they mostly gather to sing "hymns to Christ as a god." These people are oath-bound, not into a criminal conspiracy, but precisely *not* to rob or defraud anyone. They do, however, quite obstinately refuse to sacrifice to the gods. Should Pliny execute them solely for being Christians, he asks, or only if they have committed some crime? Or should they be executed if, offered a second chance, they continue to refuse to sacrifice? Trajan and Pliny agree that former Christians (those now willing to offer sacrifices) should not be killed, that no anonymous accusations should be credited, and that Christians should not be actively hunted down. A known and unrepentant Christian should of course be executed. Nowhere in their correspondence do Pliny or Trajan entertain the possibility that Christians might share in *Jewish* exemptions from worshiping the gods. Nor, apparently, are the Christians themselves making this claim. To these early second-century Roman rulers, gentile members of the Jesus sect are simply conspicuous atheists (people who refuse to acknowledge the gods) whose neighbors are turning them in to the authorities in hopes of getting them killed.

Despite the evidence of Pliny and Trajan that neither the local populace nor the Roman authorities considered Christians a form of Jews in the early second century, the break between the traditions was by no means complete. In the same period that the Romans were deciding how to deal with gentile Christians, books like Revelation and the gospel of John indicate that *Jewish* Christian groups in Asia Minor continued to think of themselves as Jews. Over the course of the second century, however, such a view would become increasingly difficult to maintain. Christian groups began including explicitly Christian writings among their sacred texts, thus creating a different scripture from that read in the Jewish community. Christian liturgy had also come to differ from Jewish liturgy. Sometime before 150 C.E. the gentile Christian Justin recorded a debate (whether fictional or actual is disputed) with a Jewish interlocutor, proving that Christians alone constituted "*verus Israel*," the true Israel. By the middle of the second century relatively few Christians—and even fewer Jews—would have assumed that "Christianity" was one way among many of being a Jew.

THE ORIGINS OF THE NEW TESTAMENT

WHEN JESUS' FOLLOWERS first began to "search the scriptures" for help in understanding the messiah, it was the Jewish scriptures that they searched. They used a version called the Septuagint (abbreviated LXX), a Greek translation of ancient Hebrew scriptures, together with more recent texts, some of them originally composed in Greek. Because most Jews no longer spoke or read Hebrew, the Septuagint was widely used throughout the Jewish world. No formal Jewish "canon," or set list, yet existed; the Septuagint included texts (like the Torah) long considered sacred, plus others (like 1 and 2 Maccabees) whose status was less firmly established. In addition, among those texts widely read in Jewish circles were several, such as 1 Enoch, that foretold both the coming of the messiah and the end of the world. Christians, when they decided on a canon, would canonize the Septuagint as their "Old Testament." When the Jewish community later decided on its own formal list or canon, it chose only texts that had been written in Hebrew or Aramaic and excluded many later writings, including some (such as Sirach) that had been immensely popular even in rabbinic circles. So, in its "Old Testament," Christianity actually preserves an early stage of Jewish religious life, one that was largely forgotten by Jews after the rabbis created a formal (and shorter) Jewish canon.

As Jesus' followers spread their message, they supported their claims not only on the basis of their experience, but also by interpreting Jewish scripture, particularly texts from the Torah, the prophets, and the psalms, as prophecies of his suffering, resurrection, and exaltation. The writers of the canonical stories about Jesus, the gospels, seem to have used both collections of Jesus' teachings (like the hypothetical collection known as "Q"), and at least one "passion narrative," the story of his suffering and death. It would surely have been his resurrection that convinced them of the approaching "last days" and gave urgency to their preaching. Ultimately, the Jesus movement would be propelled, not by the teachings of a great master, but by his disciples' belief that Jesus was risen Lord.

Although early Christian teachers would surely have focused on the message of Jesus' death and resurrection, the earliest known Christian

FIRST ENOCH

First Enoch has the distinction of enormously influencing the thought of people who have never heard of it. Consisting of sections written (probably in Aramaic) between the fourth and first centuries B.C.E., 1 Enoch purports to be a series of visions recorded by Enoch (see Gen. 5) for those living in the last days. The work was a favorite among apocalyptic Jews; it appears to be quoted in such diverse works as Jubilees, Daniel, and Jude. Copies of 1 Enoch were also found among the Dead Sea Scrolls. First Enoch elaborates many of the distinctive ideas that would form the core of Jewish apocalyptic thinking, among them the resurrection of the dead followed by judgment performed by a preexistent, celestial messiah; and the idea that "fallen angels" form a cosmic opposition to God. In short, Enoch is essential to understanding the Christian scriptures. Many beliefs that contemporary Jews and Christians alike consider distinctly Christian were developed and popularized in early Jewish circles by 1 Enoch.

writings are neither teachings of nor stories about Jesus, but letters. As
the missionary community expanded, crossing geographic, ethnic, and
social boundaries, many questions arose: How should the relationship
between Jew and Gentile be understood in the new age? Does Jesus'
resurrection affect our lives (and deaths) now, or only our hope for the
future? When Christians die, do they get resurrected right away, or do
they have to wait for the end of the world? And just exactly when *is* the
end of the world coming, anyway?

Christian expectations of an any-minute-now end time also raised
problems about how to carry on in the meantime. Because the group
combined a relatively egalitarian ethos with a mixed socioeconomic
makeup in a fashion unprecedented in antiquity, endless questions
arose about which of the old rules still applied, here at the end of time.
Often, confused or conflicted groups turned to their founders, itinerant missionaries, for advice. They did so both by means of personal
messengers and by letter. Scores of letters must have circulated among
the far-flung groups of Jesus-followers during the first years of their existence. Of these, a handful remain, most of them by a missionary
named Paul.

During the mid-first century, then, two types of documents circulated among Jesus-following groups: letters from founders and other
missionaries, and writings preserving sayings of and stories about Jesus.
Within a generation or two, however, congregations began to feel the
need for a fuller account of their own origins. The generation of eyewitnesses had died and the end had not yet come: the very continuation
of history seemed in need of explanation. In addition to the delay of
God's judgment, the destruction of the Jerusalem temple in 70 caused
profound trauma throughout the Jewish world. Some interpreted this
cataclysmic event in apocalyptic terms. Like others whose relationship
with the temple cult was less than positive, some Christians would have
read the temple's fall as the beginning of God's judgment against a corrupt system. Mark, the first of the four canonical gospels, was produced
during the immediate crisis of 66–70 C.E. It portrays a brusque and confrontational Jesus who announces both the coming destruction of the
temple and his own coming "on the clouds" as God's agent in the last

days. Over the following decades the authors of Matthew, Luke, and John would develop and refine the story of Jesus, shaping it to meet the specific needs and concerns of the communities for which they wrote.

By the early second century not only these four gospels, but several more, some still known and some now forgotten, had been composed. These vary widely in both tone and content. In one, the Infancy Gospel of Thomas, Jesus is given a childhood, and delights in causing miraculous mischief. Caught in the sabbath violation of forming clay into the shape of birds, the young Jesus simply claps his hands and the "evidence" flies chirping away. By contrast, a separate, Coptic gospel also named after Thomas consists of a compilation of Jesus' sayings intended to lead the reader to *gnosis,* or the saving knowledge of truth: "Whoever finds the interpretation of these sayings will not experience death" (v. 1). This gospel contains no stories or morals, only a set of cryptic vignettes pointing to the divine life within the reader. Several gospels, now known only as they are quoted in other texts, were written for Jewish congregations and reflect a Jewish Christianity that maintained the validity of Jewish ritual and rejected Jesus' divinity. These lost Jewish gospels, the Gospel of the Ebionites, the Gospel of the Nazareans, and the Gospel According to the Hebrews, were composed in communities that may have stayed especially close to the teachings and practice of Jesus, only to be later declared heretical by a church that had grown in other directions. In an entirely different mode, the Gospel of Peter seems utterly remote from the Jewish community: here Pilate washes his hands of guilt for Jesus' death, but "none of the Jews washed his hands." The variety of gospels conveys a hint of the diversity of belief and practice among early Christian communities.

Additional types of literature were circulated and read at Christian gatherings. The Didache, an instruction manual written around 100 C.E., reveals Jewish aspects of early Christian liturgy, a heritage of which its users may or may not have been aware. The Didache's instructions for the grace following meals, for example, and for performing baptism in running water, are recognizable to modern Jews, as they were to ancient ones. The instruction regarding food purity—"undertake what you can"—could have been lifted from a Reform Jewish platform. But, as in the gospels, so also in other early Christian works, the Jewish-friendly ethos of one text is countered by the fierce anti-Judaism of the next. The Epistle of Barnabas, for example, provides an extended "proof" of Christianity's superiority over Judaism. Torah and prophets are quoted endlessly, always to demonstrate that the Jews have misunderstood, misused, and forfeited their part in God's promises to Israel. Christian texts, like the communities that wrote them, were anything but unified in their teachings.

By the end of the first century, Paul's letters had taken on the status of scripture (see Ignatius, *Eph*. 12.2; 2 Peter 3:15–16) in some circles, and readings from a gospel would soon become part of the church's Sunday worship. Most churches seem initially to have used only one gospel. In fact, around 170 C.E. Tatian produced a harmonization of Matthew, Mark, Luke, and John into a single gospel that would prove immensely popular in Syria as late as the fourth and fifth centuries. Depending on regional, ethnic, and theological factors, different Christian groups developed different traditions of which books were read and taught in the assembly. For the most part, churches tended to consider authoritative those texts that were most ancient, and that were compatible with their beliefs. Paul's letters enjoyed early and widespread acceptance (except in some Jewish-Christian circles, where his stand against circumcision was rejected), but it was not until the beginning of the third century that the four now-canonical gospels became accepted as a group in most regions. The non-Pauline epistles, apocalyptic visions such as the Apocalypse of Peter, and writings such as the Didache remained the most fluid, accepted by some groups and rejected by others as late as the sixth century.

The factors that led to the adoption of a uniform canon are not fully known. One influence may have been the fourth-century development of technology that allowed the entire canon to be bound together into a single codex. Ironically, the emperor Diocletian's order of 303 C.E. that Christian books were to be burned probably stimulated discussion of which books really counted as scripture (and were thus subject to confiscation and burning). Another factor was surely the emperor Constantine's conversion to Christianity, with the attendant boost to a developing "orthodoxy" within a still-diverse Christian community. The limitation of acceptable texts went hand in hand with the limitation of acceptable beliefs. The first known canon lists, from the fourth century, show considerable unanimity in accepting only the four now-canonical gospels and the letters of Paul. The Epistle to the Hebrews, in contrast, is missing from the Muratorian Canon, an important early list, and listed by Eusebius in the early fourth century as "disputed." The Apocalypse of Peter appears in the Muratorian Canon but is not considered "genuine" by Eusebius. The discrepancies go on, with Jude, James, Hebrews, 1, 2, and 3 John, and 1 and 2 Peter each left out of at least one of the existing lists. As late as the sixth century the canon of Claromontanus includes Barnabas, the Acts of Paul, the Shepherd of Hermas, and the Apocalypse of Peter. And because texts produced by culturally dominant groups were far more likely to survive than the texts of marginalized or suppressed groups, the available sample can be assumed to underrepresent the diversity of early Christian texts and communities.

The first known list of precisely those twenty-seven books that now constitute the New Testament was included by Bishop Athanasius of Alexandria in his paschal letter of 367 C.E. Athanasius mentions that the Didache and the Shepherd of Hermas are useful for instruction, but apparently he does not intend them to be read as "scripture" in the assembly. Athanasius's canon did not enjoy more than regional authority, though his ban on "heretical" books seems to have prompted the Egyptian gnostic communities to hide their manuscripts, thus preserving them for later generations. Many such banned manuscripts contained texts that would be forgotten until their rediscovery in the twentieth century. Church councils in 393 (Hippo) and 397 (Carthage) affirmed the twenty-seven-book list, but custom would continue to vary for some time.

The church's self-definition over a period of almost six hundred years resulted not only in lost texts but with them, in Bart Ehrman's phrase, lost Christianities. The diversity of early Christian voices has been narrowed; only those that can, at least in principle, be reconciled remain. Nonetheless, the documents preserved in the New Testament

WHY DIFFERENT CHRISTIAN GROUPS HAVE DIFFERENT CANONS OF THE OLD TESTAMENT

The earliest Christian Old Testament differed from the Jewish Bible in that it included books (the Apocrypha) excluded from the Hebrew Bible, was based on a Greek translation, and moved the "latter prophets" (all the books named for prophets) from the middle of the Bible to the end, pointing forward to the messiah. This remained the case until the Protestant Reformation of the sixteenth century, when Martin Luther, in a move "back to the sources," advocated that the Old Testament be based on the Hebrew rather than the Greek, and that the Apocrypha be excluded. Most Protestant Christian bodies follow Luther's preference, reading the text of the Jewish Bible arranged in the Christian order. Catholic, Eastern Orthodox, and Anglican Christians continue to include the Apocrypha.

represent substantial diversity. The four gospels differ (as those who preferred Tatian's harmonization were clearly aware) not only in their details, but also in their understanding of who Jesus was. Other writings differ as well. The Jesus of Hebrews, for example, who "learned obedience through what he suffered," is a far cry from John's "man who came down from heaven."

The generations during which the Jesus sect moved from an exclusively Jewish membership to a majority gentile membership were fraught with tensions. The texts of what is now the New Testament reflect a period when extraordinary pressures, from the destruction of the Jerusalem temple to the founding of all-gentile communities, pressed the group's leaders to rethink and rearticulate their relationship to the Jewish people. The distinctively Jewish voice of the New Testament seems not to have been preserved for its own sake, but neither was it systematically excised. For almost two millennia, that Jewish voice lacked readers who could or would hear it. These writers spoke, after all, not with the voice of Judaism as it has grown and developed over the centuries, nor with the voice of Christianity as it was soon to grow. Rather, the New Testament's Jewish voice is a haunting echo of first-century apocalypticism, of Jews who awaited the end of the world, and hoped to see it in their lifetimes.

THE ORDER OF THE NEW TESTAMENT CANON

IN THEIR CANONICAL FORM the books of the New Testament are arranged in rough chronological order in terms of the events they relate. Thus, we begin with the life of Jesus in the gospels, move to the story of the first generation of his followers in Acts, and then proceed to Paul, the great teacher of the first generation. Next comes the work of Paul's contemporaries, James, Jude, and Peter. The book of Revelation, describing the end of the world, comes, appropriately enough, at the end. This semi-historical arrangement of the canon creates the impression that the works placed earlier in the canon (the gospels) were written before the "later" ones. That impression is false. Paul's letters were written before any of the gospels, whereas some of the letters following Paul's were written between the composition of Mark, the earliest gospel, and John, the latest. Some of the letters attributed to Paul may have been written by others at a later date. The order in which the books appear in the canon thus bears no relation to the order in which they were written.

Theoretically, we should be able to trace the development of the Jesus movement (or at least those branches of it whose writings were preserved in the New Testament) by reading the books in the order in which they were composed. This, unfortunately, is not possible, simply because so much uncertainty exists about the dates of the books. As an introduction to the New Testament, this book will follow the approximate order of the Christian canon. A few exceptions are as follows: Mark, the earliest-written of the canonical gospels, precedes Matthew and Luke. The Acts of the Apostles follows the gospel of Luke. Luke-Acts was originally composed as a two-volume work and only later separated in order to create a compendium of four gospels. The gospel of John, meanwhile, bears a strong family resemblance to four other books, 1, 2, and 3 John and Revelation. These "Johannine" books will be examined in a separate section. In the New Testament, Paul's letters to his congregations appear approximately in order of length, from longest (Romans) to shortest (Philemon), followed by 1 and 2 Timothy and Titus, letters to his assistants in the field. I have chosen to group the letters in approximately chronological order. Issues of date and authorship will be included in the discussion of each book.

THE
SYNOPTIC GOSPELS

By 70 c.e. Jesus-revering groups had flourished—and been centers of controversy—for forty years. A generation earlier, Paul had followed other missionaries across the Mediterranean, teaching and preaching the messianic message. He wrote letters instructing congregations and their leaders, supplementing the message—"the gospel"—of Jesus' resurrection with new interpretations of Torah and guidelines for behavior and belief. Gentiles began joining the community; indeed, they did so in such numbers that their presence became a source of tension and adjustment for the young sect. In the 60s a bitter and prolonged revolt against Rome tore through Judea. Families were divided; fear and suspicion grew; Jesus' followers hoped that this at last might be the beginning of the end-time struggles that would vindicate them and usher in God's reign on earth.

Stories of Jesus continued to circulate among his followers, some by word of mouth, others in written form. The collected sayings of the Lord became standard in some circles, as did an account of the trial and death, or "passion" (from the Latin *passus,* suffering), of Jesus. With the passion account, Christian scribes created something new. Not a simple compilation of sayings or stories, the passion account was a sort of midrashic reflection on Jesus' death, a retelling of the story that included interpretive citations from scripture and added portentous symbols.

The reason for this early focus on Jesus' death was simple. Whereas Jesus' deeds and sayings could be treasured and remembered for their own sake, his death was an embarrassment, and as such a major obstacle to those who proclaimed him messiah. No texts and no traditions predicted anything but triumph for the messiah. Opposition, yes, but always opposition followed by victory. A messiah crucified by Rome was the very type of the failed messiah. And not only was he failed, he was still a liability. Roman soldiers continued to "keep the peace" in every land in which Jesus' followers gathered, and crucifixion was still a favored form of punishment. Jesus' crucifixion was thus the great conundrum, as Paul called it, the "stumbling block" of the earliest Christians. The need to finesse this embarrassing event fostered scriptural reflection and strategic interpretation from the very outset of the Christian experience.

To bridge the gap between messianic expectations of glory and the irreducible horror of Jesus' death, Christian scribes sought biblical images of righteous suffering, especially images that might link such suffering to the messiah. Several texts — texts that had long been associated with the suffering of Israel itself — were now interpreted by the Christians as messianic prophecies. The suffering servant songs of Isaiah 52–53 offered a model of God's servant despised and abused by all but exalted by God; Psalm 22 provided a detailed vignette in which evildoers taunt and torment the righteous one; and Zechariah 1:9–10 described a ruler who was humble and lowly. Such texts would have provided a conceptual lifeline for Jesus' followers: what happened was *not* unthinkable but had been foretold by the scriptures. God's chosen servant had suffered, but he had done so *according to a divine plan* and *for the sake of the people.* "He was wounded for our transgressions . . .; upon him was the punishment that made us whole" (Isa. 53:5).

· And so, in the decades following Jesus' crucifixion, unknown Christian scribes set about composing a midrashic, interpretive account of his death, representing his trial and suffering as the fulfillment of prophecy: the passion. Detail upon detail — spitting, striking, mocking, the dividing of his garments, his cry of desolation — were culled from ancient texts and woven into a densely symbolic narrative that ceaselessly pointed to Jesus as God's suffering, righteous one. Unlike true midrash, the rabbinic embellishment of biblical texts, the passion narrative is not a reworking of an original text. Rather, the "text" behind the passion account is the church's memory of Jesus' death. No one has preserved an unembellished version of the facts of Jesus' death. The lack of any ideologically neutral narrative means that we have no way of getting behind the symbolically rich narrative to a potential historical core. It may be, for example, that Jesus *did* cry out the words of Psalm 22, "My God, my God, why have you forsaken me?" If so, then this cry could have encouraged an author to add other details from the same psalm—the mocking and the divided garments. Alternatively, perhaps his garments *were* divided, and this led the author to focus the narrative on Psalm 22. No one knows how much of the passion account is symbolic and how much is literal. We know only that Jesus was crucified, and that his followers soon interpreted this profound abjection as his willing self-sacrifice, a sacrifice made "according to the scriptures."

Scholars generally consider the passion narrative one of the earliest Christian compositions (it is the only section of text shared almost word for word by Matthew, Mark, and Luke). Mark, the author of the earliest gospel, inherited this text and built his account around it. His gospel narrative continues the technique employed by the passion author, using biblical allusions to interpret the events of Jesus' life. The result is a seamless symbolic biography in which the distinction between event and interpretation is (quite intentionally) lost. This symbolic biography is called a *gospel,* literally the "good news" about Jesus. The "true" story of Jesus, from the Christian perspective, is precisely this midrashic interpretation, a story that explains not only what happened but why it matters.

Each of the canonical gospels combines three elements. First, and most simply, each incorporates what was known or presumed true about Jesus' life and death, including sayings and stories already preserved elsewhere in written form. Second, the gospels include scriptural (Septuagint) quotations and allusions crafted to reveal the significance of Jesus' deeds and words. Finally, they contain teachings specifically shaped, not for Jesus' original hearers, but for a later generation, the readers and hearers of each gospel account. This last, context-specific aspect of the gospels is plainly stated in the gospel of Luke. Luke announces that although many have, by his day, already written accounts of Jesus' life, his own account will provide "security" (*asphaleia*) for his patron, Theophilus. Luke's unselfconscious claim to have shaped his narrative according to his reader's needs makes it clear that the work was never conceived of as "just the facts." The gospel writers wrote for communities in crisis—one reeling from the events of the Roman war; one stinging from the larger Jewish community's rejection; one groping to articulate the role of Gentiles in God's new kingdom. Each gospel, while proclaiming a universal message, is simultaneously responding to the concerns of particular and diverse audiences. The authors of Matthew and Luke depended on a version of Mark's gospel for their basic story. Each, however, expanded Mark's gospel with additional material, and each shaped the narrative to address the specific concerns of his own community. Matthew, Mark, and Luke therefore contain highly interconnected narratives, and are generally referred to as the synoptic gospels, the gospels that see things together, or that invite comparison.

THE GOSPEL ACCORDING TO MARK

CHURCH TRADITION ASSIGNS each gospel to someone who knew Jesus personally, in Mark's case, to John Mark, the apostle Peter's assistant. Although this attribution is ancient, no substantial evidence supports it; the author is unknown. Scholars have long disputed the provenance of Mark's gospel, with Rome, Syria, and Galilee vying as probable locations. Mark's awareness of details connected with the Roman war, together with his insistence that the risen Jesus has gone to Galilee and must be sought there, has led scholars in recent years to favor a Galilean setting. The date of composition is either shortly before or shortly after the destruction of the temple in 70 C.E. The temple is the clear focus of Mark's apocalyptic expectation: all that Jesus suffered, all that his followers have undergone, and all that the Jewish people have endured will come to a head in the wake of the temple's destruction. Then the "Son of Man" will come in clouds "with great power and glory" (13:26) and begin God's just reign over the earth. This apocalypse is imminent. "There are some," says Jesus, "standing here who will not taste death until they see that the kingdom of God has come in power" (9:1). Apparently Mark writes at a time when some of Jesus' associates are still alive, and he expects the end before their death. The gospel attributed to Mark is stark, abrupt, and enigmatic. It resists understanding, and it does so by design. In Mark Jesus is followed by disciples who consistently earn his anger and frustration. They, as much as the enemies they fear, are hard of heart, blind, and faithless. Ultimately, they desert and deny him in his hour of need. The gospel writer seems to expect no better from his readers. "What I say to you," says Mark's Jesus, "I say to all: Keep awake! . . . Watch! . . . Let the reader understand!" Mark's gospel is permeated with warnings against the reader's all too apparent weakness. Whether in Jesus' hour of trial or in the desperate struggle against Rome, "You will all," says Jesus, "become deserters." Mark has not composed a pretty story but a tale in which divine power must tear apart the heavens, struggling against enemies human and divine to establish God's kingdom.

This dark writing begins as good news: "The beginning of the good news of Jesus the Messiah, the son of God" (1:1). The word *euangelion,* translated "good news" or "gospel," is superficially positive but is laden with intimations of the conflict to come. In antiquity the term was commonly used in official pronouncements—specifically, announcements of the birth or accession of an emperor. The birth of Augustus, for example, was hailed as the beginning of the *euangelion* of the son of God and savior of the world. People in the Roman world knew where to look for "saviors"—either to the gods or to the emperor, whom the gods sponsored. Mark's joyful announcement of a savior's birth is thus a confrontational opening. In the historical context of Roman domination, the plot has already been announced: the divine savior must contend against the human, the embodiment of worldly power. If Mark wrote at the height of the Jewish revolt against Rome, then his reader would readily have seen the implications of his announcement: the current war is the inevitable outcome of Jesus' birth a generation and more ago.

Mark's opening verse proclaims that God's power and presence have been authoritatively manifested in the world. This intrusion of God's power, says Mark, occurs in fulfillment of scripture: "as it is written in the prophet Isaiah" (1:2). In fact, the scripture Mark "cites" is an amalgam of texts from Exodus, Malachi, and Isaiah combined into a single oracle. The oracle announces that God's messenger is coming, a voice crying in the wilderness, "Prepare the way of the Lord." The texts Mark combines were already recognized as messianic prophecies in the first century, and so, when John the Baptist appears "in the wilderness," we understand him to be the forerunner of the messiah. In fact, John is depicted as the specific forerunner anticipated by Malachi: Elijah. We know this because we are told that John is "clothed with camel's hair, with a leather belt around his waist." He is, as it were, wearing an Elijah suit (2 Kings 1:8). And he announces that one "more powerful" than he is coming. The theme of "the stronger man" will dominate Mark's gospel, as Jesus proves stronger, not only than Elijah, but than Rome, Satan, and finally, death itself.

Son of God in Jewish Traditions

In the Hebrew Bible the phrase *son of God* can designate angels or lesser divinities (as in Gen. 6:1–4), but as a title it is used, as it was throughout the ancient Near East, to designate the ruling monarch. In 2 Samuel 7 God promises that an heir of David will reign perpetually and will be a "son" to God. Thus, any Davidic monarch could claim the titles son of David, messiah (or "anointed one"), and son of God—all titles ascribed in the gospels to Jesus. The king's divine sonship was not understood as a physical reality but as adoption or even rebirth, as indicated in the enthronement ritual of Psalm 2:7: "You are my son; today I have begotten you." Much early Jewish literature referred to the messiah as God's son—not surprisingly, given the messiah's role as king. In early Christian thought, traditions of the messiah as God's adopted son soon melded with Hellenistic traditions in which kings and heroes might be either literal children of gods and goddesses or human beings divinized after death. This hellenization of the ancient Israelite notion opened the way for the Christian understanding of the Trinity, in which Jesus shares God's personhood as "son."

Mark next introduces Jesus, who comes south from Galilee to be baptized by John. As Jesus comes up out of the water, the heavens are torn apart and we hear the first of three solemn announcements of his identity: a heavenly voice proclaims, "You are my beloved Son; with you I am well pleased" (1:11). Inexplicably, no sooner is Jesus told how pleased God is than "the Spirit" drives him out, like some unclean spirit, into the wilderness. Jesus spends forty days in the wilderness, an image evocative of Moses and Elijah, each of whom spent forty days in the wilderness preparing to meet God. Jesus, says Mark, was tempted by Satan. The nature of Satan's temptation is left unstated, but the reader understands that at the end of forty days Jesus, ministered to by angels, has emerged the victor. Already he is proving himself "the stronger man" and is equipped to prevail against the powers of Satan in this world.

Jesus returns to Galilee where, entering the synagogue on the sabbath, he astounds the people with his teaching and by performing exorcisms. The people wonder where he gets such power, but the demons already know: "What have you to do with us, Jesus of Nazareth? Have you come to destroy us? I know who you are—the Holy One of God!" (1:24). Spiritual powers, from God to the demons, recognize Jesus' authority, but earthly powers are not so inclined. Jesus goes to Capernaum, where some scribes (experts in Jewish law) accuse him of blasphemy, others, of eating with unclean companions, and the Pharisees, of breaking the laws of the sabbath. Jesus claims authority as the "Son of Man" to do good in any circumstances—healing in God's name, eating with sinners who repent, and picking grain to eat on the sabbath. New cloth, says he, should not be used to patch an old garment, lest the patch tear the garment when it shrinks. New wine demands new wineskins, lest the newly fermenting vintage burst the seasoned skins, which cannot expand to accommodate it. Jesus' analogies are vivid but puzzling, since it is not clear that he is teaching anything that should be called "new."

In the context of Mark's developing Christianity, however, the analogies of the cloth and the wineskins are highly provocative. Have the messianic communities already begun to "tear away" from the

fabric of Jewish life? Have older forms of Judaism proved unable to accommodate the heady mix of Christian proclamation? Jesus' analogies
suggest irreconcilable differences between the Jesus movement and the
rest of the Jewish world. New wine, says Jesus, *bursts* the old skins, so
that "the wine is lost and *so are the skins.*" Like the opponents he portrays, so Mark also sees a potential for Christian belief and practice to
destroy the tradition. Mark's point is not that Jesus is opposed to Torah
or tradition. On the contrary, he will later show Jesus advocating even
more stringent divorce laws than those of the Pharisees. When community leaders challenge Jesus again in chapters 10 and 11, he gives extraordinarily strict legal opinions. Mark's Jesus is not *opposed* to the law.
His position is more subversive than a simple abrogation of the law:
Mark claims that Jesus' authority actually outweighs that of the law.

The lines have been drawn between Jesus and those who claim authority over the Jewish community. Jesus next enters a synagogue
where a man with a withered hand awaits. "They watched him," says
Mark, "to see whether he would cure him on the sabbath, so that they
might accuse him. . . . Then he said to them, 'Is it lawful to do good or
to do harm on the sabbath, to save life or to kill?' " (3:3–4). Jesus heals
the man. In consummate irony, the Pharisees "immediately" conspire
with the Herodians (an otherwise unknown group) to "destroy him."
Mark none too subtly distinguishes between Jesus and the powers of
this world: Jesus' power to do good incites the leaders to use their
power to kill. Mark places the leaders on the side of the demons.

The demons, meanwhile, fall down before Jesus, shouting, "You are
the Son of God!" Jesus' family disagrees, siding instead with those who
say he is out of his mind, that is, possessed by a demon. The reader
knows that the demons, not the family, are correct. At this point some
otherwise unidentified scribes come up with their own interpretation
of Jesus' power: he can cast out demons because he is working for
Beelzebul, the prince of demons. This explanation seems plausible
enough on the face of it, since the demons are on a first-name basis with
Jesus. Jesus counters that if Satan is working against himself, then he is
about to fall, since neither a kingdom nor a house divided can long
stand. The saying would have carried a special sting in the Palestine of

Jesus' Siblings

All four canonical gospels make reference to Jesus' siblings, either his brothers (Mark 3:31–32; Matt. 12:46; Luke 8:19–20; John 2:12) or his brothers *and sisters* (Mark 6:3; Matt. 13:55–56). Only the brothers—James, Joseph, Judas, and Simon—are named (some gnostic texts also name Thomas as a brother of Jesus). All the gospel accounts suggest tension between Jesus and his family. Many later church traditions, as well as Paul (in 1 Cor. 9:5 and Gal. 1:19) and Acts (1:14), include Jesus' brothers, particularly James, as leaders in the early church. The New Testament texts seem to assume that Jesus' siblings are the sons and daughters of Mary and Joseph. As early as the second century, however, the view that Jesus' siblings were Joseph's children from an earlier marriage developed as a means of affirming the perpetual virginity of Mary. Modern Catholic interpreters generally translate the Greek *adelphos* as "cousin" for the same reason.

70 C.E., where disastrous infighting among the leaders of various rebel factions led to the fall of the "house" of God, the temple.

Beginning in chapter 4, Mark intersperses stories of Jesus' power and the leaders' opposition with scenes focusing on the twelve "disciples," Jesus' inner circle of followers. In Mark as elsewhere in the New Testament, the twelve disciples are also called apostles, or those who are sent as Jesus' emissaries. Chosen to participate in Jesus' mission, the disciples fail repeatedly. Nor is their failure unexpected, as Jesus makes clear in his first parable (4:3–9): the word of God, says Jesus, is like seed, some of which is sown on a path, some on rocky soil, some among thorns, and some on good soil. The seed sown on the path is snatched away by crows as soon as it falls, and represents listeners from whom Satan "takes away" the word. The rocky soil symbolizes those who cannot allow the word to take root, and who quickly fall away under persecution. The seed among the thorns represents believers whose worldly desires choke off the growth of God's word. Finally, the seed falling on good soil represents believers in whom God's word endures, grows, and bears fruit. The implications of this first parable are clear: simply hearing the word, however willingly, does not make one a follower. On the contrary, many factors, from wealth to persecution, will intervene to keep the number of true followers small. The disciples, as it turns out, will prove to be "rocky soil" in which Jesus' teachings must struggle to take root.

Repeatedly, Jesus calms a storm with a word or comes out walking on the water, and the disciples recoil in fear and confusion: "Who then is this, that even the wind and the sea obey him?" (4:41). Any demon could have told them, but they seem determined not to know. Jesus, however, continues to perform healings, exorcisms, and miracles designed as symbolic representations of his identity. He feeds a crowd of four thousand from a few loaves of bread, recalling Elijah's similar miracle. Next he feeds five thousand "in the desert," a setting that suggests Moses and the manna in the wilderness. Like Elijah, he raises a child whom others had thought dead. Repeatedly, the disciples fail to comprehend what he is about. "Do you still not perceive or understand? Are your hearts hardened? Do you have eyes, and fail to see? Do you have ears, and fail to hear? And do you not remember?" (8:17–18). Those with the most reason to see and accept Jesus have become dull of hearing and incapable of remembering his signs of power.

The identity of Mark's congregation—the dull-eared followers for whom the book was written—is tantalizingly obscure. They are often assumed to be Gentiles because in 7:11 Mark explains a Jewish custom for his readers. Mark's subtle and allusive use of biblical texts, however, suggests an audience capable of following his nuanced references to the Bible. Moreover, Jesus says his followers will be handed over to councils and beaten in synagogues, a prophecy apparently describing the experience of Mark's own community. A person beaten in the synagogue was a person subject to Jewish communal discipline, that is, a Jew. Mark's distinctive portrayal of the disciples as failures and deserters also seems to require a Jewish audience. Mark writes his gospel in a time of terror and confusion, when brother will betray brother, a time when messianic hopes foster vainglorious images of triumph—and when messiahs are routinely being wiped out. He writes to followers who seek a soft and reassuring way, who, like Jesus' original disciples, would rather decide who gets which throne in heaven than remain faithful to the messiah here on earth. Writing for the fearful and faithless followers of his own day, Mark writes a gospel in which Jesus' original disciples are as bad as Mark's readers.

The plight of the disciples would seem hopeless were it not for hints of redemption that Mark builds into the narrative. The theme of Jesus healing the blind, in particular, serves as a key to the disciples' (and the readers') condition. Throughout Mark's narrative, blindness symbolizes obtuseness and opposition to the gospel. Jesus depicts those "on the outside" as blind, but the disciples, too, are regularly castigated for their failure to see the obvious: "Have you eyes and fail to see?" Over the course of the story, Jesus gives sight to many blind people, but one in particular deserves closer attention. In 8:22 a blind man is brought to Jesus for healing. Rather than healing him by word or by touch, as in other passages, Jesus puts his own saliva on the man's eyes. The man, however, is only partially healed. Asked whether he can see, he responds, "I can see people, but they look like trees walking." Jesus lays his hands on the man's eyes a second time, the man's sight is restored, and he sees "everything clearly." Some, it seems, require more than a single miracle.

Mark's story of the twice-healed blind man is located strategically between two accounts of the disciples' obtuseness. In 8:13–21, they fail to comprehend either Jesus' miracles or his teachings. Then, in 8:31 they refuse to hear the one thing they most need to understand: "He began to teach them that the Son of Man must undergo great suffering, and be rejected by the elders, the chief priests, and the scribes, and be killed, and after three days rise again." The disciples, however, had signed up to see "the Son of Man coming in the clouds" with the angels, not suffering and dying. Peter "rebukes" Jesus for his talk of suffering and death—this is no way for the messiah to act. Jesus, however, responds that any who want to be his disciples must "take up their cross and follow." Discipleship involves suffering. Those who are ashamed of Jesus' degradation will be rejected when the Son of Man "comes in the glory of his Father with the holy angels." The gospel is about both humiliation *and* exaltation. Nor are the disciples offered a "take it or leave it" sort of deal. It is too late to back out. Those who are ashamed of Jesus' suffering now will face his judgment when he comes in glory.

At this point Mark has laid out his essential claims about Jesus: he is sent to be both the earthly messiah and the apocalyptic "Son of Man" whose coming will herald the end of the world. Of the two main streams of Jewish expectation of divine intervention, Mark has chosen to employ both. Jesus is both the son of David whom tradition claimed would be heralded by Elijah, and at the same time the cosmic Son of Man and judge of the world. Mark concludes the first half of his gospel with a vision that consolidates this image of Jesus' identity:

> Jesus took with him Peter and James and John, and led them up a high mountain apart, by themselves. And he was transfigured before them, and his clothes became dazzling white. . . . And there appeared to them Elijah with Moses, who were talking with Jesus. . . . Then a cloud overshadowed them, and from the cloud there came a voice, "This is my Son, the Beloved; listen to him!" Suddenly when they looked around, they saw no one with them any more, but only Jesus. (Mark 9:2–8)

Like Moses and Elijah before him, Jesus ascends a mountain where he encounters God. And indeed, Moses and Elijah are already there waiting for him. The presence of the two prophets confirms Jesus' identity as the messiah. Although Elijah was designated as the messiah's forerunner, Moses was to be the messiah's model. Moses predicted that after his death God would "raise up a prophet like me" (Deut. 18:15), a statement that in Jesus' day was considered a messianic prophecy; the messiah would be the prophet like Moses. And just as Moses had prophesied that the people would listen to this later prophet, so God commands the disciples, "This is my Son, the Beloved; listen to him!" It is hard to imagine a clearer message.

The disciples, however, don't get it. Twice more they refuse to hear Jesus' straightforward announcement that he will be killed, turning instead to arguments over which of them will have the greatest honor when Jesus is glorified. Mark's point, of course, is not really what dunderheads the original disciples were. He is writing not only *for* his readers but *about* them as well. The foibles of Jesus' first disciples become an object lesson for Mark's beleaguered community. Mark's community seems to be losing heart over its suffering—rejected by other Jews, in danger from Rome, and with no cosmic triumph in sight. Just as Mark's Jesus must teach his disciples to endure the hardships ahead, so Mark is training his own disheartened followers to keep the faith.

In 10:46 Mark begins his account of Jesus' last days. The narrative is dense with messianic symbolism. Jesus approaches Jerusalem "lowly, seated on an ass," as foretold by the prophet Zechariah. The crowds spread palm branches on the road and call out the blessing of Psalm 118, "Blessed is the one who comes in the name of the Lord," and they cry "Hosanna" (Hebrew *hoshianu*), literally, "Save us!" Arriving in Jerusalem, Jesus enters the temple and begins to drive out those who are "selling and buying" there. Jesus' action is extreme, since some form of exchange was necessary if worshipers were to obtain the requisite animals for sacrifices. The exchange, however, created an opportunity for temple officials to gouge worshipers. Jesus overturns the money-changing tables, quoting segments from Isaiah and Jeremiah, "My house shall be called a house of prayer for all the nations" (Isa. 56:7), but "you have made it a den of bandits" (Jer. 7:11). The prophetic quotation situates Jesus in a number of respects. First, his anger over abuse of the temple mirrors that of Jeremiah, thus aligning him with the great tradition, rather than casting him as a rebel against it. Second, his use of the Isaiah passage strategically points out that Isaiah had already foreseen that "all nations" would come to participate in Israel's worship. That is, Jesus' followers, by including Gentiles in their number, were fulfilling the temple's role in a way that the temple itself had not. Finally, the reference to the temple as a house of "bandits" was surely a pointed one in the wake of the first revolt. The first century, particularly the late first century, was a time in which bandits and revolutionaries were nearly interchangeable categories in Palestine. In fact, Eleazar ben Simon, whose rebel faction occupied the temple from the winter of 68 until its destruction in 70, had been the leader of a group of Galilean bandits. Jesus' charge that the temple had become a den of bandits could not have failed to remind Mark's readers of the temple under literal bandits in their own day.

Mark goes on to describe Jesus' disciples, Galileans in the big city, admiring the grand buildings of the temple complex. The disciples' impressionability sets up Jesus' prediction of a grim future. "Not one stone," says Jesus, "will be left here upon another; all will be thrown down!" (13:2). Whether Mark is writing at a time when Roman victory has become inevitable, or in the immediate aftermath of the temple's destruction, Jesus' prophecy cuts to the heart of Mark's audience. Jesus now begins an extended discourse describing the events of "those days"—Mark's days—in apocalyptic terms. They will hear of "wars and rumors of war," earthquake and famine, the sun will be darkened, and false messiahs will lead many astray. Moreover, Jesus' followers will be "handed over to councils" and "beaten in synagogues," put to death and hated. "But the one who endures to the end will be saved" (13:13). As a final sign, "the desolating sacrilege will be set up where it ought not to be." Mark's aside, "Let the reader understand," suggests that Jesus' message was all too clear in his own day.

Whatever specific abomination Mark equates with "the desolating sacrilege" (possibly Roman standards bearing the image of the emperor), the phrase is taken from Daniel's vision of the last days (9:27; 11:31; 12:11). Daniel, says Jesus, was correct. When the desolating sacrilege is set up, then "they will see 'the Son of Man coming in clouds' with great power and glory. . . . Truly I say to you, this generation will not pass away until all these things have taken place." The very immanence of Roman victory and the suffering of Mark's community serve to confirm Jesus' words. Now more than ever they must follow him through suffering and on to glory.

Mark moves immediately from Jesus' explicit predictions of apocalyptic glory to the account of his death, an account he overlays with biblical symbolism in order to argue that Jesus did not die because of the systematic cruelty of the Romans; rather, he went "according to the scriptures." Jesus celebrates the seder meal with his disciples, employing the symbols of the exodus to represent his own sacrificial death: his blood, not that of the lamb, will serve as a sign of the covenant. Jesus observes that his betrayer is "dipping bread into the bowl with me," thus fulfilling the psalmist's prediction that "one who ate of my bread has lifted the heel against me" (Ps. 41:8). "For," says Jesus, "the Son of Man goes *as it is written of him.*" So also at the meal's conclusion, Jesus announces, "You will all become deserters." Why? Because "it is written, 'I will strike the shepherd, and the sheep will be scattered' " (14:27). Jesus goes off to pray, the Romans arrest him, and the disciples flee, becoming deserters.

At the moment of Jesus' arrest, Mark alone of all the gospels mentions "a certain young man" who "was following him, wearing nothing but a linen cloth. They caught hold of him, but he left the linen cloth and ran off naked" (14:51–52). The young man is unnamed, and his presence unexplained, at least for the moment. His naked panic could represent that of any of Jesus' followers, whether of Jesus' own day or of Mark's.

Jesus next goes through a series of trials before the high priest, the Sanhedrin, and Pontius Pilate. The legal irregularities and historical improbabilities of the trials as portrayed in the gospels (including the trial's highly unlikely setting on the first day of Passover) are well documented, and each gospel depicts Jesus undergoing a different combination of hearings, floggings, and humiliation. Mark begins with a trial before the high priest, "all the chief priests, the elders and the scribes," and "the council" (Sanhedrin). Only false and conflicting accusations can be found, until the high priest himself asks, "Are you the Messiah, the Son of the Blessed One?" Mark's reader is already aware of the answer, since God has named Jesus his beloved son, not once but twice in the narrative. Jesus answers, "I am," but then quotes Daniel's apocalyptic vision of "the Son of Man" coming with the clouds and seated at God's right hand. At this, the high priest tears his robes as a sign that he has just witnessed blasphemy. The notion that Jesus' claim to be God's earthly agent constitutes blasphemy is puzzling, since Jewish tradition includes many such agents, among them Moses, Elijah, and the prophets. The charge of blasphemy seems to amount to nothing more than the high priest taking offense at what he sees as Jesus' false presumption.

The council rules that Jesus deserves death and refers his case to the Roman prelate, Pilate. Pilate is not interested in Jesus' putative blasphemy, asking instead, "Are you the King of the Jews [or Judeans]?" (15:2). Pilate's concern is whether Jesus has set himself up in opposition to Rome. Rome has dealt with such kings of the Jews before. Jesus gives an enigmatic answer, or perhaps one whose meaning has become obscured over the centuries: "You say so." The answer may be either affirmative ("You said it!") or evasive ("*You* say so [but not I]"). In either case, the proper response from Rome is clear. The native leadership accuses a popular figure of instigating sedition against Rome, and he does not deny the charges. Crucifixion, the standard punishment for sedition, is in order.

Curiously, Mark shows a more tempered Pilate than one might expect—certainly a milder character than that described by the first-century chroniclers Josephus and Philo. Mark claims that Pilate was accustomed to *release* a prisoner by popular request every year at Passover. Passover, the festival of liberation, was the most volatile time of the year, when Roman troops were in Jerusalem in force to "keep the peace." Pilate's "custom," which is attested nowhere outside the gospels, seems unlikely in the extreme. Pilate suggests to the crowd that he release Jesus, but they call instead for a certain Barabbas, whose name, ironically, means "son of the father," and who is said to have "committed murder during the insurrection." Barabbas is almost certainly inserted as a sort of anti-Jesus, a true seditionist but a false "son of the father." Throughout his trial scene, Mark exonerates both the crowds and Pilate, stressing that it was the chief priests who instigated the crowd to call for Jesus' crucifixion. In a move entirely out of character for either Roman prelates in general or Pilate in particular, Pilate bows to pressure from the priests. Jesus is flogged (a standard prelude to crucifixion) and crucified. The *titulus,* the sign designating the crime for which Jesus is crucified, reads, "The King of the Jews," ironically labeling him with his correct messianic title.

Mark's portrayal of the crucifixion makes continual allusions to Psalm 22—the mocking of the crowds, their sarcastic suggestion that God should deliver him, the casting of lots over his garments, and Jesus' cry to God, "Why have you forsaken me?" all find their parallels in the psalm. Mark uses the psalm to send two messages to the reader. First, Jesus' death happened "according to the scriptures," as a part of God's plan. Second, anyone familiar with this psalm (or who takes the trouble to look it up) knows that the sufferer's cry of abandonment is not the end of the story. On the contrary, God hears the cry of the sufferer, at which point "all the families of the earth" turn to God in worship (Ps. 22:27). Jesus' death in agony was merely the prelude to God's deliverance of "all the families of the earth."

At the point of Jesus' death the curtain separating the Holy of Holies (the inner sanctum) from the rest of the temple is torn in two. The episode is clearly symbolic, though exactly what it symbolizes is not clear. The tearing of garments in mourning is an ancient Jewish practice (see, e.g., Job 1:20), and the torn curtain may represent God's own grief at the death of his chosen one. Alternatively, because the curtain formed a barrier separating the divine presence from the mundane world, the tearing of the curtain could represent the end of any separation between God and the people. Finally, the destroyed curtain has been understood as prefiguring the destruction of the temple in 70 C.E. Whatever its precise significance, the torn curtain recalls the "tearing open" of the heavens at Jesus' baptism. Like the darkness at noon and the earthquake accompanying Jesus' agony, the curtain attests that Jesus' death is of cosmic significance.

Mark reports that one Joseph of Arimathea goes to Pilate to request permission to bury Jesus. The request would have been extraordinary, since one of the goals of crucifixion was to dishonor the body and display it, as a deterrent to future rebellions. Mark is careful to note that Joseph is "a respected member of the council," perhaps by way of explaining Pilate's acquiescence. Jesus is buried in a rock-hewn tomb, with a stone rolled against the opening.

The ending of Mark's gospel (at 16:8) is undoubtedly strange. In antiquity its strangeness resulted in the addition of various alternative endings designed to bring Mark into line with the other gospel accounts. Modern scholarly consensus is that the ending's strangeness is intentional. Jesus dies and is buried on Friday, before the beginning of the sabbath. On Sunday, after the sabbath has ended, three of Jesus' women followers arrive with spices to perform a rudimentary embalming and so complete the burial process. When the women arrive at the tomb, they find it already opened. Within is "a young man, dressed in a white robe, sitting on the right side; and they were alarmed" (16:5).

Who is this mysterious young man? Is he related to the "young man" who left his linen cloth and ran away naked at the time of Jesus' arrest? Or is he meant to recall the demon-possessed man of Mark 5 who, being healed, is found "sitting, clothed and in his right mind"? Fear, nakedness, insanity, desertion—all emblems of our human frailty—have been transmuted into an image of wholeness. Jesus, however, is not here. The young man tells the women that Jesus is going before them into Galilee, and that they in turn must go tell the disciples. But, says Mark, "they went out and fled from the tomb, for terror and amazement had seized them; and they said nothing to anyone, for they were afraid." Following an initial image of healing, the gospel ends in fear unconquered and a commission unfulfilled. The final irony, of course, is that although the last we see of the women is their mad flight, we know that somehow, somewhere, they too came to "their right minds," fulfilled their commission, and told the story. The existence of Mark's gospel is the proof.

What has Mark accomplished in this first of the full-scale gospel narratives? He tells a dark tale, in which a stark and unapproachable Jesus gathers a band of followers, knowing from the outset that they will prove faithless. Proclaiming the "good news" that the kingdom of God has drawn near, first John, the herald of the kingdom, then Jesus himself are slaughtered by the authorities. It is a brutal yet mundane story, given the repeated and ruthless dashing of Jewish hopes under Roman rule. Messianic hopefuls appear, gather a following, and suffer a shameful and agonizing death. Why do we need to hear this tale?

For Mark's gospel to have been "good news" to his community, they must have been in desperate straits indeed. Most likely they had already fulfilled Jesus' prediction that his followers would be "handed over to councils" and "beaten in synagogues," even tried "before governors and kings" (13:9). That is, members of the community had undergone discipline within their synagogues and, at times, been turned in to the secular (Roman) authorities. And, we may infer, their loyalty under pressure had been less than exemplary. "You will all become deserters" (14:27). The disciples have proved unworthy of their master. Small wonder that Mark's gospel ends with doubt rather than certainty, and with fear instead of joy. Nor, in the last days of the revolt, would Mark's followers have been alone in their fear and despair. Revolutionaries, Pharisees, Sadducees, Essenes, and the sect called Christians all were powerless to stop the bloody chaos of ongoing revolt and Roman reprisals.

In the maelstrom of the First Revolt, Mark writes to create a new coherence, a new symbolic world wrought from the symbols of the world's end. The heavens have been torn open, the temple destroyed. But far from signifying the end of God's reign, these are the very portents of its beginning. The human world is blind to God's work in its midst, but human blindness, even hatred and desertion, are powerless to impede his coming. The stronger man has arrived; Satan has been bound; the one who fled in fear is healed and seated at the right hand. Jesus' followers need only to abandon their fear and follow the one who goes before them into God's kingdom. Like the rabbis, who would spend the next two centuries reclaiming and reshaping Jewish symbols in the wake of the temple's fall, so Mark also salvages the Jewish symbolic world in the wake of the same disaster. Unlike the rabbis, Mark is not creating a vision for the long run. On the contrary, the messiah has come and the days are short.

THE GOSPEL ACCORDING TO MATTHEW

THE GOSPEL ACCORDING TO MATTHEW is frequently considered the most Jewish of the four gospels. The author was Jewish, the congregation was either predominantly or exclusively Jewish, and the community's members seem to have been concerned with how they were perceived in the synagogues they evidently continued to attend. Yet Matthew's gospel comes as something of a shock for the Jewish reader. In Matthew Jesus not only spars with Pharisees; he calls them children of hell, blind guides, blind fools, and hypocrites. Jewish crowds urge Pontius Pilate to crucify Jesus, wildly calling for his blood to "be on us and on our children!" (27:25), a cry that would echo through generations of Christian persecution of Jews. It is hard to imagine a more *anti-*Jewish account than this "most Jewish" gospel.

What can account for the harshly anti-Jewish tone adopted by the thoroughly Jewish community in which this gospel was written? The answer takes us to the heart of early Christian experience. Matthew's community, more than that of any other gospel, is enraged at the larger Jewish community precisely because it feels (probably correctly) that it has been disowned by other Jews. Matthew's gospel sounds so anti-Jewish not because the author sees Jews as evil, but because it represents a volley in an ongoing battle over whether Jesus' followers have forfeited their identity as Jews. Matthew's harangues against "the Jews" express his community's pain over the widening separation threatening an unwanted divorce between them and the rest of the Jewish world.

The location and date of Matthew's composition are usually surmised on the basis of his apparent engagement with both Gentiles and "the synagogue next door." Matthew's gospel seems to reflect an urban environment with significant populations of both Jews and Gentiles. Syrian Antioch is the most common guess, although northern Galilee is equally possible. The date is around 85 or 90 C.E., after the destruction of the Jerusalem temple but before a definitive parting of the ways between Judaism and Christianity.

More than any other gospel, Matthew singles out the Pharisees as the archenemies of Jesus. Pharisaic teachings and conduct are dissected, opposed, and challenged. The Pharisees are above all condemned as hypocrites. Matthew's preoccupation with the Pharisees implies that his community lived in an area where the Pharisees exercised considerable influence. Community members have been "flogged in their synagogues"; that is, they have undergone corrective discipline *as members of Pharisaic synagogues.* As in all the gospels, the ceaseless antagonism between Jesus and the Pharisees is anachronistic, a retrojection of conflicts between Jesus' followers and the Pharisees after the fall of the temple in 70 C.E. It is, however, equally anachronistic to see in Matthew a conflict between "early Judaism" and "early Christianity." Matthew presupposes Christians and Pharisees as two Jewish sects competing to offer the most authentic version of Jewish life and belief. Matthew's rhetoric against the Pharisees is fierce for this reason, and for one other: Matthew realizes that Christians have already lost the battle. All Matthew's threats and fulminations, culminating in an announcement that the kingdom of God will be taken away from this nation and given to another, acknowledge that, in the end, his community's future will lie among the Gentiles. The parting is no less bitter for being inescapable.

Christian tradition attributes the gospel's writing to Matthew the tax collector, one of Jesus' original disciples mentioned in 10:3. This eyewitness attribution, together with the gospel's extensive sections of Jesus' teachings, made Matthew the favorite gospel of many early church fathers. The church's privileging of Matthew included its wholesale acceptance of both the author's brutal excoriation of the Pharisees (generalized to include all Jews) and his claim that responsibility for the death of Jesus lay upon the Jews and their children. The gospel most intent on defending the young sect's Jewishness has probably contributed most to Christianity's abuse of the Jews.

Matthew begins his gospel with a rather quaint nod to tradition: a genealogy of Jesus modeled on the "begats" of the Hebrew Bible. Matt. 1:2–16 is based loosely on 1 Chron. 3:1–3, but with the generations juggled in order to divide Jewish history into three distinct, fourteen-generation epochs: from Abraham to David, from David to the exile, and from the exile to the birth of the messiah. Matthew seeks to demonstrate numerologically (a practice called *gematria* in Hebrew) that the moment for the messiah's birth has arrived.

In addition to demonstrating the cosmically correct timing of Jesus' birth, Matthew's genealogy includes a bit of damage control. Traditionally, such a list included only fathers and sons. Matthew inserts the names of four *mothers:* Tamar, Rahab, Ruth, and "the wife of Uriah." All four are known in biblical tradition as foreigners who had suspect sexual liaisons with Israelites—Tamar, a Canaanite, who posed as a prostitute and slept with her father-in-law, Judah; Rahab, another Canaanite, who *was* a prostitute; Ruth, a Moabite, who spent the night with Boaz on the threshing floor; and Bathsheba, "wife of Uriah the Hittite" and lover of King David. Four mothers of the Jewish people (in tradition Rahab marries Joshua), all of disputed virtue but honored in Jewish tradition, pave the way for the birth of Jesus—to Mary, a suspected adulteress. Unlike Luke's account, which centers on God's promises to Mary, Matthew's story focuses on Joseph and his all-too-reasonable suspicions about Mary's unexplained pregnancy. Ultimately, Joseph's doubts are assuaged by an angel, who reassures him that the child is of divine origin and instructs him on how to proceed. The gospel's careful defense of Mary's virtue suggests that rumors about Jesus' illegitimacy circulated in Matthew's day.

The Virgin Birth

Matthew's and Luke's gospels preserve the tradition that Jesus' mother was a betrothed virgin who became pregnant by means of God's spirit. Matthew stresses Joseph's incredulity, perhaps as a means of addressing the reader's own natural doubts, but presents the birth as the fulfillment of prophecy: "A virgin shall conceive and bear a son" (Isa. 7:14, LXX). Early Christians, reading the Septuagint of Isaiah, would readily see it as prophesying a future miracle. In fact, however, the Septuagint does not follow the Hebrew, which reads, "The young woman is pregnant [or 'will conceive'] and will bear a son." That is, whereas Isaiah was referring to a young woman (presumed not to be a virgin) of his acquaintance, the Septuagint posits an as-yet-unknown virgin. In the Hellenistic context of the first century, portents and miracles (including divine impregnation of otherwise virgin women) were frequently said to accompany the birth of great sages and leaders; Isaiah's prophecy, in the Septuagint form, was therefore appropriated as a prophecy of Jesus.

Every important event in Matthew takes place "to fulfill the scripture." By far the most prolific quoter among the gospel writers, Matthew is intent on certifying that Jesus is, beyond any possible doubt, the messiah foretold by the prophets. Writing as a Jew, for Jews, he seeks to bolster the identity of a sect that finds itself increasingly at the margins of Judaism. His birth narrative, for example, includes a series of vignettes unique to his gospel and designed to place Jesus squarely at the center of Jewish messianic expectations. Jesus was born at the right time (fourteen generations after the exile) and under the right circumstances ("Behold, a virgin shall conceive . . ."). Already at his birth the Gentiles, wise men from the east, found it written in the very stars that a new "king of the Jews" had been born. Asked where the messiah was to be born, Israel's own "chief priests and scribes" testified that Bethlehem, Jesus' birthplace, was the spot designated by the prophets.

Building on his presentation of the birth of Jesus as the birth of the messiah, Matthew introduces a new theme: Jesus as a second Moses. When Herod the king hears from the Babylonian wise men (magi) that a new king has been born, he emulates the pharaoh of the exodus story, ordering all the young children of Bethlehem to be killed. Herod may be evil, but he is no fool; *he* is wise enough to believe the story the wise men bring him. Jesus' parents must save their infant from the evil pharaoh *redivivus*. Ironically, they do so by fleeing to Egypt. Why Egypt? To fulfill (of course) what had been spoken by the prophet, "Out of Egypt I have called my son" (Hos. 11:1). Like Moses, the messiah must come out of Egypt to save the people. Herod soon dies, and Mary and Joseph return home, moving north to Nazareth. Why? To fulfill the saying that "he will be called a Nazorean" (Matt. 2:23).

Matthew now introduces John the Baptist (or baptizer), who "appears" in the wilderness, fulfilling Isaiah's prophecy about "the voice of one crying in the wilderness, 'Prepare the way of the Lord' " (Matt. 3:3; Isa. 40:3). The Lord, in this case, is not God, but Jesus. Matthew's baptism scene is based on Mark's but reworked to introduce the religious conflict that will form a leitmotif in his gospel. Both Jesus and the Pharisees come to John for baptism, here a symbol of both purification and repentance. John rejects the Pharisees' show of repentance as hypocrisy, but Jesus, *despite* his manifest purity, undergoes the ritual in order to "fulfill all righteousness" (3:15). The reader doesn't need to guess whose side Matthew is on. The putative difference between "the righteousness of the Pharisees" (5:20) and that of Jesus symbolizes the competition between Pharisees and Jewish Christians in Matthew's own day.

Having outlined his claim that Jesus is the new Moses, Matthew demonstrates Jesus' authority as a teacher of Torah. Chapters 5–7 consist of a single speech, commonly known as the Sermon on the Mount. Matthew seems to share a view expressed in the Dead Sea Scrolls that the messiah will have authority over the law. In contradistinction to the Pharisees, who were promulgating the sages' *interpretations* of Torah (the Oral Torah), Matthew presents the Torah of the messiah. "*You* follow the teachings of the sages? *We* follow the teachings of the messiah himself!" From a modern perspective, Matthew's bid to trump rabbinic authority seems almost ludicrous—placing the claims of a local messianic pretender against all of rabbinic Judaism. But such a perspective is anachronistic. In Matthew's day rabbinic tradition was very much a work in progress; rabbinic authority, even more so. Matthew was not resisting already established rabbinic authority but countering the rabbis' bid for authority as arbiters of Jewish law. In this context it is entirely plausible that Matthew's community would consider "the teachings of the messiah" more than a match for the teachings of the sages.

Jesus, the new Moses, prepares to teach the people by ascending "the mountain." From this Sinai-esque locale he presents the people with covenant blessings and with instruction. Jesus sets forth nine "beatitudes," literally, attributes that make one "happy" (Greek *makarios*). The list—blessed are the merciful, the poor in spirit, the peacemakers, the pure in heart, those who hunger and thirst for righteousness—upholds traditional biblical virtues such as mercy and righteousness but emphasizes the *internal* purity of those who receive God's favor. Jesus follows his list of blessings with a discussion of Mosaic law: "Do not think that I have come to abolish the law or the prophets" (5:17). This is precisely what many in Matthew's day *did* think (and, for that matter, what many continue to think), and beneath Jesus' words we hear Matthew's instructions to his community: "Don't buy into the accusation that we have abandoned the law and the prophets!" On the contrary, claims Jesus, "I have come not to abolish but to fulfill." Here is the core of Matthew's argument: Jesus "fulfills" the demands and the expectations of Jewish law and prophecy. Matthew has painstakingly sought to demonstrate that Jesus' birth and life take place "to fulfill what was written." Jesus himself is eager to "fulfill all righteousness." This is not, Matthew insists, an outlaw movement. Jesus fulfills all righteousness, but does so from the perspective of God's beloved son, the one who understands not only the law but the intention of the One who gave it.

Faced with Pharisaic criticisms of his community's observance, Matthew sets out to prove that it is *Pharisaic* observance that falls short

THE SYNAGOGUE ROOTS OF THE LORD'S PRAYER

The Lord's Prayer, which appears in slightly different forms in Matt. 6:9–13 and Luke 11:2–4, is the central prayer of all Christian denominations. Remarkably, this "most Christian" prayer is closely related to the central prayers of Jewish liturgy, especially the kaddish. Beginning with a call to sanctify God's name ("hallowed be thy name") and continuing with a request for God's will to be done and God's kingdom established on earth, the Lord's Prayer closely follows the contours of the kaddish: "May [God's] great name be hallowed, in the world whose creation He willed; May His kingdom soon prevail, in our own day." While the kaddish itself was and is a communal prayer, similar prayers (some including the request to "deliver us from evil") are recommended for private devotion in the Palestinian Talmud.

of God's standards. "Unless your righteousness exceeds that of the scribes and Pharisees," says Jesus, "you will never enter the kingdom of heaven" (5:20). Jesus illustrates this "greater righteousness" by interpreting five central tenets of biblical law: "You shall not kill," "You shall not commit adultery," "You shall not bear false witness," "An eye for an eye and a tooth for a tooth," and "You shall love your neighbor as yourself." In each case Jesus makes the commandment *more* demanding by requiring not only purity of actions but purity of motive as well. Thus, one must not even *feel* anger or lust, far less commit the actual crimes of murder or adultery. On the contrary, if someone strikes your right cheek, you must offer your left; if someone compels you (as Roman soldiers had the right to do) to carry a burden for one mile, you must carry it for two. If someone takes your coat, you must give your cloak as well—quite possibly leaving you stark naked! Jesus concludes his call to absolute virtue by restating the levitical basis of purity: "You shall be holy, for I, the Lord, am holy" (Lev. 19:2). Even this demand is sharpened in Jesus' reformulation: "Be perfect, therefore, as your heavenly Father is perfect" (5:48).

If this is what Jesus taught, one could hardly accuse him of abrogating the demands of Torah. Well might Jesus claim that such righteousness exceeds that of the scribes and Pharisees; it exceeds all limits of human virtue. But why teach unattainable ideals? In fact, Jesus' teachings are not much different from those of other Jewish sages of his day. Jesus' elder contemporary, the rabbi Hillel, taught, "What is hateful to you do not do to your neighbor; that is the whole Torah . . . go and learn it" (*b. Shabb.* 31a). Jesus' summary of "the law and the prophets" is similar: "Do to others as you would have them do to you" (7:12). Hillel's comment on the whole Torah, while simple on the surface, carries a barb—"go and learn it." The rabbi's point is not merely that one should *study* the Torah but that one's life must be spent "going and learning" how to treat others both justly and kindly. Anyone who has learned this has learned "the whole of Torah." Jesus' teaching carries a similar simplicity and a similar edge: merely be perfect, as God is perfect. If God "sends rain on the righteous and on the unrighteous," you must do likewise. What else can it mean to give to others as you would have them give to you? Both Jesus and Hillel offer impossible teachings to foster both good deeds and humility.

Matthew's connection between the teaching of Hillel and that of Jesus is striking. While any historical relationship between Hillel and Jesus is unlikely (Hillel probably lived earlier than Jesus), the relationship between Hillel and *Matthew* seems clearer. Hillel was one of the sages upon whose teachings the rabbis (in Matthew, the Pharisees) sought to build. As such, one might expect Matthew to pit Jesus' authority *against* Hillel's (as others may well have done). Matthew, however, wants to make the case that Jesus contradicts neither the law nor the prophets, *nor even the highest ideals of Pharisaism.* "Do whatever they teach you," says Jesus, "but do not do as they do, for they do not practice what they teach" (23:3). Matthew wants to show that Jesus and Hillel taught the same thing—that "knowing" the law is easier than living it. "Not everyone," says Jesus, "who says to me, 'Lord, Lord,' will enter the kingdom of heaven, but only the one who does the will of my

Father in heaven" (7:21). Matthew's goal is not to disprove Pharisaic teaching but to discredit the Pharisees around him as hypocrites and, in the process, to co-opt their growing influence. Everything the Pharisees teach, says Matthew, Jesus taught better. Matthew's conclusion to Jesus' teaching underscores the point: Jesus taught the crowds "as one having authority, and not as their scribes."

Whereas the Sermon on the Mount (a text unique to Matthew, but with a loose parallel in Luke's Sermon on the Plain) was designed to demonstrate Jesus' *authority* as a teacher of Torah, in chapters 8–16 Matthew relates healings and other miracles that emphasize his divinely given *power*. As soon as Jesus descends from the mountain, he is met in rapid succession by a leper, a man whose servant is ill, the apostle Peter's sick mother, two demoniacs, and a man who is paralyzed. All are healed "to fulfill what had been spoken through the prophet Isaiah, 'He took our infirmities and bore our diseases.' " The Pharisees accuse him of blasphemy, which, in the context of Jesus' acts of power and compassion, has the ring of sour grapes. Jesus goes out and eats with "tax collectors and sinners," offering them healing in the form of acceptance, and providing the Pharisees with another chance to grumble. "Go," Jesus says to his critics, "and learn what this means, 'I desire mercy, not sacrifice' " (9:13). Jesus is quoting Hos. 6:6, a verse he will cite again in Matt. 12:7 in a dispute over sabbath observance. Hosea's call for "mercy, not sacrifice" is also cited in the rabbinic *Aboth de Rab. Nathan* (11a) in a discussion of how to compensate for the lack of sacrifices after the destruction of the temple. Like the citation of Hillel above, Jesus' use of the verse demonstrates that he *agreed* with Pharisaic principles: the point is not ritual observance but human compassion. Jesus follows up this teaching by going out and healing another five people.

As in the other gospels, Jesus continues for several chapters healing, teaching, and having caustic exchanges with the Pharisees. Matthew's account, however, includes several distinctive features. First, Jesus moves from being the authoritative *teacher* of Torah to being its virtual embodiment. Claiming that "no one knows the Father except the Son and anyone to whom the Son chooses to reveal him," he proclaims:

> Come to me, all you that are weary and are carrying heavy bur-
> dens, and I will give you rest. Take my yoke upon you and learn
> from me; for I am gentle and humble in heart, and you will find
> rest for your souls. For my yoke is easy, and my burden is light.
> (Matt. 11:28–30)

Jesus' call is a striking amalgam of the claims made by personified
Wisdom in the book of Proverbs and in the noncanonical Sirach and
Wisdom of Solomon. In these books Wisdom is portrayed as a woman
who, having participated along with God in creation, calls humans to
come to her, take on her "yoke," and gain life and blessing through her
teaching (see Prov. 8; Sirach 6; Wisd. of Sol. 7). Here Jesus speaks as
Wisdom incarnate. Matthew's gospel is sprinkled with such claims: in
18:20 Jesus announces that "where two or three are gathered in my
name, I am there among them," paraphrasing *Pirke Aboth*'s claim (3.2)
that "if two sit together and words of Torah are between them, the
Shekinah [the divine presence] rests between them." Is Jesus, then,
both the wisdom of and presence of God? In 12:6 he claims that "something greater than the temple is here"; in 12:41, "something greater than
Jonah"; and in 12:42, "something greater than Solomon." Matthew has
portrayed Jesus as both fulfiller of Torah and teacher of Torah; now he
suggests that Jesus is "something greater" than Torah as well.

It is no coincidence that Matthew's extravagant assertions of Jesus'
authority are placed in the context of confrontations with the Pharisees. Matthew's claims about Jesus—he is the preexistent Wisdom of
God, the means to experience God's Shechinah, the deepest meaning
of the Torah itself—are precisely the claims the early rabbis (Pharisees)
were making for the Oral Torah. Matthew is equipping his community
to go head-to-head against Pharisaic teachings. Small wonder that
Matthew's Jesus calls his disciples "scribes" in emulation of the legal
scholars who helped develop rabbinic Judaism: "Every scribe who has
been trained for the kingdom of heaven is like the master of a household who brings out of his treasure what is new and what is old" (13:52).
Matthew himself is such a scribe, searching ancient prophecies even as
he records the new teachings of the messiah.

Matthew includes seventeen parables in his gospel—more, even, than the parable-loving Luke. The parables focus on three topics—the nature of God's kingdom, the opposition to God's kingdom, and the coming divine judgment. The parables are arranged topically, with those describing "the kingdom of heaven" in chapter 13. The kingdom of heaven is the hallmark of the messianic age. If the messiah has come, then the kingdom of heaven, God's rule on earth, should be evident. The fact that the world seemed not to have changed much was a major objection to claims that Jesus was the messiah. Matthew's parables of the kingdom address this problem. God's kingdom, says Jesus, will appear in unexpected ways—like a mustard bush that grows from a tiny seed, or like bread dough that is leavened from a "hidden" bit of yeast. The location and value of this kingdom are also unexpected—like finding buried treasure or a rare pearl. Why don't we see God's kingdom around us? Because it's hidden! Like wheat growing together with weeds, it appears in the *midst* of an evil world, to be separated only at the final harvest. In contrast to Mark's thickheaded disciples, Matthew's disciples understand these parables and their lesson. Whereas Mark sharply warned his faltering community to "keep awake," Matthew reassures his followers that they are scribes fully equipped for their task.

The stories of Matthew 14–16 follow the order of Mark 6–8 almost exactly, with a few crucial additions. Here, as in Mark, we first hear of the death of John the Baptist, after which Jesus miraculously feeds thousands of followers, walks on water, condemns the Pharisees for hypocrisy, heals a Canaanite woman, feeds another large crowd, and asks his disciples in private who they believe he is. Matthew changes Mark's account only in sharpening the critique of the Pharisees, announcing that Jesus "was sent only to the lost sheep of Israel" (rather than to Gentiles), and enhancing the image of Peter as leader of the disciples. In Matthew, Peter actually succeeds in walking out on the water to meet Jesus—at least until his faith weakens and he begins to sink. Moreover, it is Peter who recognizes Jesus as not only messiah but also "the son of the living God." In response Jesus tells Peter that he is the rock ("*petros*" is a Greek nickname, roughly equivalent to our "Rocky") on which he will build the church. Peter is given the "keys of the kingdom of heaven" (16:19), a role that resulted not only in the tradition that Saint Peter was the first "bishop of Rome," or pope, but in countless jokes in which Peter stands at the heavenly gates screening angelic hopefuls.

"From that time on," says Matthew, "Jesus began to show his disciples that he must go to Jerusalem and undergo great suffering . . . and be killed, and on the third day be raised" (16:21). From 16:21 onward, Matthew's gospel occupies itself with questions related to Jesus' death and resurrection. Chapters 16–18 closely follow the text of Mark, with a few additions unique to Matthew. In Matt. 17:24 Peter is challenged by those in charge of collecting the temple tax. Does Jesus pay the tax or not? Unlike the question about paying taxes to Caesar, which appears in all three synoptic gospels, the question about the temple tax appears in Matthew alone, and focuses on the question of Jewish identity. Do Jesus and his followers (represented by Peter) continue to pay a tax levied on Jews alone? Jesus responds pointedly that a king's own children do not pay him taxes; that is, as God's son Jesus is exempt from taxes owed to God. But rather than give offense to the temple authorities, Jesus pays the tax by means of a miracle. He sends Peter out to catch a fish; Peter does so, and in the fish's mouth is the shekel needed to pay the half-shekel tax for both of them.

In 18:15–20 Matthew adds a section on community discipline. Jesus advises his followers on how to settle internal disputes: first confront the person in private, then (as rabbinic law would also direct) return with one or two witnesses. As a last resort, bring the case before the entire "church" (*ecclesia*) or assembly. Finally, "if the offender refuses to listen even to the church, let such a one be to you as a Gentile and a tax collector." The teaching, unremarkable in itself, reveals a great deal about Matthew's community. Perhaps more than any other passage, Matthew's dismissive "Let such a one be to you as a Gentile" displays the community's unselfconscious self-identification as Jews. The group inhabits the cusp between an exclusively Jewish movement and a mixed Jewish-Gentile movement. Matthew knows of the church's spread to the Gentiles; later, Jesus will tell his disciples to go and make disciples of *all nations*. But unlike Luke, who expends enormous energy proving that the increasingly gentile movement really is still Jewish, Matthew simply thinks like an observant first-century Jew. How to say that a member should be cast out of the congregation? "Let such a one be to you as a Gentile."

As Jesus draws ever nearer to Jerusalem, he tells several parables unique to Matthew's gospel. The first, in 20:1–16, describes the "unfairness" of the coming kingdom. The kingdom of heaven, says Jesus, is like a landowner who hires day laborers to work in his vineyard. Some are hired at six A.M., others at nine, more at noon, three, and finally, at five o'clock—literally "at the eleventh hour" of the twelve-hour workday. At quitting time the landowner calls in the laborers, beginning with the *last* hired. All the laborers—those who worked twelve hours and those who worked only one—receive the same, standard day's wage. Those who worked the entire day are understandably resentful, but the owner (obviously, God) claims his right to be generous as he chooses. Matthew's parable suggests that one way for Christian groups to deal with Jewish opposition was simply to write off Jewish objections as sour grapes. Other Jews are unhappy with the new sect only because they resent God's generosity toward sinners and Gentiles.

As Jesus enters Jerusalem he continues to tell parables illustrating the conflict generated by the coming of God's kingdom. The harshest of these is the story of the wicked tenants (21:33–44), a parable taken from Mark, in which vineyard workers repeatedly abuse the servants (prophets) sent by their master (God), until at last he sends his own son (Jesus), only to see him killed by the evil servants. The parable's plot is unchanged from Mark's version, but Matthew draws a new conclusion: "The kingdom of God will be taken away from you [the chief priests and elders] and given to a people [*ethnos*] that produces the fruits of the kingdom." Matthew's use of the term *ethnos,* nation, is particularly harsh. Who is this new "people" who will replace the current Jewish leadership in God's kingdom? The Gentiles? A mixed gentile-Jewish church? In his own day, Matthew wrote to resist attempts to disenfranchise his own, marginal form of Jewish belief. In the course of history, he turned out to have written the prescription for the church's disinheriting of the Jews.

Matthew's account of Jesus' arrest and crucifixion highlights his bit-
terness toward the Pharisees. In chapter 21 Jesus arrives in Jerusalem.
Matthew makes surprisingly clumsy use of Zech. 9:9, "Behold, your
king comes to you, humble, and mounted on a donkey, on a colt, the foal
of a donkey." Misreading the parallelism of the original, which says that
the king rides a donkey—that is, a colt, the foal of a donkey—Matthew
solemnly informs us that Jesus enters the city riding both a donkey and
a colt. The crowd, seemingly oblivious to the messiah's awkward posture, shouts out, "Blessed is he who comes in the name of the Lord!"
Rather than "purging" the temple by driving out the money changers,
as in Mark and Luke, here Jesus engages in a series of debates with as-
sorted leaders—"priests and elders," "Herodians," "scribes and Pharisees," and "Sadducees"—culminating in a lengthy speech against the
Pharisees in chapter 23.

Jesus' seven "woes" against the Pharisees, unique to this gospel, vividly
express the bitter animosity that had grown up between at least some
Pharisees and some Christian groups by the late first century. Jesus begins
by acknowledging the Pharisees' authority. They "sit on Moses' seat," he
says. "Therefore, do whatever they teach you and follow it" (23:2–3).
Whether "Moses' seat" designates a place or an office is both unknown
and irrelevant: Jesus is granting the Pharisaic claim (*m. Pirke Aboth,* 1.1) to
be the authoritative transmitters of Moses' law. Just as elsewhere
Matthew tries to ally himself with Pharisaic teaching by allusions to Hillel
(in 7:12, and again in 22:34–40), so here he deferentially acknowledges
Pharisaic authority. Then he attacks. "Do whatever they teach you and
follow it; but do not do as they do, for they do not practice what they
teach." The charge of hypocrisy, ever popular among Greco-Roman
philosophical schools, is Matthew's leading complaint against the arbiters
of righteousness of his day. They lay burdens of ritual observance on
others that they themselves refuse to bear, "they do all their deeds to be
seen by others," they tithe the tiniest portion of their produce while
avoiding the more substantial issues of justice and mercy. They are
"whitewashed tombs, which on the outside look beautiful, but inside they
are full of the bones of the dead and of all kinds of filth." It seems as if
Matthew has been waiting the entire gospel to vent this load of spleen.

The passage is disturbing in its rancor and has long provided fodder to those seeking proof that Jews are legalistic, hypocritical, and self-serving. If one reads between the lines of Matthew's invective, however, the passage is a surprisingly rich source of information about the Pharisees of the first century. The Pharisees, for example, have "the place of honor and the best seats in the synagogues" and love to be called "rabbi" (23:6–7). Matthew's diatribe gives us our earliest evidence of when the title *rabbi* came into use, and of the status held by Pharisees in at least some synagogues of the period. "You cross sea and land," says Jesus, "to make a single convert, and you make the new convert twice as much a child of hell as yourselves" (23:15). Jews crossing land and sea to make converts? Though surely exaggerating, Matthew suggests that in the first century Judaism was a proselytizing religion. And, finally, "I send you prophets, sages, and scribes, some of whom you will kill and crucify, and some you will flog in your synagogues and pursue from town to town." What prophets, sages, and scribes will the Pharisees persecute? Members of Matthew's own community, surely. Once worshiping in the same synagogues where the Pharisees have "seats of honor," now Matthew's followers have been flogged and driven from town to town. Although Romans alone practiced crucifixion in this period, Matthew accuses the Pharisees of having handed his companions over for execution. Matthew's diatribe reveals both the status that the rabbis enjoyed, at least on a local level, and his own shock at having been made an exile from the Jewish community.

Matthew's Jesus follows up his venomous harangue with the prophecy that the Jerusalem temple will soon be "thrown down." The disciples are eager to hear, "When will this be, and what will be the sign of your coming and of the end of the age?" (24:3). The tirade against the Pharisees, of course, reflects heightened tensions between Jesus' followers and the Pharisees in *Matthew's* period, not Jesus'. But the prophecy of the temple's demise—an event that had taken place within the reader's memory—serves to underscore Jesus' credibility in the debate: he was right about the temple, and he was right about the Pharisees, too. In light of God's "obvious" rejection of both the temple hierarchy (the Sadducees) and the Pharisees, when will God reveal that

Jesus was his true agent? First, answers Jesus, "they will hand you over to be tortured and will put you to death. . . . [M]any will fall away, and they will betray one another and hate one another. . . . Then the end will come" (24:9–14). The worse things become, the greater their hope should be.

Read through the lens of Christianity's triumph over the entire Western world, Matthew's predictions appear grandiose and self-serving. Anything Christians suffer is proof of their righteousness and a prelude to eternal exaltation over everything and everyone else. Such a reading, however (and it is easy enough to read Matthew in this way), ignores the reality of Matthew's original social and historical setting. In the wake of centuries of Christian ascendancy, it is difficult to picture Matthew the persecuted sectarian, a man who really *didn't* know what would become of his community. Pharisees and Romans seemed equally determined to eradicate them, and God was not exactly intervening to help them out. This apparently self-confident "gospel of the church" began as the exhortation of a frightened leader comforting an equally frightened flock. One can sympathize with Matthew the embattled community leader (which he was), however, without accepting his portrait of the Pharisees as self-serving religious bullies (which they were not). Matthew is filled with such tensions, all the more so for its two-thousand-year-old role in the history of religious persecution.

As Matthew's gospel moves closer to Jesus' arrest and execution, Jesus begins to tell the disciples parables emphasizing preparedness. "You must be ready," he says, "for the Son of Man is coming at an unexpected hour" (24:44). "Keep awake therefore, for you know neither the day nor the hour" (25:13). At the climax of these exhortations, Jesus describes the moment for which the early church was waiting—"when the Son of Man comes in his glory, and all the angels with him." Matthew's depiction of the last judgment is unique in the gospels, and it is not at all what his vituperative rhetoric would lead us to expect. When the Son of Man (Jesus) sits on the throne of his glory, says Jesus, he will first separate the people of the world into two groups, "as a shepherd separates the sheep from the goats."

> Then the king will say to those at his right hand, "Come, you that are blessed by my Father, inherit the kingdom prepared for you from the foundation of the world; for I was hungry and you gave me food, I was thirsty and you gave me something to drink, I was a stranger and you welcomed me, I was naked and you gave me clothing, I was sick and you took care of me, I was in prison and you visited me." (Matt. 25:34–36)

The righteous are surprised, and ask when they saw him in any of these conditions. The king answers that whenever they did these things for the least of his brothers, they did so for him. To the "goats" he says, "You that are accursed, depart from me into the eternal fire prepared for the devil and his angels; for I was hungry and you gave me no food, I was thirsty and you gave me nothing to drink . . ." The unrighteous are unaware of having mistreated their Lord, but he tells them, "Just as you did not do it to one of the least of these, you did not do it to me" (25:45).

The language of judgment is as harsh as anything in the gospel of Matthew. Remarkably, however, reward and punishment are not meted out on the basis of religious beliefs, but in response to people's actions. Those in "all the nations" who have been merciful and generous will be blessed; the callous are sentenced to eternal fire. Matthew's judgment scene has, in fact, a very Jewish feel to it. The threat of hellfire shows up in a number of early Jewish texts, but judgment is never based on religious affiliation. As it is stated in the Talmud, "the righteous of every nation have a place in the world to come" (*b. Sanh.* 105a). Matthew apparently did not allow his anger at "the scribes and Pharisees" to blur his vision of what counts in the eyes of God.

Matthew's passion account follows Mark's, but with additions tailored to emphasize Matthew's distinctive concerns. First and foremost, Matthew insists that *everything* about the crucifixion took place to fulfill scriptural prophecy. Jesus has already told his disciples no fewer than four times that "the Son of Man must suffer and die" in accordance with scriptures—no bitter twist of fate this, but the hand of God. Now Matthew informs us that if the disciples fled, it happened only because the scripture had to be fulfilled—in contrast to Mark's account, where it is the disciples' own fault. Why didn't Jesus call upon his divinely given powers to resist arrest? "How then would the scriptures be fulfilled, which say it must happen in this way? . . . All this has taken place, so that the scriptures of the prophets may be fulfilled" (26:54, 56). Even Matthew's story of how a "potter's field" was bought using the blood money returned to the priests by a repentant Judas, includes a note that this happened to fulfill the prophecies of Jeremiah. Strangely, Jeremiah's prophecies include no passage even vaguely resembling the quotation Matthew attributes to him (though the prophet does visit a potter and is instructed to buy a field). But Matthew would seemingly rather make up his own prophecy than recount events *not* "foretold by the prophets."

In addition to Matthew's concern to prove that Jesus' death took place entirely according to scripture, he is eager to exonerate the Roman authorities and to place the blame for Jesus' death entirely on the Jews. Here it becomes more difficult to sympathize with Matthew's plight; in attempting to discredit his Jewish opponents he seemingly vilifies the entire Jewish people. Pontius Pilate, infamous among Jews and Romans alike for his brutality and capricious rulership, is expressly cleared of responsibility for Jesus' death. Pilate's wife is granted the gift of prophecy, warning her husband to "have nothing to do with this innocent man." Consequently, Pilate tries to release Jesus. Constrained by the crowds, he agrees to Jesus' crucifixion, but only after publicly washing his hands to indicate his innocence in the matter. "The people as a whole" have no such compunctions but shout out, "His blood be on us and on our children!" (27:25). And so the fantasy of Jews rabidly intent on destroying the son of God is born.

Matthew next relates a Jewish conspiracy in an addition almost certainly devised to counter Jewish claims of a *Christian* conspiracy. After inciting the Jewish people to take responsibility for Jesus' death, the "chief priests and the Pharisees" come to Pilate with a new concern: the resurrection. After all, this imposter predicted his own resurrection in three days' time. We'd better set a guard at the tomb to make sure the disciples don't come steal the body! Pilate agrees and guards are posted, but of course they are of no avail; Jesus is resurrected in spite of them. At this, the chief priests make their most cynical move. Confronted with the guards' direct testimony of the resurrection, the priests bribe them to say that they fell asleep on the job, allowing the disciples to steal the body. "This story," says Matthew, "is still told among the Jews to this day" (28:15). On this point it seems reasonable to take Matthew at his word. It would be surprising if no one had suggested that the resurrection had been faked. (In fact, some scholars continue to advance this explanation for the birth of Christianity.) But Matthew deftly turns the story back on itself: it is not the Christians who are circulating lies, but the Jews. The chief priests, feeling themselves threatened by evidence that God had resurrected Jesus, preferred an elaborate cover-up. Non-Christian Judaism, Matthew implies, was rotten to its very core.

Matthew concludes his gospel with Jesus' dramatic appearance on a mountain in Galilee. Commanding the disciples, "Go therefore and make disciples of all nations," Jesus authorizes the spread of Christianity beyond a hostile Jewry and to "all nations," that is, the Gentiles. "Remember," says Jesus, "I am with you always, to the end of the age." The baby called Immanuel, God-is-with-us, at his birth, now promises his own presence among his followers. The teacher who interpreted Moses' commandments in the Sermon on the Mount now calls the disciples to obey *his* commandments. And Matthew adds the command, unique in the New Testament, that future followers should be baptized "in the name of the Father, and of the Son, and of the Holy Spirit" (28:19). This formula need not imply (as it came to do in later Christian thought) that Matthew conceived of God as a "trinity," with the Son and Spirit as equal partners with the Father. As messiah and son of David, Jesus was also a son of God. But Matthew's vision of Gentiles baptized in Jesus' name tacitly acknowledges the spread of this messianic sect far beyond the Jewish environment in which Matthew's own followers sought to understand their new identity. At the conclusion of Matthew's rancorous sparring with his Pharisaic peers, he seems almost to concede defeat. While still arming his own followers to defend their legitimacy as Jews, Matthew also provides the vision of a future among the Gentiles.

THE GOSPEL ACCORDING TO LUKE

THE GOSPEL OF LUKE might be considered the fraternal twin of Matthew's gospel. Like Matthew, Luke wrote around 85–90 C.E., using as sources both Mark's gospel and the collection of Jesus' sayings known as Q. Luke, however, adds distinctive and distinctly charming elements, making his gospel one of the best-loved parts of the New Testament. Luke alone tells of an angel announcing Jesus' birth to a startled Mary, of Jesus' birth in a lowly stable, and of angels and shepherds gathering to celebrate his birth. Luke is the "Christmas pageant gospel," but its influence goes far beyond its role as the source of a million crèche scenes. Along with the gospel's companion piece, the Acts of the Apostles (together known as Luke-Acts), Luke's work makes up fully one-fourth of the New Testament, and its impact has been commensurate with its length. Luke-Acts provides the foundation story for all of Christianity—from Jesus' birth and life through the birth and growth of the Christian church. Even Christians who have never read Luke's narrative know its plotline, which is widely accepted as "the gospel truth" about early Christian history. In his brief introduction, the author of Luke-Acts promises to give an "orderly account" (1:3) of Christian beginnings; his well-constructed narrative has remained the paradigm for Christian self-understanding ever since.

Luke's gospel was written after the destruction of the temple in 70 C.E. and during the decade or so in which Gentiles were beginning to form a majority in the Jesus sect. During this same period, the Pharisees (soon to be known as "the rabbis") were beginning to stake their claim as the rescuers of Judaism following the destruction of the Jerusalem temple; thus, as in Matthew, tension between the Pharisees and Jesus' followers is evident. The physical location of Luke's community is not known, although the thriving metropolis of Antioch in Syria is a reasonable possibility. Far more certain than its geographic locale is the community's ethnic and social location. Luke addresses his gospel to someone he calls Theophilus. The name literally means "God-lover" and is probably a cipher for *God-fearer,* a term for gentile adherents to Judaism who had not undergone full conversion. Luke may be writing to an individual, most likely his patron, or he may be addressing an entire category of readers toward whom his history is especially directed: gentile "God-fearers," probably of some social standing, who are now participating in Judaism through their involvement with the Jesus sect. Luke acknowledges that "many," including eyewitnesses, have already produced accounts of the community's beginnings. His goal is a narrative that will provide "security" to his reader, Theophilus. But why would Theophilus, a well-placed Gentile (Luke addresses him as "your Excellency"), require reassurance? What kind of *insecurity* would plague such a patron, creating the need for Luke to write his gospel? The answer is not one that would occur to most modern Jews, or even to most modern Christians: Luke-Acts addresses the insecurity of gentile converts who are worried about whether they as Gentiles should be allowed to join the Jesus community, a community they understood as—and that understood itself to be—the true Israel.

God-fearers were a natural source of converts for the Jesus sect, which in the late first century was unique as a form of Judaism in which Gentiles could participate as full members without undergoing circumcision. While the opportunity for full inclusion would have been welcomed by Torah-adherent Gentiles, such a liberal inclusivity would naturally raise the question of whether this sect was *really* Jewish at all. The fact that few *Jews* were joining would have added to the confusion.

(Some early Christian congregations did require circumcision for membership, but these were soon eclipsed by the quickly growing "liberal" wing.) Writing to assure his anxious God-fearer, Luke needs to demonstrate that (1) Jesus' life and resurrection constituted "the next chapter" in the ongoing history of Israel, and (2) gentile membership was legitimate even without full conversion to Judaism. Luke writes to prove both that the sect is authentically Jewish and that Gentiles may become members of this Jewish sect. An additional theme, that with the messiah's arrival Israel has become divided between those who accept God's actions and those who reject them, allows Luke to address the relative *absence* of Jews from the new sect.

Christian tradition identifies Luke as a physician and companion of Paul, but no firm evidence supports this. Scholarly tradition has considered Luke himself a gentile convert to the Jesus sect, but no evidence beyond his excellent Greek and knowledge of the Roman world (skills any well-educated diaspora Jew might have displayed) supports this assumption. Luke's narrative task of reassuring gentile readers about the sect's Jewish legitimacy suggests that Luke was the Jewish leader of a gentile congregation. To establish that Jesus and the resulting church are the legitimate continuation of biblical Israel, Luke organizes his work as if it comprised volumes two and three of a three-volume history of Israel. Volume one, the Hebrew scriptures, recounts the history of Israel before the birth of the messiah. Volume two, the gospel of Luke, describes the messiah's life and death. Acts, the third volume, recounts the story of the early church as the story of Israel in the messianic age. This three-part scheme allows Luke to construct a seamless story running from Abraham and Moses through Jesus and his first disciples, all the way to the apostle Paul.

Luke opens his story by introducing Elizabeth and Zechariah, an elderly Jewish couple who are "righteous" and "blameless" before God but, due to Elizabeth's barrenness, childless. Any reader who has heard of Sarah and Abraham recognizes the reference, and expects God to bless the couple with a child. Luke provides the requisite miracle: An angel appears to Zechariah and prophesies the birth of a son. This son, moreover, will act with "the spirit and power of Elijah . . . to make ready a people prepared for the Lord" (1:17). Why Elijah? Elijah's role of returning to herald the coming of the messiah was already established in first-century Judaism (and see Mal. 4:5–6). Luke's reader, who has gotten the message that Israel's history is being replayed, recognizes that the upcoming miraculous birth will presage the messiah's arrival. Luke's compelling reuse of biblical themes has enabled readers for almost two thousand years to make a seamless transition from the "Old Testament" to the new, and to see in Jesus the obvious continuation of Israel's story.

Luke positions the reader in a world in which God's prophecies are being fulfilled. Consequently, he next announces that, just as the angel predicted, Elizabeth has indeed become pregnant. God then sends the angel to a betrothed virgin named Mary, who learns that she will become pregnant through the direct action of God's spirit; her son will be given the throne of David and be called the son of God. Just as Luke's earlier prophecy recalled Abraham and Sarah, so this story of a woman startled by an angel announcing the birth of a "savior" closely parallels the story of Manoah's wife (Samson's mother) in Judges 13. Luke has rendered a narrative world in which things happen "just like in the Bible"—a world in which miracles are to be expected.

Mary responds to the angel's announcement by quoting Abraham's words of acceptance, "Here am I" (Gen. 22:1; see also Moses in Exod. 3:4). Mary's response is crucial to Luke's narrative scheme: like Abraham and Moses, Mary accepts both God's work and her place in it. *Faithful* Israel believes in God's promises and awaits their fulfillment. Elizabeth praises Mary, saying, "Blessed is she who *believed* that there would be a *fulfillment* of what was spoken to her by the Lord." Mary responds with the "Magnificat," a song based closely on Hannah's song in 1 Samuel 2, praising God for rescuing the lowly while casting down the powerful (1:46–55). Luke's lengthy first chapter closes with the birth of John, the fulfillment of the book's first prophecy.

In chapter 2 Luke recounts the birth of Jesus in Bethlehem, "the city of David." Jesus is born in a stable and acknowledged only by shepherds, but his birth is greeted with joy by the angels in heaven. Luke is eager to demonstrate not only Jesus' Jewish pedigree but his continued

Jewish legitimacy; thus Luke alone recounts both Jesus' circumcision (2:21) and his "presentation" (the rite of *pidyon ha ben*) at the temple (vv. 22–38; cf. v. 39). Jesus' presentation is witnessed by a "righteous and devout" Jew named Simeon, and by Anna, a prophet. God has promised Simeon that he will live to see the messiah. He, of course, recognizes Jesus, proclaiming him not only the salvation and glory of Israel but also "a light for revelation to the Gentiles" (2:29–32). Luke first demonstrates Jesus' Jewishness—his family performs "everything required by the law." Then he announces that the messiah has come to fulfill God's promises to *Gentiles* as well as to Jews (cf. Isa. 49:6). Finally, Simeon adds a more somber note: Jesus is "destined for the falling and the rising of many in Israel." Israel will become divided over Jesus.

In chapter 3 John ("the Baptist") appears as a prophet, proclaiming that "all flesh" will soon see God's salvation. As in Mark's gospel, Jesus comes to John for baptism. Luke next provides a genealogy (vv. 23–38) tracing Jesus' ancestry through David and Abraham, back to Adam, the original "son of God." In contrast to Matthew (whose genealogy extends back only to Abraham), Luke wishes to demonstrate that the messiah belongs to all of humankind, and not to Israel alone.

Luke's universalism—his eagerness to include the gentile world in his story—is matched by his sensitivity to those he considers outsiders: the poor, the ritually unclean, and, especially, women. Only Luke gives Mary a starring role in his narrative, and throughout the gospel important male figures are provided with female counterparts (for example, the two prophets, Simeon and Anna). Luke alone includes the story of the sisters Martha and Mary, one consumed with the work of hosting Jesus while the other "sits at his feet" to be trained as a disciple. Luke's awareness of women and their often invisible roles seems to embody his claim that, in Jesus, God "has put down the mighty . . . and exalted the lowly."

Luke begins his account of Jesus' ministry with a story demonstrating both the inclusion of Gentiles and the division of Israel. Jesus appears in his hometown, teaching in the synagogue on the sabbath. He chooses his own *haftarah* (prophets) reading (which may have been common practice in first-century synagogues), unrolling the scroll of

Isaiah to read, "The spirit of the Lord is upon me, because he has anointed me to bring good news to the poor. He has sent me to proclaim release to the captives and recovery of sight to the blind" (Isa. 61:1). "Today," says Jesus, "this scripture has been fulfilled in your hearing." Jesus is the fulfillment of God's promises; Israel must now accept or reject this fulfillment.

Upon hearing Jesus' claims, the people are divided. First they speak well of him, hoping that he will perform miracles such as those he did in the largely gentile city of Capernaum. Jesus rather rudely points out that Elijah's and Elisha's greatest miracles were performed on behalf of Gentiles. Not surprisingly, the people are offended, and drive him out of town. Jesus, however, proceeds to make good on his promise to fulfill Isaiah's prophecy. Returning to Capernaum, he heals the sick and frees those possessed by demons. Already Luke foreshadows his version of the later experience of the church: first Jesus teaches in the synagogue, announcing himself to be the messiah. This is exactly what Paul will do in Acts—and what many of Jesus' followers must have done in the years after Jesus' death. The people are interested, but take offense at the suggestion that Gentiles may be more open to or deserving of God's favor than they are. They then drive Jesus (or his followers, or Paul) out of the synagogue. Jesus (or his followers, or Paul) then goes among the Gentiles, where he demonstrates divine power and authority. Jesus' power, Luke says, is real, but Israel has rejected God's work in him.

After Jesus' first demonstrations of his power, he enters into a series of conflicts with the Pharisees. The Pharisees are always defined by Luke as "insiders" and therefore always at least potentially hostile to Jesus' mission of calling in those who have strayed. The Pharisees challenge Jesus for eating with sinners, for allowing his disciples to pick handfuls of grain on the sabbath, and finally, for healing a man with a chronic illness on the sabbath. The rabbis argued that work required to save a life is legal on the sabbath but that other forms of healing are forbidden (*Aboth de Rab. Nathan* 31). Jesus insists on focusing on the man's needs rather than the letter of the law: "Is it lawful . . . to do good or do harm . . . to save life or destroy it" on the sabbath? The Pharisees make no comment. Jesus performs the healing and they are enraged.

Ritual Purity

In ancient Israel, the world as a whole was divided into three categories: holy (God and things or people pertaining to God), clean (or "neutral"), and unclean (things that caused ritual defilement). God was understood to reside in the midst of the people, who must therefore maintain the greatest possible degree of ritual holiness. Ritual impurity, however, was inescapable—the result of natural causes such as disease or contact with a corpse, as well as of serious crimes. Persons who had become "unclean" were therefore required to undergo purification before coming into potential contact with the realm of the holy. In the postexilic period the concept of ritual holiness was broadened so that entire categories of people (Samaritans or Gentiles) might be considered "unclean." Some Jewish groups forbade or limited contact with such "unclean people." In Luke 7 the host assumes that the prostitute is ritually unclean, though biblical law does not specify this.

Luke repeatedly portrays the Pharisees as people whose observance serves no greater purpose than to make them feel righteous, even as they ignore or look down on those who are suffering. Historically, there is no reason to believe that the Pharisees were any more or less self-righteous than any other religious group. Luke, however, is concerned to justify his own movement's more lenient interpretation of Jewish law. As the advocate of a group that has chosen to include Gentiles, "outsiders" to Judaism by definition, Luke shows a special sensitivity to the ways in which "insider" status can be abused.

In chapters 7–8 Luke turns to stories in which Jesus' power is exercised on behalf of Gentiles, beginning with an expanded version of Mark's story of the Roman centurion. The centurion sends a message to Jesus, asking to have his slave healed, and the Jews who relay his message affirm that this man "loves our people, and it is he who built our synagogue for us" (7:5). The centurion is both a God-fearer and a patron of the Jewish community. At his request, Jesus heals the slave, saying, "Not even in Israel have I found such faith." The centurion's story recalls Jesus' first appearance in the synagogue at Nazareth, where he asserted that Elijah and Elisha had performed their greatest miracles for Gentiles. The story also speaks directly to "Theophilus," the God-fearer-turned-Christian who doubts his legitimacy as a member of Israel. Faith, says Luke, is the only credential needed.

Luke uses Jesus' success among the Gentiles to set up his theme of division within Israel. In a terse summary in 7:29–30 Luke announces that "all the people" acknowledged God's work, but "the Pharisees and the lawyers rejected God's purpose for themselves." Ironically, we next see Jesus dining as a guest in the house of a Pharisee; the setting cries out for controversy. Sure enough, a woman who is a "sinner" (presumably a prostitute) and therefore ritually unclean arrives and approaches Jesus. Jesus, with no apparent concern for his own purity or that of his host's house, allows the woman to touch and kiss him. The host concludes that Jesus cannot be a *real* prophet (let alone the messiah), since

THE TAX COLLECTOR, THE PHARISEE, AND THE HISTORY OF INTERPRETATION

The story of the tax collector and the Pharisee is a tale of two Jews. Neither says or knows anything about Jesus. Ironically, in the history of Christian interpretation the tax collector has been taken as a type of the repentant *Christian*, while the judgmental Pharisee has been seen as representative of Jews and Judaism. The parable has thus been interpreted as a story of Jewish hostility toward Christians, who are understood to be humble, self-effacing, and thus morally superior to "self-justifying and legalistic" Jews. The story exemplifies the ease with which the New Testament's inter-Jewish commentary becomes anti-Jewish critique when read in the context of the now-gentile church.

a prophet "would have known what kind of woman this is." Jesus, however, proves himself a prophet by knowing the Pharisee's thoughts. He rather tartly observes that unlike "the one to whom little is forgiven" (the upstanding Pharisee), the woman, who has experienced forgiveness commensurate with her many sins, expresses correspondingly great love. Those with no need of Jesus' healing express no gratitude for his gifts.

In chapter 9 Luke reports Jesus' transfiguration on the mountain. As in Mark, Jesus is revealed in conversation with Moses and Elijah, but Luke adds to Mark's account by informing the reader of the substance of their discussion: they are talking of Jesus' departure, which he will soon "accomplish" at Jerusalem. Luke places Jesus' crucifixion firmly within the divine purview: God has already planned for Jesus to be crucified, and Jesus is prepared to accomplish God's will. In 9:51 Jesus "sets his face" for Jerusalem and death. Over the next ten chapters, Luke reminds us that whatever Jesus says and does, he does so "on his way." Most of what Jesus does on the way is teach, and in Luke Jesus' distinctive mode of teaching is the parable, several of which are unique to Luke's gospel. Both the parables and the miracles in chapters 9–19 emphasize the division between the rich, the self-righteous, and the Pharisees, all of whom oppose Jesus, and the poor and humble, who welcome him.

In 10:25–37 Jesus is addressed by a "lawyer," a scribe or expert in Jewish law, who asks, "What must I do to inherit eternal life?" As in Mark and Matthew, the young lawyer asserts that the heart of the law is found in Deut. 6:5, the verse following the *shema,* "You shall love the Lord your God with all your heart," together with Lev. 19:18, "You shall love your neighbor as yourself." Jesus agrees and, citing Deut. 30:19, says that this Torah gives life. The lawyer, however, presses the point, asking, "So, who is my neighbor?" Jesus responds with the story of the so-called good Samaritan. As the story opens, a man is going down from Jerusalem to Jericho. The traveler is beaten, robbed, and left for dead. A priest sees the man but crosses the road to avoid him, and travels on. A Levite does the same. The priest's and Levite's motivations here depend on the direction (unspecified) in which they are traveling. If they are heading toward Jerusalem they are presumably concerned with maintaining their ritual purity in order to remain eligible for temple service. Hence they give a wide berth to what may be a defiling corpse in the road. If they are returning home *following* temple duty, then their actions seem entirely callous. In either case, Luke presents the priest and the Levite, guardians of the Torah, as ignoring the man's desperate situation and the clear mandate of Torah to help those in need. Luke next introduces a Samaritan, a person inherently unclean and himself a stranger in hostile territory. The Samaritan gives his time, attention, and money in order to help the injured Judean. Responding to the

SAMARITANS

The Hebrew Bible traces the origins of the Samaritans to 722 B.C.E., when the Assyrians decimated the northern Israelite capital of Samaria, sending much of the northern population into exile (thereby creating the fabled "lost tribes" of Israel) and replacing it with a population drawn from other parts of the Assyrian empire. This new population is portrayed in 2 Kings 17 as both ethnically and religiously mixed: "So they feared the Lord but also served their own gods." The new population, called Samaritans by the Judean (southern) authors of the Bible, developed a distinctive version of Israelite beliefs, with a canon limited to the Torah and a central sanctuary on Mount Gerizim, near Shechem (modern Nablus). According to Nehemiah 6, following the Babylonian exile the Samaritans were eager to help rebuild the Jerusalem temple, but the Judean leadership excluded them. Relations between Samaritans and Jews continued to be strained, with the Samaritans claiming descent from the northern tribes, and Jews viewing them as non-Jewish descendants of foreign settlers. Two small communities of Samaritans continue to live in Israel today, where they are recognized as citizens by the state of Israel.

question "Who is my neighbor?" Jesus asks who acted like a neighbor to the injured man. The answer reflects Luke's larger theme: the one on the margins of Israel, someone with no ritual purity to protect, was the one person available to become a neighbor.

Luke continues his critique of self-righteousness in his parable of the prodigal son (15:11–32). The younger of two brothers asks his father for his share of the inheritance, and promptly wastes everything in dissolute extravagance. When, however, the son returns home begging his father's forgiveness, the father is so relieved that his only concern is to celebrate. The responsible elder brother, who has stayed home behaving all this time, is less than delighted with the lavish celebration over the manifestly undeserving younger brother. Luke applies this tale of sibling rivalry to the situation of the Jewish people. Jesus has gone about announcing God's forgiveness to prostitutes and tax collectors (the prodigals), and respectable, elder-brother types (like the Pharisees) are offended. The parable, however, makes an even more pointed comment about Luke's historical situation than about Jesus'. Whereas the religious leadership of Jesus' day may have been disturbed by his easy acceptance of *Jewish* outcasts (tax collectors and prostitutes), by the late first century it was the easy inclusion of *Gentiles* that gave offense. Luke may have been commenting on later Jewish (and even Jewish-Christian) indignity over the inclusion of Gentiles in the sect. Remarkably, the elder brother is neither rejected nor even severely criticized within the story. "You," says the father, "are always with me, and all that is mine is yours." Luke's affirmation of the Jewish people—specifically of Torah-observant Judaism—is striking. While Luke clearly approves of the welcome God offers the "bad" younger brother, he seems also to respect the position of more conservative Jews. The conflict over who is in and who is out has done nothing to damage God's regard for more observant Jews, who are "always with him" and will inherit their share of God's blessing.

Luke's parables exemplify his theme of a divided Israel: as Mary predicted, God "has exalted those of low degree, but the rich he has sent empty away." In yet another depiction of the gap between the humble and the proud, in 18:9–14 Jesus tells of a Pharisee and a tax collector praying at the temple. The Pharisee's prayer is a virtual parody of the Pharisaic ideal. Apparently playing on the section of the Shemoneh Esreh prayer that thanks God for not making one a Gentile, a slave, or a woman, the Pharisee simply gives thanks that he is "not like other people": thieves, rogues, and adulterers, "or even like this tax collector." The Pharisee fasts *twice* a week (surpassing the more common practice of a weekly fast) and he donates a tenth of his income to the poor. He lacks no virtue but humility. The tax collector, by contrast, has no virtue *except* humility, and beats his breast saying, "God, be merciful to me, a sinner." But, says Jesus, it was the tax collector who returned home "justified" before God. The vignette is humorous (unless, of course, the reader is a Pharisee), and programmatic for Luke's gospel: those with much—even much virtue—risk excluding themselves from God's new order, simply because they have much to lose. Those with little, whether little status, little wealth, or even little virtue, are able to rejoice in the new order God is initiating.

Luke concludes his many parables with two encounters illustrating the divisions Jesus has described in the parables. Jesus meets with a "ruler" who, like the lawyer of 10:25, asks how he may inherit eternal life. Jesus answers that in addition to keeping the commandments, he must sell his possessions and give to the poor. At this, the ruler "becomes sad" but does nothing. By contrast, Zacchaeus, the chief tax collector, welcomes Jesus into his home, spontaneously announcing that he will give half of his possessions to the poor. The *virtuous* rich man proves unable to follow Jesus, while the despised Roman collaborator (also rich) acknowledges his unworthiness and gives up his wealth. Having concluded his extended discussion of rich and poor, insider and outsider, in 19:28 Luke returns to his narrative of Jesus' final journey.

In 19:29 Jesus rides into Jerusalem. For Luke, Jesus' arrival in Jerusalem is a great moment in Jewish history—the messiah's coming and the inauguration of the age to come. Throughout the gospel Luke has finessed the problem of Jewish antagonism toward the Jesus movement by his theme of division within Israel: The Jewish people were not hostile to Jesus and his message. On the contrary, Israel was *already* divided between the humble, who were open to God's message, and the proud, who rejected it. In his version of the passion narrative, Luke brings the theme of division to the fore. Jesus, says Luke, taught daily in the temple, with the result that "all the people" were spellbound, while "the chief priests, the scribes, and the leaders" sought to kill him. Luke thus frees "the people" from blame for Jesus' death; after the crucifixion they will leave "beating their breasts" in grief and repentance.

Luke's presentation of the Last Supper (22:1–38) follows Mark's closely, but with emphasis on Jesus' death as the fulfillment of God's will, and on Jesus as God's willing and faithful servant. As in Mark's gospel, the Passover seder is shaped to reflect the meal's significance within the *Christian* community. Thus, Jesus says that the matzoh, which in the seder serves as a reminder of slavery and redemption, will be eaten by Jesus' followers in remembrance of him. The cup of thanksgiving after the meal (the fourth cup, or *hallel*) becomes a symbol of a "new covenant," sealed with the blood of Jesus (cf. the original "blood of the covenant" in Exod. 24:8).

JEWS FOR JESUS AND MESSIANIC JEWS

Not unlike the ancient Ebionites and Nazarenes, some modern Christians of Jewish descent combine faith in Jesus as messiah with Jewish religious observance. Jews for Jesus (founded in 1973) and the Union of Messianic Jewish Congregations (founded in 1979) are the most prominent organizations for ethnically Jewish Christians. Both groups give high priority to converting other Jews; both affirm the literal truth of the New Testament and consider Jesus the "fulfillment" of Judaism. All major branches of Judaism have declared such "Hebrew Christian" associations to be exclusively Christian and in no sense Jewish, and have protested their efforts to evangelize Jews to Christianity. Luke-Acts, with its careful anchoring of Christian identity in Jewish tradition, has been a favorite resource for these groups.

In Luke's crucifixion account, the theme of Israel's division reaches its climax. The "chief priests and rulers" hand over Jesus to the Romans, but "a great multitude of the people" follow weeping as he goes to the cross. Two Jewish criminals are crucified alongside Jesus. One mocks him; the other reveres him, thereby gaining a place in paradise. Luke uses the crucifixion to sharpen the image of Jews and Judaism he has been developing since the beginning of the gospel. In general, "the people" follow Jesus and those in authority despise him. Luke is careful, however, not to exclude everyone of rank or wealth from "the kingdom" (after all, many gentile God-fearers were of high social standing). The case of Joseph of Arimathea serves to demonstrate that even Jews of high standing may by their faithfulness be included in God's kingdom. Joseph is "a good and righteous man . . . waiting expectantly for the kingdom of God." Joseph honors Jesus by requesting his body at the end of Jesus' life, thereby recalling Anna and Simeon, the righteous prophets who hailed the infant Jesus at his dedication. Luke concludes his account of Jesus' death with the notice that at the onset of the sabbath, Jesus' followers returned and "rested according to the commandment." Luke makes it utterly clear that Jesus' followers continued to live as a faithful remnant of Israel—pious and humble Jews.

Unique to Luke's resurrection account are stories of Jesus' appearances while on the road to Emmaus (a town outside Jerusalem) and, later, at a private home. As the risen Jesus walks and talks with his disciples, he is at great pains to point out to them that everything that happened to him (including resurrection) had been foretold by the prophets. Indeed, when they do not recognize him he chides them for not believing "all that the prophets have declared" (24:25). If they had paid attention to scripture, they would have foreseen both his death and his resurrection. "Then, beginning with Moses and all the prophets, he interpreted to them the things *about himself* in all the scriptures." "Everything," says Jesus, "*written about me* in the law of Moses, the prophets, and the psalms must be fulfilled" (24:44). Here is Luke's strongest statement in favor of the Jesus movement as a legitimate, indeed, *the* legitimate expression of Judaism. Luke began his gospel with vignettes of pious Jews whose experience, like that of the barren Elizabeth, recalls the experiences of the patriarchs. Soon, these devout Israelites hear that ancient prophecies are about to be fulfilled among them. Jesus is born and is portrayed fulfilling various biblical prophecies. Now Jesus, having been both killed and resurrected *as a fulfillment of prophecy,* shows the disciples where to find the "parts about him" in the scriptures. Luke's rhetoric is a tour de force of the first order. He has moved from arguing that Jesus fulfills the biblical prophecies about the messiah (one can understand *Jesus* by seeing how he conforms to the model of *scripture*) to having the resurrected Jesus explain the "prophecies about him" in the Bible (one understands *scripture* when one sees how it conforms to the model of *Jesus*).

Luke's narrative brilliantly strives to give the gentile reader security that the Jesus movement is the true inheritor of God's promises to Israel. Millions of Luke's gentile readers have accepted his assurance that in becoming Christians they are also fulfilling "the law and the prophets." In the book of Acts Luke will address his gentile reader's remaining problem (a problem of little or no concern to modern Christians): what is the status of uncircumcised Gentiles in this new "Jewish" community? The Jesus movement may be legitimately Jewish, but are *they?*

The Acts

of

the Apostles

L IKE LUKE'S GOSPEL, Acts is addressed to Theophilus. Luke opens the narrative by reminding his reader of all that Jesus said and did "in the first book," that is, in the gospel. Acts is volume three in Luke's story of Israel that began with the Hebrew scriptures, continued with the story of the messiah, and now describes the beginnings of the messianic age. It is also the only extant account of the years immediately following Jesus' death. In 1:1–7:60 Luke will seek to demonstrate that after Jesus' death and resurrection his followers, empowered by the spirit of God ("the Holy Spirit"), became the core of "faithful Israel"—those who understood that the messiah had come, and lived accordingly. This rump quorum of the Jewish people soon begins to recapitulate the life of Jesus, performing miracles like his but suffering persecution like his as well.

In 8:1–15:41 Luke turns to the new sect's "gentile problem." His discussion of what to do about "Gentiles for Jesus" is probably his most important contribution to Christianity. His conclusion: "God has made no distinction" between Jew and Gentile. Gentiles may therefore be included in the sect without undergoing formal conversion to Judaism. In the final section of Acts, chapters 16–28, Luke recounts the journeys of the apostle Paul, describing the course of the new sect as it spreads across the Roman empire. Paul speaks about "the messiah" in synagogues throughout the diaspora, but his message is accepted by vastly greater numbers of Gentiles than of Jews. Always in tension with the synagogues and always welcomed by the Gentiles, Paul eventually becomes discouraged with the Jewish community. Ultimately he announces that "this salvation of God has [now] been sent to the Gentiles; *they* will listen" (28:28). The book of Acts thus takes us from a group of Judeans struggling to make sense of Jesus' postresurrection appearances to the establishment of a new religion—a "gentile Judaism" spreading rapidly across the empire. The rest, we may say, is history.

As he does in the gospel, in Acts Luke continues to reassure his gentile reader on two points: first, that the Jesus community is truly a *Jewish* community. The Gentiles among whom Christianity first spread were predominantly those already attached to synagogues—students and admirers of Judaism as an ancient and venerable tradition. Such "half converts" had no interest in joining an ersatz Judaism, let alone a new religion. Much of Judaism's appeal lay in its antiquity, and Luke's readers wanted to be sure—particularly in light of the sect's relative failure among Jews as a whole—that the new sect was legitimately Jewish. Second, Luke's gentile reader needed reassurance that he or she could legitimately join a Jewish community. After all, gentile hangers-on had grown accustomed to participating on the margins of Jewish life and understood that without full conversion (including circumcision for males) they could not become members. If, as Luke argued, the Jesus sect was truly Jewish, then an informed Gentile would *expect* to be excluded. Acts 1–15, Luke's answer to these gentile anxieties, is so deftly argued that it has proved definitive in shaping the Christian worldview to the present day.

Luke's narrative in Acts opens with his gospel's closing image: Jesus ascending into heaven following his postresurrection appearances. The disciples choose Matthias as a replacement for the traitor Judas, so that the "new Israel" can have a full complement of twelve patriarchs, representing the twelve tribes of Israel. Chapter 2 begins at the feast of Pentecost (Shavouoth). Shavouoth, a harvest festival in ancient Israel, was by Jesus' time a pilgrimage festival associated (as it is today) with the

The Holy Spirit/*Ruach*

In both the Hebrew Bible and the New Testament, the divine presence is described as an agent that acts upon human beings with transforming power. Both the Hebrew *ruach* the Greek *pneuma* refer primarily to wind, moving air, or breath; and the use of these terms to describe God's presence is essentially metaphorical, a way of portraying a nonphysical entity that acts on the physical world. In the Hebrew Bible the *ruach elohim*, the spirit of God, is regularly said to rest upon individuals and groups, bestowing either superhuman strength (Samson in Judg. 14:6) or the power of prophecy (Saul in 1 Sam. 10:10). Some of the later prophetic books (see Joel 2:28 [Hebrew, 3:1]; Ezek. 36:26-27) foresee an end-time "outpouring" of the divine spirit that will permanently transform human hearts. Jewish apocalyptic literature expected the coming messiah to be endowed with God's spirit (1 Enoch 49:3; 62:2). New Testament literature continues this understanding of God's spirit as an illuminating and transforming presence; as messiah, Jesus is filled with God's spirit. After Jesus' death, the divine spirit empowered his followers. The doctrine that the Holy Spirit is, along with the Father and the Son, a member of the Trinity, was not fully developed until the fourth century.

giving of the Torah. Luke makes full use of Sinai imagery in describing the scene: the disciples experience a wind from heaven, then fire, and then the presence of the Holy Spirit. The sequence of wind, fire, and divine presence echoes the experience of Elijah on Mount Horeb (1 Kings 19), which in turn alludes to Moses on Sinai. In his gospel Luke has already shown us Jesus "on the mountain" with Moses and Elijah. Now the disciples have their own mountaintop experience. Following in the steps of Moses, Elijah, and Jesus, the disciples are touched by God's spirit and empowered to speak God's word to the people.

Tongues of heavenly fire touch them and they speak "in other languages"—indeed, in every language represented by the great collection of diaspora Jews who hear them.

Peter announces that the descent of the Holy Spirit fulfills the prophecy of Joel: "In the last days . . . I will pour out my Spirit upon all flesh, and your sons and your daughters shall prophesy" (Joel 2:28). That's the good part. Peter then accuses his fellow Israelites of crucifying Jesus, killing him "by the hands of those outside the law" (the Romans). Quoting several psalms in succession, Peter argues that Jesus, now raised from the dead, was the messiah foreseen by David. "Therefore," says Peter, "let the entire house of Israel know with certainty that God has made him both Lord and Messiah, this Jesus whom you cruci-

GLOSSOLALIA

The practice of "speaking in tongues," which has been controversial for centuries, continues in some modern Christian circles. Glossolalia is difficult to define, mostly because the two New Testament examples, Acts 2:4–8 and 1 Cor. 14:2, 6–11, clearly describe different phenomena. In Acts the disciples speak in "different languages," that is, in human languages that are understood by the international crowd of bystanders. In 1 Corinthians, however, Paul objects to the congregation's emphasis on Spirit-induced speech that cannot be understood by listeners. This latter phenomenon seems to resemble the practice suggested in the Testament of Job 48:1–50:3 (and probably assumed in the angelic liturgies of Qumran), in which human beings join the angels, praising God in an angelic language. As in the Hellenistic tradition of "mantic" (ecstatic) prophecy, the speech is unintelligible and must be interpreted by a prophet. Both Charismatic and Pentecostal Christians continue to value the experience of speaking in a "spiritual language."

fied." Peter's Jewish listeners are "cut to the heart" by this speech; thousands, says Luke, are baptized in response to this first Christian sermon. To the modern reader it seems extraordinary that a sermon accusing the Jews of crucifying Jesus should meet with such a positive response from the Jewish community. But the text is not written for Jewish readers. Peter may address a crowd of Jews, but Luke's true audience remains Theophilus, the gentile reader. Reading that thousands of Jews have come to "know with certainty" that God has exalted Jesus as Lord and messiah, Theophilus can have certainty as well.

In chapter 3 Luke demonstrates the disciples' newly given ability to work miracles in Jesus' name. Peter and John are accosted on their way into the temple by a lame man begging at the temple gate. Peter heals the man, who enters the temple, praising God. Peter then delivers another interpretive speech, claiming that the Jews did kill "the Author of life" but did so in ignorance. This time, however, Peter includes a threat: Jesus was the "prophet like Moses" foretold in the Torah, and "everyone who does *not* listen to that prophet will be utterly rooted out of the people." The Jews can either accept Jesus as messiah or be "rooted out." Despite Peter's acerbic accusations and threats, Luke again paints a rosy picture of Jewish response: an additional five thousand Jews are baptized into the sect.

Soon, however, trouble arises: not all Jews agree with Peter. "The priests, the captain of the temple, and the Sadducees" (that is, the leaders, but not the people) object to Peter's claims on the basis that he asserts the reality of resurrection. Most Jews of the first century believed in a future resurrection, and would have sided with Peter on this question. The temple leadership, however, are resurrection-denying Sadducees, and they arrest Peter and John. Peter makes yet another speech. The "chief priests and elders" are enraged but dare not punish Peter and John "because of the people." The two are released.

The stories of Peter's early preaching allow Luke to make several key points. First, both Peter's miracles and his quotations from Torah are intended to prove that Jesus was the messiah. Second, by performing miracles in Jesus' name, Peter demonstrates that God now works through the community just as he formerly worked through Jesus.

Finally, by showing that the Jewish people are convinced by Peter's preaching (only the leadership is threatened), Luke reassures his gentile reader that the Jesus movement is a credible form of Judaism. At the same time, however, Luke explains the animosity between Jesus' followers and other Jews—something that Luke's gentile reader would have witnessed: just as the Jewish people were divided over Jesus in his lifetime (as demonstrated in Luke's gospel), so now they will be divided over the church.

Jesus' disciples continue to work miracles and to preach, and in chapter 5 the chief priest has them arrested. They are freed by an angel, leaving the guards to find an empty cell, an obvious allusion to Jesus' empty tomb. Being excellent citizens, the disciples allow themselves to be recaptured and taken before the Sanhedrin for trial. The Sanhedrin want to have them killed but are dissuaded by a certain "Gamaliel, a teacher of the law" (5:34). Though no external evidence suggests that Gamaliel (the elder) had any contact with the early Christians, Luke employs him to bolster Christian credibility: no less a figure than the rabbi Gamaliel intervened on behalf of the apostles. The sage does not actually *support* the messianists; on the contrary, he compares them (probably anachronistically) with Theudas, another messianic revolutionary (see Josephus, *Ant.* 20.97–98) who was killed by the Romans. Gamaliel counsels that the Jesus movement be allowed to die a natural death—unless it should indeed be "of God," in which case even the Sanhedrin would be unable to destroy it. Gamaliel's practical solution carries the day; the apostles are flogged and released.

Luke's case that Jesus was the messiah reaches its climax in chapters 6–7 with the martyrdom of the apostle Stephen. Stephen, his accusers claim, says that Jesus "will destroy [the temple] and will change the customs Moses handed on to us." Luke, of course, is writing *after* the temple's destruction, and responding to charges that the Christians had rejoiced in its demise. Luke needs to prove that Jesus' followers, far from exhibiting hostility to Jews or Judaism, embody God's will for the Jewish people. Stephen responds to the charges against him by giving a lengthy recital of Israel's past. Beginning with Abraham, he creates what became a phenomenally popular take on Jewish history: the history of Israel was all a preparation for Jesus. Luke's powerful recasting of Israel's story has become deeply rooted in the Christian consciousness and continues to contribute to misperceptions about Judaism. The life of Jesus, says Stephen, was foreshadowed by the biblical Joseph—hated by his brothers and handed over to suffer at the hands of strangers. After this abuse Joseph was rescued by God and raised to an exalted position, at which point he "made himself known to his brothers." Joseph, it turns out, can be made into a pretty good model for Jesus. Joseph, however, is only the warm-up act; the true model for Jesus is Moses. Stephen retells the Moses story, embroidering it with references to *Luke's* version of Jesus' life. The Israelites' challenge to Moses, for example—"Who made you a ruler and judge over us?" (Exod. 2:14)—parallels Jesus' own encounter with his people: "Friend, who set me to be a judge or arbitrator over you?" (Luke 12:14). Like Jesus, Moses was rejected after his first attempt to help his people but was sent back a second time by God (in Jesus' case, after his resurrection), this time with power to deliver them. Throughout Stephen's speech, "this Moses whom they rejected" (7:35) prefigures "this Jesus whom you crucified" (2:36). Turning the tables on his accusers, Stephen claims that it is *they* who are a "stiff-necked people, uncircumcised in heart and ears, . . . forever opposing the Holy Spirit, just as your ancestors used to do." Like the worshipers of the golden calf, it is *they* (and not the Christians) who are abandoning the law of Moses, who have "received the law" but have not kept it.

The Sanhedrin, of course, are not at all pleased at Stephen's comparisons. Upon concluding his speech Stephen sees a vision of the opened heavens, where Jesus, "the Son of Man," stands at God's right hand. Stephen's listeners promptly stone him to death for blasphemy. By becoming the first Christian martyr, Stephen quite dramatically illustrates Luke's contention that the church now replicates the life of Jesus. After working miracles and teaching the people on God's behalf, he is killed as an enemy of the Jews. At this point in the narrative Luke has effectively concluded his argument that Jesus and his followers represent God's fulfillment of the promises made to Abraham, and as such are the true Israel. Luke's defense of the movement's Jewishness includes a built-in explanation of why most Jews will fail (and Luke does present it as *failure,* not "disagreement") to accept Jesus as messiah: Israel has been divided, and only some are able to perceive and accept God's new work in their midst.

The next section of Luke's narrative (chapters 8–15) addresses the reader's second anxiety: how can Gentiles be full members of a Jewish sect if they do not undergo circumcision? Here Luke makes a brilliant end run around what had by his day become a glaring problem for the Jesus sect, namely, that a predominantly gentile group claimed to be the one true embodiment of *Judaism.* Rather than confronting this issue head-on, Luke presents a developmental view of the movement. A group of devout Jews following Jesus, the messiah, becomes the true continuation of the people Israel. Soon this true (and Jewish) Israel finds that Gentiles are flocking to join them. What to do? By framing the question as a legitimate problem facing a devout Jewish community, Luke deflects the question of whether the sect is "still Jewish" if it includes unconverted Gentiles, perhaps even as a majority. Instead, he focuses on a more neutral problem: what is the proper status of God-fearing Gentiles in the messianic age?

Chapter 8 opens with a notice that, "scattered" by persecution, Jesus' followers went and preached throughout Judea and Samaria. The apostle Philip, having been received with "great joy" by the Samaritans, is sent by an angel to Gaza, on the Judean coast. There he finds an Ethiopian eunuch (apparently a Jew) puzzling over Isaiah's prophecies regarding God's suffering servant: "Like a sheep he was led to the slaughter, and like a lamb silent before its shearer, so he does not open his mouth" (Isa. 53:1; Acts 8:31). The servant in Isaiah's prophecy (whose identity remains a scholarly conundrum) is cruelly abused, suffering "for our sins." Philip explains that the servant is Jesus; the eunuch is baptized on the spot. Isaiah's suffering-servant passages had never been read as messianic prophecies in Jewish antiquity, and Luke demonstrates the movement's strategy of choosing passages that could plausibly be applied to Jesus, and then interpreting them as *messianic* prophecies *fulfilled* by Jesus. Luke's purpose in this section is to depict the sect's movement outward from the center of the Jewish people (in

Jerusalem) to the margins, to those—Samaritans and a diaspora Jewish eunuch—who have a claim to Jewish identity but an ambiguous legal or ritual standing among the Jewish people. Having introduced the topic of those on the margins of the Jewish community, Luke has moved that much closer to the real subject at hand: those with no Jewish status at all.

Acts 9 opens with an abrupt "meanwhile," as Luke redirects our attention to Saul (later, Paul), the Pharisee who will head up the sect's mission to the Gentiles. Saul, it seems, has been busily persecuting the Jesus sect (a fact he confirms in his letters) and has just been sent by the high priest to Damascus, where he is to search synagogues for followers of Jesus. (Luke's image of a central Jerusalem authority policing Jews in Damascus is highly implausible.) Saul is accosted en route by a blinding light and a voice from heaven. "Lord," he asks, "who are you?" The "Lord" whom Saul addresses is, of course, none other than "Jesus, whom you are persecuting." Saul now has to do some serious theological backpedaling, and soon he is in the synagogues of Damascus, not persecuting Christians, but confounding "the *Jews* who lived in Damascus by proving that Jesus was the messiah" (9:22).

Luke returns in chapter 10 to Jesus' original followers and introduces the figure of Cornelius, a God-fearing centurion whose story, told and retold over the next five chapters, will form the core of Luke's case for the inclusion of Gentiles in the sect. Cornelius was "a devout man who feared God . . . [and] gave alms generously to the [Jewish] people." Here is a well-placed gentile patron of the local Jewish community—someone with whom Theophilus can identify. Cornelius has a vision in which an angel commands him to send to the coastal city of Joppa for Peter, the leader of the apostles. He does so, and as his messengers approach Joppa, Peter also has a vision:

> He saw the heaven opened and something like a large sheet coming down, being lowered to the ground by its four corners. In it were all kinds of four-footed creatures and reptiles and birds of the air. Then he heard a voice saying, "Get up, Peter; kill and eat." (Acts 10:11–13)

Peter has no intention, even in a vision, of eating all that *tref* (ritually forbidden food), but the voice insists: "What God has made clean, you must not call profane." This scenario is repeated no fewer than three times when Cornelius's messengers appear at the door. Peter gets the point; the gentile Cornelius, the human equivalent of *tref,* has been declared clean. Peter travels to Cornelius's house, announcing that by so doing he is breaking Jewish law in response to a direct command from God. Although it is by no means certain that any law of the period forbade Jews from entering the homes of Gentiles, Peter is clearly portrayed as transgressing the custom of observant Palestinian Jews.

Cornelius greets Peter and tells him of his vision. At this Peter announces, "I truly understand that God shows no partiality, but in every nation anyone who fears him and does what is right is acceptable to him." The principle that God is not partial (Deut. 10:17) but accepts those who are righteous (Prov. 15:8) was well established within Jewish tradition, but here Peter extends its application beyond the boundaries of the Jewish community: God is "not partial" to the Jews. The force of Peter's claim in the context of first-century Judaism is difficult to assess. The Babylonian Talmud states that the righteous of every nation have a place in the world to come (*b. Sanh.* 105a), but Acts predates the Talmud. And Luke goes beyond even the Talmud, claiming that because righteous Gentiles are "acceptable" to God, they may be included not only in the world to come but also in the Jewish community. Peter's announcement that "God is not partial" will result in radically new boundaries for the messianic sect.

As Peter is speaking, the Holy Spirit descends upon Cornelius and his household, who are thereupon baptized. The giving of the Spirit *before* baptism is of crucial importance to Luke. Baptism, the *mikvah,* was the primary (perhaps only) conversion ritual for *Jews* joining Luke's branch of the Jesus sect. To join other forms of Judaism, Gentiles would have been not only baptized but also circumcised. Cornelius and his household, however, have undergone no conversion rituals at all when they are directly validated by the descent of God's spirit. Luke will make Cornelius's inclusion by divine fiat into the precedent for the entire movement's acceptance of Gentiles without circumcision.

Peter returns to Jerusalem, where he is criticized, not for converting "uncircumcised men," but for merely *eating* with them. Peter proceeds to repeat his vision almost verbatim but with the addition that the Spirit expressly instructed him to "make no distinction between them and us." This claim is, in a Jewish context, astonishing. The entire question of whether the messianists are or are not still members of historical Israel (a question Luke purports already to have answered in the affirmative) hinges on this point. Beginning at Sinai the Israelites are repeatedly commanded to "make a distinction" between clean and unclean, "because of the tabernacle in your midst" (Lev. 15:31). God's presence in the midst of the people Israel requires that they maintain levels of ritual purity not required for "the nations." Ultimately, the very identity of Israel as partner in a covenant with God depends on the command "You shall make a distinction." Now, Peter is told, God has changed his mind.

Small wonder that Luke has argued so painstakingly that the messianists were faithful members of the Jewish community, or that he repeats three times Peter's claims that *God* told him to eat *tref, God* told him to visit Cornelius, *God* bestowed the Spirit on an uncircumcised Gentile. Yes, it's contrary to Torah and tradition, but don't blame the Christians; God did it! "Who," asks Peter, "was I that I could hinder God?" This is the climax of Luke's argument, an argument that would prove pivotal in Christian self-understanding: that, as prophesied in the scriptures, God had changed the rules for inclusion in the Jewish people, making "no distinction" between Jew and Gentile. The rest of the Jewish people, including many Jewish members of the Jesus movement, would disagree. Witnessing an increasingly gentile association that ignored Jewish practice and tradition, most Jews would simply conclude that the movement had ceased to be Jewish.

Having established through the Cornelius story that Gentiles were joining the messianists because of God's direct intervention, Luke turns his attention back to Paul. At Antioch in Pisidia (in Asia Minor, not the larger Antioch in Syria), Paul attends sabbath services in the synagogue and is invited to speak. He directs his comments to "you Israelites and others who fear God," that is, to Jews and gentile God-fearers.

Paul proceeds to give the by now familiar narrative proof that Jesus is messiah, but "because the residents of Jerusalem and their leaders did not recognize him or understand the words of the prophets that are read every sabbath, they fulfilled those words by condemning him" (13:27). Paul suggests that every Jew who paid any attention to scripture recognized Jesus as messiah; only a few who hadn't been listening had wanted him killed. "But God raised him from the dead. . . . And we bring you the good news that what God promised to our ancestors he has fulfilled for us, their children." It is hardly surprising that Luke should be the New Testament author most quoted by modern Jews for Jesus; he makes the strongest case possible that Jesus is "good news" for Jews. Paul wins converts among both Jews and Gentiles and is invited to speak in the synagogue again. On the next sabbath, however, "when the Jews saw the crowds, they were filled with jealousy" and opposed him. Paul, in turn, announces that because the Jews have rejected the word of God, "we are now turning to the Gentiles" (13:46). Paul's—and for that matter, the entire movement's—turn to the Gentiles is not portrayed as a result of the movement's unpopularity among the Jews but as the fulfillment of prophecy: "I have set you to be a light for the Gentiles, so that you may bring salvation to the ends of the earth" (Acts 13:47; Isa. 49:6).

In Acts 15 the issue of gentile conversion comes to a head. Luke presents the problem succinctly: "Certain individuals came down from Judea and were teaching the brothers, 'Unless you are circumcised according to the custom of Moses, you cannot be saved.' " (The precise meaning of salvation is not spelled out, but in Luke's context it means full inclusion in the messianic community, acceptance by God, and, after death, resurrection.) The community's response to those who required gentile circumcision will provide a resolution to Theophilus's anxiety: on what basis can God-fearing Gentiles participate in "the new Israel"?

A meeting, the so-called Council of Jerusalem, is held to address the question of gentile circumcision. The first position presented is that of "believers who belonged to the sect of the Pharisees," that is, Christian Pharisees: "It is necessary for them to be circumcised and ordered to keep the law of Moses." Luke opens with the conservative position: full conversion is required. Aware of Pharisaic/rabbinic criticism of the Jesus sect's practice, Luke anticipates and neutralizes the Pharisaic position by presenting it as a position already addressed by Pharisees *within* the community. Peter responds by recounting his experience with Cornelius: God himself has already included Gentiles without circumcision, "and in cleansing their hearts by faith he has made no distinction between them and us." The Gentiles, says Peter, are being purified "by faith" rather than by baptism (the *mikvah*) or circumcision. Peter, of course, is arguing, not about a new religion called "Christianity," but about the correct way to practice *Judaism*. This, he says, is how we must structure Jewish observance in light of the messiah's arrival. In the matter of Gentiles, God is bypassing Mosaic law. As faithful Jews, we need to follow suit. This principle is immediately confirmed by James, Jesus' brother, who quotes the Septuagint version of Amos 9:11–12: "I will rebuild the dwelling of David . . . , so that all other peoples may seek the Lord—even all the Gentiles over whom my name has been called." The inclusion of Gentiles, argues James, has always formed part of Israel's messianic expectation. James then decrees that gentile believers should observe a simplified version of what were later called the Noahide laws—prohibitions against acts such as adultery and murder that the rabbis considered binding on the entire human family. The Jerusalem elders agree, and send out letters and apostles to relay the news to gentile adherents in the diaspora.

The historical accuracy of Luke's account cannot, of course, be verified. Paul, in Gal. 2:1–10, refers to a meeting with similar results but differing in details. In the context of Luke's narrative, however, the Council of Jerusalem marks the crowning moment in his quest to provide "security" for an anxious gentile reader. God has taken the lead in purifying those Gentiles who seek to serve him, and no further sign of the covenant is necessary. Luke continues to depict the Jesus movement as the obvious next step in the life of the Jewish people—the arrival of the messiah, when "Gentiles shall come to your light" (Isa. 60:3). Christianity, Luke argues, is Judaism, pure and simple. And because God is Lord of all, Gentiles may be included on whatever terms God

CHRISTIAN VIEWS OF JUDAISM AS "TRIBAL" AND "EXCLUSIVE"

Luke asserts that only Christian Pharisees wanted Gentiles to undergo full conversion before joining the Jesus sect. Here, Pharisees (the forebears of the rabbis) are depicted as *marginalized* members of the community who refuse to accept that God has no need for everyone to become Jewish in order "to be saved." Luke's contrast between the ungracious requirements of the Pharisees and the liberal openness of God paved the way for later Christian assumptions that Judaism is "narrow," "tribal," or "exclusive" whereas Christianity is "open," "universal," and "accepting." Such characterizations have proved remarkably resilient, even among otherwise liberal Christians, and despite rabbinic Judaism's claim that the righteous of all nations have a place in the world to come, or many Christians' claim that non-Christians are doomed to hell.

dictates. Jews who raise objections are demonstrating a basic hostility toward God.

It is hard to overestimate the impact of Luke's narrative scheme on the Christian imagination. In all fairness, the general outline of events as he portrays them is entirely plausible: Christianity began among Jews who believed that the messiah had been killed but resurrected by God, that he had returned to empower his followers, and that their faith had been enriched and transformed in light of the messiah's advent. When these Jewish messianists were faced with the interest of gentile God-fearers, they were pressed to consider how the community might best structure itself in the messianic age. Such an outline of Christianity's early development is reasonable enough. Luke's task, however, was not to provide a historical outline but to reassure a well-placed gentile Christian. He therefore needed to argue both that Christianity is the purest and highest form of Judaism and that, all Jewish tradition to the contrary, the purest Judaism is one that welcomes Gentiles without conversion. And Luke succeeded. Millions have accepted Luke's invitation to include themselves as members of this new "Israel." Luke offers outsiders a warm welcome into a new and joyful Jewish community. Sadly, he offers this welcome at the cost of discrediting the Jewish community as a whole. The second half of Acts will concern itself with Paul's missionary journeys, and with the disastrous break between Paul and the Jews.

Luke lays out a pattern whereby Paul goes to speak at synagogues throughout the eastern Mediterranean world and experiences spectacular success among God-fearers and modest success among Jews, followed by persecution at the hands of those Jews who do not convert. Luke's repeated descriptions of Paul preaching in the synagogues serve to demonstrate the movement's good-faith effort to maintain itself as a legitimate Jewish community. At the same time, the pattern of success among the Gentiles and rejection by the Jews allows Luke to account for the movement's increasingly gentile makeup. The overall effect of Acts 16–28 is to build upon claims Luke has laid out in the first half of the book: that the Jesus sect is the legitimate continuation of the people Israel and that the inclusion of Gentiles in the sect is likewise legitimate, the fulfillment of God's promises to Abraham and the prophets. Paul's journeys will not be dealt with in detail here; only episodes bearing directly on the Jesus movement's embattled Jewish identity will be discussed at length.

After the Council of Jerusalem in Acts 15, Paul travels to Derbe and Lystra in central Asia Minor, where he encounters a believer named Timothy (16:1–3). Paul wishes to enlist Timothy, the uncircumcised son of a Jewish mother and a Greek father, as a missionary assistant, but before doing so, he has Timothy circumcised. Paul is depicted as eager to fulfill all appropriate Jewish rituals—he respects the Jewish community's norms and strives to maintain the Jewish legitimacy of his mission. Remarkably, the account of Timothy's circumcision appears in the chapter immediately following the ruling that gentile Christians need *not* undergo circumcision. Luke is clearly making a case that Jewish Christians continue to be good Jews—in the case of Timothy, better

Jews than they had been previously! The same point is made in 21:17–26, when Paul's loyalty to Jewish law is challenged by "many thousand" Jewish Christians in Palestine who are "all zealous for the law." These observant members of the sect are under the impression that Paul has been teaching "all the Jews living among the Gentiles to forsake Moses, and . . . not to circumcise their children or observe the customs." Paul's prior circumcision of Timothy has, of course, already shown the reader that the accusation is false, but Paul is now given an additional opportunity to demonstrate his loyalty to Torah: he pays the expenses of four Jewish Christians who are undergoing a Nazirite vow, an act of special devotion as described in Numbers 6. Ironically, the existing evidence suggests that lax observance of Mosaic law (or none at all) was not uncommon among diaspora Jews of the first century. Luke's point, however, is that the Jews who followed Jesus remained faithful to Torah, perhaps even more so than some other diaspora Jews.

Luke's insistence on the messianists' Jewish legitimacy is overshadowed by his accounts of Paul's suffering at the hands of the Jewish majority, and by Paul's announcements that God's offer of salvation, having been rejected by the Jews, has now gone to the Gentiles (13:46; 18:6; 28:25–28). As it turns out, not only has God's offer gone to the Gentiles; it seems to have gone especially to Gentiles of high standing (10:1; 13:7; 17:12). Luke repeatedly emphasizes that the Gentiles among whom the movement takes root are not, or not exclusively, the miracle-hungry crowds of the Roman metropolis but people of standing: centurions, wealthy merchants, and government officials. Having addressed Theophilus's theological anxieties, Luke seeks to assuage his social anxieties as well. Luke takes pains to show that the sect is admired by wealthy and sophisticated Romans.

As Paul journeys through the Roman world he repeatedly demonstrates the miracles that are the hallmark of divine power at work in the community, thwarting the efforts of Jewish enemies and impressing both synagogue-going God-fearers and the gentile officials before whom he must repeatedly testify in his own defense. Paul is shown in Athens engaging in dialogue with devotees of the Athenian philosophical schools, all of whom admire his message. In Ephesus, home of a popular cult of Artemis, Paul bests Artemis's followers with his preaching of Christ. Our hero can go head-to-head with any religion of the day. But even as Christianity spreads across the gentile world, hostility toward Paul grows. Finally, while he is on a visit to Jerusalem, the crowds accuse him not only of "teaching everyone everywhere against our people, our law, and this place" but of the specific crime of bringing a Gentile into the temple. Paul is arrested. Brought before the Sanhedrin, Paul provokes a scuffle between Pharisaic and Sadducean members by claiming, "I am on trial concerning the hope of the resurrection of the dead" (23:6–10), a hope the Pharisees affirmed but the Sadducees denied. His case is brought to the Romans, but the procurator Festus throws up his hands, saying that it amounts to a Jewish "disagreement . . . about their own religion" (25:19). Paul ultimately requests that his trial be heard in Rome, and once there, he continues to preach to the Jewish community, emphasizing that "it is for the sake of the hope of Israel that I am bound with this chain" (28:20). The Roman Jews are divided in their response, but in his final speech Paul condemns them, saying that they have fulfilled the words of the prophet by growing so callous that they cannot turn to God and be healed. "Let it be known to you," Paul concludes, "that this salvation of God has been sent to the Gentiles; they will listen." The book ends with Paul under house arrest in Rome, awaiting trial.

The figure of Paul effectively represents Luke's view of Christianity itself: devoutly Jewish, steeped in Torah, misunderstood by the Jewish community and moving in increasingly gentile circles, but facing an uncertain future at the hands of Roman authorities. The unknown author of Luke-Acts effectively provided the "security" needed by thoughtful Gentiles in the new sect. Luke's image of a humble and devout people, called and empowered by God, has remained at the heart of Christians' self-image, even when the religion has wielded imperial power. And his image of a failed Judaism that stood by, smug, judgmental, and legalistic, willfully excluding itself from God's blessings, has had an equally enduring legacy.

THE LETTERS OF PAUL

F OR MUCH OF THE twentieth century, Paul of Tarsus was considered the founder of a new religion, Christianity. Jesus had been a Galilean teacher, but Paul, a hellenized Jew of Asia Minor, brought Jesus' message, both physically and philosophically, to the Gentiles. In recent years the image of the "Christian Paul" has fallen out of favor. Just as in the nineteenth and twentieth centuries scholars rediscovered the Jewishness of Jesus, so now they have begun to reclaim the Jewishness of Paul. The reality of a Jewish Paul—a Paul who never dreamed that his missionary endeavors would spread anything but a new stage in Jewish belief—carries a particular poignancy in light of later Christian history. Whatever his intentions, Paul remains the founder of Christianity as a thought system that could continue to grow without the participation of Jews; this is the use to which Paul's writings have been put. If Paul can still be said to have founded Christianity, however, it is now clear that he did so unintentionally.

Thirteen books of the New Testament are attributed to Paul; another, Acts, is largely concerned with his biography. Despite this relative abundance of material, no detailed reconstruction of his life is possible. The difficulty lies in the nature of the sources. Paul's letters were composed as guidance to individual congregations; any information they contain about Paul is incidental. Acts's portrayal of Paul is fuller, but even more selective. Paul is the hero of Acts and, as such, epitomizes those themes and virtues that Luke, the author, wishes to highlight. Thus, in his letters Paul stresses his independence from the Jerusalem church and his deficiencies as a speaker, whereas Luke's Paul is bold and eloquent, and above all, a delegate of Jerusalem. Reliable information about Paul is scarce, and only a tenuous biography is possible.

According to Acts, Paul was born sometime around 5–10 C.E. in Tarsus, a cosmopolitan city of southeast Asia Minor. Acts says that as a young man Paul came to Jerusalem, where he studied with the Pharisaic teacher Gamaliel (the elder). Paul mentions only that he was a zealous member of the Pharisaic sect. Sometime in the 30s he was engaged in persecuting Jesus' followers (the reasons are not stated) when he had a vision of the risen Jesus (here Acts and Paul's letters agree) and was divinely commissioned to become Jesus' "apostle to the Gentiles." Paul's conversion into the Jesus sect was a departure from his Pharisaic allegiance, but not from Judaism per se. On the contrary, Paul saw Jesus as God's promised messiah and himself, like Jeremiah, as having been set apart from before his birth to be "a prophet to the nations [*goyim*]" (Jer. 1:5). Paul's missionary activity fulfilled biblical expectations for the end time.

Although Paul describes several years spent in Damascus and Arabia (Gal. 1:17), his missionary work seems to have begun in Syrian Antioch, the capital of the Roman province of Syria-Palestine and an early center of the Jesus movement. While in Antioch, he appears to have been at the center of the dispute between traditionalist members of the sect—those who favored the circumcision of gentile converts—and those who, like himself, believed that Gentiles were to be included *as Gentiles* rather than through conversion to Judaism. Both Paul and Acts report a meeting held in Jerusalem to resolve these matters (Gal. 2:1–10; Acts 15:1–29), but Acts's picture of a happy resolution does not match Paul's account of ongoing conflict within the community. The Antioch leadership seems to have favored circumcision of converts, and Paul soon moved his mission westward, founding and visiting congregations in Asia Minor, Macedonia, and Greece (see the map of the Eastern Roman Empire in the First Century C.E., p. vi).

Acts portrays Paul as seeking converts in diaspora synagogues, where his message proves more attractive to gentile God-fearers than to Jews, but Paul does not mention such a pattern. Some of his congregations seem to consist of former pagans, rather than of Gentiles with a previous Jewish affiliation.

From the late 40s to the early 60s C.E. Paul traveled, taught, and wrote letters to congregations across the Aegean basin. Most of the letters respond to crises arising in congregations that Paul had founded but could not visit in person, either because he was working in another region or because he was in prison. Acts reports imprisonments in Philippi, Caesarea, and Rome; Paul himself suggests that such imprisonments were frequent. Christianity had not been outlawed in the 50s, but the movement transgressed social and religious norms in ways that Romans were bound to find suspect. Roman law did not typically use imprisonment as a punishment; rather, an accused criminal was imprisoned while awaiting trial. Paul may have been tried on a number of charges, from disturbing the peace to disrespecting the gods. If, as Luke portrays it, the Jewish community found that his teaching or practices violated Jewish law, the Jewish community could also have imprisoned him. Five letters, Philippians, Ephesians, Colossians, Philemon, and 2 Timothy, include the claim that they were written from prison.

With the exception of Romans, Paul's letters are addressed to congregations located in large cities across the Aegean basin: Corinth, Ephesus, Philippi, Thessalonica. Romans is addressed to a group Paul had never met, and would meet only later, as a prisoner, at the end of his life. Sometime in the late 50s Paul wrote a letter of self-introduction to the Roman congregation, seeking their support for a proposed westward expansion of his missionary activities. Instead of expanding his efforts westward, however, Paul was arrested and sent to Rome for trial. Acts reports that he lived in Rome under house arrest for more than a year; tradition holds that he was martyred there in the early 60s.

Founding and nurturing Jesus-following communities, writing letters of exhortation and sending out co-workers to follow up on his work, Paul may have been typical of many who traveled in service of the fledgling sect. Paul's letters, however—preserved, collected, and circulated among his churches—soon came to be regarded as scripture, as essential writings, first in only some branches of the sect, and eventually throughout the church. Already 2 Peter refers to Paul's letters as guides, and Luke's portrayal of the apostle in Acts sets him apart as the premier teacher of the early church. Paul's influence on the early church, if not necessarily in his own lifetime, then soon after, was profound. But if Paul was not the "founder" of Christianity, the one who (as tradition would have it) moved beyond a narrow Jewish legalism to a universal religion based on faith, then who was he? What, if not the rejection of Judaism, did he teach?

Perhaps not surprisingly, Paul taught different things in different circumstances. He wrote no treatises on Christian belief, only responses to specific problems that arose in individual congregations. In general, Paul's writings reflect his belief that God had raised Jesus from the dead and exalted him as Lord and messiah. All of scripture must accordingly be reinterpreted in light of this central reality. He himself had been singled out by Jesus to carry God's word to the Gentiles, an event anticipated by the biblical prophets. Both Paul's claim that Jesus was the messiah and his extension of the movement to the Gentiles, while defensible in terms of Jewish belief, were controversial. Paul's letters thus frequently center on the defense of Jesus' messiahship, and on arguments against gentile circumcision. The latter take the form of the impassioned condemnations of "the law" for which he is famous among Christians and infamous among Jews. It is crucial, however, to understand that Paul condemns ritual observance (including circumcision) only as a requirement imposed on Gentiles. When Paul writes to other Jews he assumes the validity of the law (Torah) while allowing for discretion in ritual observance, particularly in settings that include both Jewish and gentile sectarians.

According to Acts Paul offers sacrifice at the Jerusalem temple and circumcises his Jewish assistant Timothy. In Romans, he defends the Jewish people against the developing notion that Christians have replaced the Jews as the people of God. On the contrary, Paul's entire work derives from the proposition that the inclusion of Gentiles has taken place only as part of the messianic age. Gentiles, in the last days, have been grafted into the great tree that is Israel. They are newcomers to, not supplanters of, the Jewish people. Paul continually seeks the common ground between Jewish and gentile—or, more important, between anti-Jewish and anti-gentile—Christianities.

A final difficulty in reconstructing Paul's life and thought is the status of the so-called disputed letters. Six of his letters, 2 Thessalonians, Ephesians, Colossians, 1 and 2 Timothy, and Titus, have often been attributed to a Pauline "school" writing in the apostle's name years or even generations after his death. Pseudonymity, writing in the name of an earlier and well-known figure, was widely practiced in both Jewish and Hellenistic circles as a way of claiming continuity with or authority from an illustrious predecessor. On the basis of perceived differences in content and language usage, the disputed letters have frequently been assumed to represent such later adaptations of Paul's thought. Such perceptions are, however, highly subjective, with those letters in which Paul champions "justification by faith" granted a higher claim to authenticity than those that deal, for example, with church administration. But of course Paul might have written differently on different subjects or in different periods of his life.

A further complication in the search for Pauline authenticity arises from the customs of letter production in antiquity. Contrary to contemporary notions, one did not have to have written something in order to be its author. Authors often dictated to amanuenses, sometimes assigning them to write on a given subject but leaving the wording to them. Disciples might also be assigned to write in the master's name. Four of Paul's letters, for example, are said to come from "Paul and Timothy" (2 Corinthians, Philippians, Colossians, and Philemon) and two from "Paul, Silvanus, and Timothy" (1 and 2 Thessalonians), with the division of labor left unstated. Given the possibility that Paul could have commissioned his letters but not have written *any* them in the modern sense, the entire category of "authenticity" begins to lose meaning. As helpful as it might be to separate out the genuine Paul from his later interpreters, such a division is rarely possible.

The New Testament canon orders the letters on the basis of length, from longest (Romans) to shortest (Philemon). In this book, Paul's letters to congregations are discussed according to a rough approximation of chronological order, from 1 Thessalonians (widely considered the earliest of Paul's letters) to several letters written in the mid- to late 50s, and concluding with Romans, in which Paul proposes a journey he did not live to make. The so-called pastoral epistles, letters to Paul's associates, are discussed after his letters to congregations. Questions regarding the authenticity of the disputed letters will be dealt with on a case-by-case basis.

FIRST THESSALONIANS

THE CONGREGATION AT Thessalonica was apparently founded by Paul and his associates in the late forties. Thessalonica was the capital of the Roman province of Macedonia, a thriving port located on the main east-west highway of the empire. Details of the church's makeup and early history are made more rather than less murky by Luke's discussion of the Thessalonian church in Acts 16. Luke provides a lively narrative in which Paul preaches in the synagogue at Thessalonica, gaining some converts among the Jews and many among the God-fearers, but is run out of town by jealous Jewish leaders. Luke's account, however, disagrees with what can be surmised from Paul's letter, particularly with regard to the makeup of the congregation, whom Luke would see as a mix of Jews and gentile God-fearers but whom Paul addresses as recent converts from paganism. Luke's account is suspect, first because it was written a generation later than Paul's letter, but even more so because it conforms to Luke's standard pattern in which the advent of Jesus causes joy among Gentiles and division among Jews. This is Luke's default narrative, and there is no reason to give it credence where it is contradicted by Paul's own.

The first of two letters written by Paul to the church at Thessalonica, 1 Thessalonians, composed around 50 C.E., is probably the earliest

New Testament writing. Despite its claim to temporal "primacy," it is one of the less well-known books of the New Testament. Its most distinctive feature is Paul's response to the problem that some Christians have already died, and so will miss out on Jesus' triumphant return. Two thousand years later, this once-pressing concern has lost its urgency, with the result that 1 Thessalonians makes for a somewhat less gripping read than it must once have done. The letter does, however, allow us to examine several beliefs emerging in the early church, most notably Paul's assertion that "the Jews" killed Jesus. The very ability of the Jewish Paul to write disparagingly about Jews to a group of Gentiles will provide an important key to Paul's self-understanding and to the identity he is shaping among his converts.

Paul's letter follows the standard form for a letter of *paranaesis*, roughly translated as exhortation or encouragement. A central technique of the genre is reminding the audience of what they already know to be true, something Paul does liberally in the letter. Further, he offers himself as the model for his students' thought and behavior. And, as was common in Greek rhetoric, he contrasts the purity of his own motives with those of various "flatterers" and charlatans. The letter is, in short, typical of the kind written by Greek teachers, and would have been thoroughly recognizable to an educated Greek reader.

However thoroughly Greek its form, 1 Thessalonians is surprisingly Jewish in content. Paul uses standard tools of Greek rhetoric to remind his readers that they are "chosen." They have now "turned" from idols and from sexual immorality, the two vices Jews most abhorred in Gentiles. Now they live a life that demonstrates their chosenness, as they fulfill God's desire that they be "holy" (3:13; 4:3, 7; 5:23; cf. Lev. 19:2). Holiness, however, entails separation from those who are unclean, and such separation frequently leads to persecution. Paul attempts to explain the paradoxical conjunction of chosenness and persecution, and encourages his converts not to abandon their new life in the face of suffering. Paul must convince his gentile converts to buy into the Jewish heritage of divine favor and human persecution. The image seems incongruous, but it is crucial to Paul's self-understanding and that of the communities he founded: Paul employs Greek pedagogy to teach Gentiles how to live—and to suffer—like Jews.

Paul writes to the Thessalonians from Corinth. Upon learning that the congregation has faced persecution since his departure, Paul has sent his assistant Timothy to check on them. Timothy has now returned with a positive report of their faith and love, and Paul writes to encourage them. Throughout the letter Paul congratulates the congregation on their "work of faith and labor of love" and their joy in the face of persecution. In fact, they are doing so well that Paul repeatedly tells them (1:8; 4:9; 5:1) that he has no need to write or speak to them at all! Over the course of five short chapters, Paul tells his readers no fewer than ten times that they already know what he is telling them. These constant reminders are a standard feature of paraenetic literature, and Paul uses them here as a morale-boosting device. The readers already know everything they need to know; Paul just wants to remind them of that fact. But what is it, specifically, that these gentile Christians know, and why do they need reminding? Paul says that just as earlier he sent Timothy, so he now writes:

> so that no one would be shaken by these persecutions. Indeed, *you yourselves know* that this is what we are destined for. In fact, when we were with you, *we told you beforehand* that we were to suffer persecution; so it turned out, *as you know*. (1 Thess. 3:3–4; italics added)

Despite Paul's insistence on his confidence, however, he is not as sure of this congregation as he claims to be. He writes to "restore whatever is lacking in [their] faith" so that they will be found "blameless before our God and Father" (3:10, 13). Something, it seems, *is* lacking in their faith, and they may not end up blameless. He is, in short, attempting to shore up a congregation in danger of buckling under pressure. But what pressure do they face? Who is persecuting them, and how?

The nature of the persecution facing the Thessalonians is almost entirely a matter of conjecture. If one credits Acts, the Jewish community of Thessalonica was exceptionally hostile to the Christian message, and so might have followed up their persecution of Paul with maltreatment of his followers. First Thessalonians, however, does not support this possibility. Paul says the Thessalonians "suffered the same things from [their] own compatriots as [the Judean Christians] did from the Jews" (2:14). Paul's assertion that the Judean churches suffered at the hands of "the Jews" agrees with the later accounts in Acts and in the gospels. To the extent that Jesus' followers sought to spread their views among the larger Jewish population, they were not welcomed. Like the Qumran sectarians who retreated to the banks of the Dead Sea, the Jesus sect was made up of Jews who vocally opposed the temple hierarchy, and whose apocalyptic messianism was bound to attract unfavorable attention from Rome. The claim, repeated in every gospel, that the Christians were beaten (that is, subjected to communal discipline) in local synagogues, is entirely plausible. But Paul's analogy, that the Thessalonian Christians are suffering from *their* compatriots the same treatment that (Jewish) Judean Christians have suffered from theirs, strongly implies that it was other Gentiles and not Jews who persecuted the Christians of Thessalonica.

Although we have no documentation of persecutions against gentile Christian communities at this early stage, we know that pagan inhabitants of the Roman world have had ample motivation to oppose such groups. Like other Jews, Jesus' followers were liable to be perceived as atheists; they did not worship the gods. Such an attitude was both antisocial (not supporting the ethos of the community) and dangerous, since the gods protected the city. The Jewish god had long been known to demand that his people worship him alone, but these gentile Jesus-followers were clearly not Jews. They had not joined the cult of the Jews but worshiped someone called Christus. Such hostility, accompanied by lethal persecution, had developed in other parts of the empire within a generation or two of Paul's letter to the Thessalonians. It seems reasonable to assume that, already in the year 50, pagan communities would have shown deep opposition to this strange new association.

Paul's analogy—that the Thessalonians suffer from their compatriots just as the Judean sectarians suffered from theirs—is unremarkable in itself. He drives this message home, however, with a vicious excoriation of "the Jews":

> You suffered the same things from your own compatriots as they did from the Jews, who killed both the Lord Jesus and the prophets, and drove us out; they displease God and oppose everyone by hindering us from speaking to the Gentiles so that they may be saved. . . . God's wrath has overtaken them at last. (1 Thess. 2:14–16)

First Thessalonians, the earliest surviving piece of Christian writing, already asserts the later church's claim that "the Jews killed Jesus." Ironically, scholars are universally agreed that Paul does not intend to slander the Jews as a whole; his other writings make it clear that he still considers himself (and the other apostles) fully Jewish. Rather, he is enraged against those Jews who "hinder [him] from speaking to the Gentiles," thus opposing "everyone" by keeping them from salvation. Paul maligns as enemies of humanity Jews who, for whatever reason, oppose the spread of Christianity. Why, then, does he call them simply "the Jews"?

Strange as it may appear, Paul may not be condemning the Jews at all, but rather "the *Judeans*." The word *iudaioi* can mean either "Jews" or "Judeans," and Paul's analogy—the Thessalonian Christians were opposed by their compatriots, just as the Judean Christians were opposed by theirs—makes "Judeans" the more likely translation. It would then be other "Judeans" who oppose the Judean Christians and the spread of their movement, and whom Paul therefore condemns. Such Judeans would, of course, be Jews, just as the Judean Christians were, but Paul's analogy (both churches experienced hostility from their own people) makes it clear that they are not condemned as Jews, but for opposing the Jesus sect.

Yet, even if Paul was condemning "the Judeans" rather than "the Jews," his charge that they "killed both the Lord Jesus and the prophets" was slanderous in its original context and, in later years, disastrous in its consequences. This passage, 1 Thess. 2:14–16, exemplifies the ambiguity inherent in early Christian literature as Jewish sectarian writing—namely, it is simultaneously Jewish and anti-Jewish. As is typical in sectarian literature, early Christian writers sought to validate their own group by vilifying and discrediting competing groups. One way to prove themselves the true embodiment of the tradition is to show that their opponents have manifestly betrayed and corrupted it. Paul uses the trope of "killing the prophets," a stereotyped charge that first appears in Neh. 9:26 and is developed in later texts such as the *Martyrdom of Isaiah*. The prophets are God's spokespersons on earth, and those who kill the prophets are by definition rebelling against God. Paul simply inserts the anti-Christian Judeans into the traditional slot of rebels who killed the prophets. Killing Jesus would merely be the most recent incident in a veritable tradition of prophet-killing. The fact that Jesus was killed by the Romans, not the Jews, was irrelevant. The Judean officials who now harassed Jesus' followers would surely have approved of Jesus' death. By itself the prophet-killing charge is formulaic and unremarkable. The deeper problem in 1 Thessalonians is that Paul employs this "insider" language with *Gentiles*.

It seems that in this first surviving Christian text we already see what would become the unchanging gentile Christian pattern of delegitimizing and disinheriting the Jews. Paul began his letter emphasizing to these newly converted pagans that they are now a chosen people, called to be holy, and also to undergo persecution. Why, if Paul had already damned the Jews as "Christ-killers," was he so carefully teaching his converts how to live and suffer as Jews? The answer is that in Paul's eyes the Thessalonians were converts to the Jewish sect to which he himself belonged, the followers of Jesus. If Paul understood himself to be teaching members of a beleaguered Jewish sect, then his link between "Judeans" who persecute Judean members of the sect and their ancestors who killed the prophets makes sense as in-house, sectarian slander. It is at least plausible that Paul, intent on teaching his converts how to "be holy, even as God is holy," also taught them contempt for those Jews who, in Paul's eyes, had turned against God by killing the prophets and harassing the sect-members of Judea. He may well have thought he was teaching converts to be good Jews rather than teaching Gentiles to hate them.

Paul concludes his letter by addressing two questions that have been troubling the congregation: first, how to understand the death of community members, and second, when to expect the end of the world. The death of community members was a special problem for a fervently apocalyptic group. First, they may have assumed that none of the "elect" would die before Jesus' return. Now that some had died, it was uncertain how they could participate in Jesus' final victory. Paul reassures the community that their hope is, after all, in resurrection and that far from having missed out on God's salvation, the deceased messianists will be the very first raised when Christ returns. The community must not be discouraged by earthly events such as life, death, and persecution; a blessedly grand finale is coming. One can almost hear Paul's audience asking, "All right, but *when* it is coming?" In 5:1–11 Paul addresses the inevitable desire to second-guess when and how such an event will occur. His answer: forget about it. As a source of hope they must keep in mind that God will soon intervene to establish his glorious kingdom, but as a matter of practicality they must live as "children of the day," that is, as worthy and responsible individuals. Paul has, in effect, returned to his emphasis of chapter 1, nurturing a Jewish ethical formation. Having "turned" from idols and sexual immorality, his converts must now strive to live lives worthy of God's chosen people.

SECOND THESSALONIANS

SECOND THESSALONIANS APPEARS to be a follow-up letter to
1 Thessalonians, conveying Paul's ever more urgent exhortations in
response to the community's ongoing persecution. Paul faces two
nearly incompatible tasks: he must establish a stable and coherent
moral order for his readers at the same time that he prepares them for
the coming end of time. As was the case in his first letter, he is committed to training these recent pagans to "hold fast to the traditions" he
has taught them, namely, the norms of Jewish moral life. At the same
time, he must address their increasing excitement about the imminent
end of the world. Paul focuses on three issues in this brief letter: how to
understand the community's suffering; how to recognize the last days,
or better, how to recognize that the last days have not arrived; and the
very practical problem of what to do about community members who
refuse to work.

Paul begins, as in 1 Thessalonians, by congratulating his readers on
their "steadfastness and faith" during their persecution (1:4). As in
1 Thessalonians, the nature, source, and extent of the persecutions are
not specified. Having congratulated the community on their steadfastness, Paul turns to teaching and reassuring them. Their suffering, he
says, is evidence of God's justice. Such a claim sounds perilously close to

blaming the victim, as if the Thessalonians deserved to suffer. Paul's reasoning, however, is more oblique, and entirely in line with that expressed in other early Jewish discussions of persecution. In 2 Maccabees, for example, the narrator reassures the reader that the Seleucid persecutions represented God's kindness, "disciplining" his people so that they might be purified and so escape full retribution at a later stage.

So also the Thessalonians learn that while their suffering will make them "worthy of the kingdom of God," their enemies will soon be subjected to "eternal destruction" (1:5, 9). This destruction awaits "those who do not know God and . . . those who do not obey the gospel of our Lord Jesus." Exactly how literally Paul means this is uncertain, but it appears to be a blanket damnation of the entire non-Christian world, Gentiles ("those who do not know God") as well as Jews ("those who do not obey the gospel"). Such wholesale condemnation of the non-Christian world is highly unusual for Paul. Indeed, some scholars take this passage as evidence of the letter's inauthenticity. In context, the absolute destruction of outsiders functions primarily to reassure the beleaguered insiders that their cause will be vindicated. By the same token, they are implicitly warned that they must remain on the "inside" if they are to avoid divine wrath.

Having addressed the outcome of the apocalypse in terms of the reward of the faithful and the "affliction of those who afflict" them, Paul turns to consider its timing. Now he approaches the heart of his concern, and he expresses anxiety that "no one deceive" the community and that they not be "quickly shaken" or "alarmed" (2:2–3). Some members are causing panic with their belief that "the day of the Lord is already here." Exactly what they mean by "the day of the Lord" is not specified, and Paul is concerned simply to tell them no, not yet. On the contrary, he says, the signs of the end are well known: a "rebellion" (against God) must be led by "the lawless one," and it must succeed to the point that he enthrones himself in the Jerusalem temple as God. Only then will God send the Lord Jesus to destroy him and end Satan's work on earth. Paul's teaching is in line with apparently widespread expectations for the last days (see, e.g., Ps. Sol. 17:11–12; 1 Enoch 91:3–10), though he adds an otherwise unknown character called "the re-strainer," who is currently keeping the lawless one at bay. In the midst of this drama, or rather, because the drama has yet to reach its climax, the Thessalonians must "stand firm and hold fast to the traditions" Paul has taught them. Despite the excitement of being on the winning side of the cosmos, the community must go about the far more mundane work of being good.

Paul concludes with advice on a problem that seems to come with the territory of apocalyptic fervor: social irresponsibility. After all, if the world itself is passing away any day now, it can seem a bit silly to do the laundry or pay for groceries. This is especially true when there are community members wealthy enough to buy the groceries for you. Thus, in the Thessalonian community some are "living in idleness." This, says Paul, is definitely not "according to the tradition" he taught them (3:6). The recipients of Paul's letter (who are not among the shirk-ers) are given two instructions. First, Paul provides a rule followed by subsequent generations of intentional communities, "Anyone unwilling to work should not eat" (3:10). Second, the idlers are to be shunned, not as enemies but in order to "shame" them back into conformity.

It is striking that these earliest documents of the New Testament deal with such mundane administrative matters. The young community has suffered persecution, and Paul must console and encourage them. But more urgent is the distortion of their current life in light of their expected spiritual transformation. Consequently, community members must be disciplined in the most rudimentary ways. They must learn to survive not only the high drama of persecution but also the mundanity of daily life. So their impassioned founder fires off a message of upper-most importance: "Strive to live quietly, to mind your own affairs, and to work with your hands" (1 Thess. 4:11). When the apocalypse arrives, you'll know.

FIRST CORINTHIANS

Pᴀᴜʟ's ꜰɪʀsᴛ ʟᴇᴛᴛᴇʀ to the Christians at Corinth has been immensely popular throughout Christian history as a resource for pastoral theology—that is, as an aid for addressing real-life problems. Its lively discussions of food, spirituality, and sex give it a perennial relevance. The letter has been influential around the world for two millennia, but it seems to have had little effect—or perhaps even to have backfired—with its original readers. Paul has a *lot* more authority with strangers who read the New Testament than he had with his own congregation at Corinth.

The city of Corinth, located on the isthmus separating Achaia (northern Greece) from the Peloponnese, had been destroyed in 146 B.C.E. and then rebuilt and colonized by the Romans in 44 B.C.E. An important shipping center, it was the easiest point of transfer between Italy and Asia. The earlier Greek city had literally been a byword for fornication (*corinthizein,* to fornicate). Whether or not the new Roman city lived up to the reputation of its namesake, it would at least have offered the variety of exotic people, beliefs, and wares available in any large port town. Paul founded the Christian community at Corinth, probably shortly after leaving Thessalonica, around 50 C.E. According to Acts 18 he spent eighteen months with his new congregation before moving on. First Corinthians, written from Ephesus, probably dates from 54 or 55 C.E. The situation at Corinth is as follows: the community has divided into factions, with various camps identified by the names of their preferred teachers: Paul's followers, Cephas's (Peter's) followers, Apollos's group, and (surely the spiritual trump card) the messiah's followers. Cephas (Peter) is not known to have visited Corinth himself, but he could easily have had associates who spread a distinctive Petrine message. Apollos, according to Acts 18, was a gifted preacher sent by some of Paul's associates to work with the Corinthian congregation after Paul's departure. The factions demonstrate by their very names that despite his status as founder, Paul was not everyone's favorite teacher.

In addition to their factional divisions, the community's behavior demonstrates a colorful range of spiritual self-expression. One case of incest is tolerated, while some employ prostitutes. Still others have chosen asceticism, advocating celibacy for the married and unmarried alike. Those favoring sexual liberation exercise a similar "liberty" in matters gastronomic, freely participating in feasts held in pagan temples. Others are horrified by such behavior. The divisions continue in the community's worship life, where those who demonstrate the most spectacular spiritual gifts constitute an elite, and at ritual meals, where the wealthy allow poorer members to go hungry. Paul attempts to curb such rampant and destructive self-seeking, and he does so by drawing on the model of the messiah, who sacrificed himself for others, and the model of Torah, which calls God's people to holiness. Messiah and Torah are, of course, the anchors of Paul's own identity; in 1 Corinthians he presents them as a model for Gentiles. Paul proposes what will become the dominant paradigm for Christian moral development: simultaneous identification with Jesus and with Israel.

Paul begins the letter in his standard mode, with greetings and thanksgivings that appear generic but ever so gently foreshadow the substance of the letter to follow. He addresses the letter to those who are "holy" and "called to be holy" in the messiah Jesus. The emphasis on the community's holiness is an indirect critique of their manifest lack of holiness, as well as an invocation of their new religious identity: "You shall be holy, for I, the Lord, am holy" (Lev. 19:2). Paul goes on to congratulate them on the very aspects of their lives on which they pride themselves, all of which he will shortly expose as self-delusion. Agreeing that the community has been "enriched in [Christ]" and is "not lacking in any spiritual gift," he then points out that they must still strive to be found "blameless" (1:5, 7, 8). It's time for religious experience to result in moral behavior.

Paul begins his critique with the community's most obvious point of vulnerability, their division into factions. He points out that all their "competing" teachers have preached the same thing, the messiah crucified. The crucifixion, of course, was not the Jesus sect's most attractive selling point. But, says Paul, "God chose what is foolish in the world to shame the wise; God chose what is weak in the world to shame the strong" (1:27). If death by crucifixion demonstrates power and wisdom, then one can safely claim that the world's values have been overturned. This transformation of power and value structures is central to the message Paul is trying to get across. Take, he says, yourselves as an example: "Not many of *you* were wise by human standards, not many were powerful, not many were of noble birth." Reminding his readers of their (mostly) lower-class origins, he reiterates his point: God is glorifying what is lowly and rejecting what is considered honorable. Their spiritual status-seeking is misguided; the one who represents "wisdom . . . and righteousness and sanctification and redemption" is the one who underwent torture and humiliation for their sake.

Having set forth his basic premise that the life of the messiah—their spiritual identity as well as his—is characterized by giving oneself for others, Paul proceeds to consider specific problems within the community. He begins with two matters concerning communal discipline: the community is tolerating an incestuous relationship, and some are suing others in secular courts. In both cases Paul issues rulings based on Jewish moral and legal norms. The case of incest involves a man living with his stepmother. (His father may be either deceased or divorced from her.) Such an arrangement is, as Paul points out, forbidden "even among the *Gentiles*" (5:1; NRSV, "pagans"). Paul apparently no longer expects the Corinthians to perceive themselves as

Gentiles. The relationship is also prohibited by Torah (Deut. 27:20; 27:30; Lev. 18:7–8). Paul first compares the Corinthians to the Israelites in Egypt who had to purge out the old yeast before celebrating the Passover. Then, quoting Deuteronomy, he commands that they "drive out the wicked person from among you" (17:7; 19:19; 22:21–24). Paul responds to the issue of secular lawsuits in a similar vein, by applying Jewish rather than Roman social and moral norms. One of the privileges granted the Jewish people as a *politeuma* was the right to maintain their own courts of law for internal communal affairs; it was considered a disgrace to involve Gentiles in the legal affairs of the community. Nor were Roman lawsuits generally perceived as just; lawsuits were typically undertaken by people of higher status against people of lower status, and judges were biased in favor of high-status plaintiffs. Why, asks Paul, should the "unrighteous" judge the "righteous"?

The Corinthians, in their spiritually exalted position, have apparently rejected both Roman and Jewish moral and legal standards. They have transcended worldly concerns, and "all things are lawful" for them, from incest to prostitution. Paul sets about reeling in these spiritual geniuses, providing a theological warrant for decent behavior. " 'All things,' " he agrees, " 'are lawful for me,' but not all things are beneficial" (6:12). The purpose of spiritual freedom is not to provide new opportunities for self-indulgence. The "new life" the Corinthians experience is precisely the life and power of the messiah, and its purpose is to transform them in accordance with his example. The gift is not private, nor is it spiritual in the sense that it is unaffected by their physical behavior. Paul employs a rather racy analogy, arguing that because Jesus has already "bought" them, their bodies cannot be employed for "fornication." Like prostitutes whose services have already been paid for, their bodies are not their own.

Paul seems to be running down a list of problems that have been brought to his attention, and he now turns to the question of celibacy. Some in the community advocate a celibate lifestyle for all, married as well as single. Paul agrees that celibacy can allow a person to focus more completely on God's work, but he commands that people already married continue to have sexual relations. Remarkably, he writes that husbands and wives have rights over *each other's* bodies, perhaps alluding to rabbinic law requiring that husbands provide wives with not only food and clothing but also sex. Single people who find themselves "aflame with passion" should go ahead and marry. Paul departs from Jewish law in prohibiting all divorce, except in cases of an "unbelieving" partner seeking divorce from a believer. His general principle is that each person should "remain in the condition in which you were called" because "the appointed time has grown short" (7:20, 29). The end of the world is a bad time to schedule a wedding.

Within his general pattern of urging all to remain in their current condition, Paul makes an exception in the case of slaves. Given the opportunity to gain freedom, Paul says, "Make use of it." Unfortunately, the Greek here is ambiguous and can be understood (as NRSV translates it) to mean "Make use of your present condition." Paul's logic, however, follows that of his earlier analogy to prostitution. Having already been "bought" by God, Christians are now slaves to God and not to any human being. The claim to be God's slave (a claim Paul himself makes frequently) is, ironically, a claim of high rather than of low status. Slaves derived honor from their masters; thus, a favored slave of the emperor held far greater status than most free inhabitants of the empire. Although elsewhere (Eph. 6:5–8; Col. 3:22–24) Paul commands slaves to continue to obey their masters, he seems to do so out of a concern that Christian groups not offend against social norms. Here he envisions a slave taking the opportunity for legal manumission, and he raises no objection.

Paul next takes up the topic of food that has been offered to idols. Some community members have been attending feasts held in pagan temples, justifying their actions on the ground that "no idol in the world really exists." Well aware that "there is no God but one" (8:4), they are not committing idolatry. The status of meat offered to idols was a sensitive issue in the early church. Gentiles of some social standing would have been accustomed to participating in festive meals held at pagan temples and hosted by the person who had provided the animal for sacrifice. Such meals were a primary means of "networking" in Hellenistic culture. To be invited was to be honored by the host; to decline was both to dishonor the host and to remove oneself from desirable social and business circles. It is hardly surprising that people would be loath to abandon such a vital aspect of civic life, particularly if they did not believe the idols represented any real power. Paul himself grants the logic of their position, and opposes it, not because it is a kind of backdoor idolatry but because of its effect on the rest of the community.

Paul agrees with those he calls "the strong" that idols are meaningless, but he points out that not everyone feels this way. Some, "being accustomed to idols," still believe in their power. If these people eat food offered to an idol, "their conscience, being weak, is defiled" (8:7). The question then becomes not what does knowledge allow, but what does the community need? "Knowledge," says Paul, merely "puffs up," whereas love "builds up." His argument is identical to the one he will make in Romans 14: communal harmony is of greater importance than individual liberty. Paul offers himself as an example of someone whose actions are not guided by his rights but by the needs of others. Rather than accepting financial support from the community, he has worked for a living, making himself "a slave to all." So also in his ritual observance he makes himself a Jew when among Jews, a Gentile when among Gentiles, "all things to all people" (9:22).

In arguing that "the strong" should devote themselves to the service of the community, Paul is also defending aspects of his own ministry that may have been contributing to the Corinthians' dissatisfaction. His refusal to accept financial support, an action that seems obviously generous to us, would probably have been taken as an insult by those in the community who wished to act as his "patrons." Nor would they have been pleased with his choice of manual labor, an activity that deprived him (and, by implication, them) of social honor. Moreover, behaving as a Jew among Jews and a Gentile among Gentiles (presumably a reference to dietary standards) clearly lays him open to charges of vacillation and hypocrisy. But no, he says, "I became all things to all people, that I might by all means save some." He will behave in whatever way allows him to spread the gospel effectively. Paul's self-defense includes an implicit critique of "the strong," to whom his letter is primarily directed. The very behaviors of which they disapprove—becoming a "slave" to all—are the behaviors that, for Paul, model the life of the messiah.

In chapter 10 Paul illustrates the status of the new believers by means of a lengthy midrash on the Exodus narrative. Addressing gentile believers as de facto Jews, Paul reminds them that "our ancestors" were all "baptized into Moses" when they crossed the Red Sea. The image of "baptism into Moses" suggests that *all* Jews, all Israel, started out as proselytes, converts to the covenant of Moses. "All ate the same spiritual food," the manna in the wilderness, and "all drank the same spiritual drink," the water Moses brought from the rock. Like the members of the Jesus sect, the early Israelites were baptized and shared in a meal (like the Lord's Supper) of spiritual food and drink. This sounds like good news for the gentile Corinthians, who have been so fully integrated into the exodus experience that Paul calls the Israelites their ancestors. So much for the good news. It turns out, however, that "God was not pleased" with most of Israel, with the result that "they were struck down in the wilderness." Eating "spiritual food and drink" does not guarantee divine favor. The people of Israel "sat down to eat and drink, and they rose up to play" (10:7). Paul refers to the golden calf incident (Exod. 32), which, coincidentally enough, involved a feast held in the presence of an idol. From the golden calf he turns to Baal Peor, where (Num. 25) the Israelites indulged in both an idolatrous feast *and* fornication, with the result that "twenty-three thousand of them fell in a single day." (Numbers actually says that twenty-*four* thousand fell, but one gets the point.) It's all very well to be "chosen," but behavior still matters.

The events of the Torah, says Paul, took place "to serve as an example." "They were written down to instruct us, on whom the ends of the ages have come" (10:11). A modern reader might be struck by the sheer chutzpah of Paul's claim that the exodus occurred to instruct his own community, but such allegorical and typological readings were practiced in many first-century Jewish circles, from Philo to Qumran to the Pharisaic Oral Law. Paul's very personal appropriation of Torah would not have been extraordinary in his day. In closing, Paul adds a concession to the effect that one may eat meat previously sacrificed to an idol if it is served in a private home, and provided no one points out its tainted status. This "don't ask, don't tell" policy is intended to "give no offense to Jews or to Greeks or to the church of God." Believe what they will, they mustn't go around *looking* like idolaters.

Chapters 11–14 are devoted to a number of conflicts related to the community's worship practices. Paul briefly gives an opinion on a controversy over women prophesying with their heads uncovered. The question seems not to have involved veils or other artificial head coverings, but whether the women wore their long hair bound, as was customary (thus covering their heads), or allowed it to flow loosely, in the manner of mantic prophetesses. Paul's arguments here are notoriously muddled. Although he clearly thinks it decent for a woman to have her head covered and to accept that "the husband is the head of the wife" (11:3), Paul expresses neither surprise nor disapproval over women prophesying in the assembly. He next turns to a subject of graver spiritual import: the Lord's Supper.

Paul has heard that at the meal commemorating the death of Jesus, wealthy community members refuse to share with poor members. "One goes hungry and another becomes drunk" (11:21). To those of us accustomed to a range of communal meals, from potlucks to coffee hours, the situation is incomprehensible. In a Roman context, however, it would not have seemed unusual. Fellowship meals were a standard part of life in a voluntary association, but they were expected to follow normal social protocol, with the highest-status members dining in a central area and receiving the largest and best portions. Lower-status members stood or sat around the periphery or in separate rooms, where they were served less elaborate meals. The arrangement would have seemed as "natural" as first-class plane passengers being seated separately and receiving superior food and drink. The Corinthians' situation was complicated by the unusually wide-ranging status of their membership. Voluntary associations ordinarily attracted members of roughly equivalent social status. The Corinthian church, however, seems to have included some high-status members (Crispus, according to Acts 18:8, was the head of the synagogue) and many of lower status, including "those who have nothing" (11:22; and see 1:26). No models existed for treating such a mixture of people as "community," and so the community has fallen back on known standards.

Status issues, clearly visible in relation to communal meals, turn out to form part of many of the Corinthians' conflicts, and it should come as no surprise that in this highly status-conscious community, spiritual attainments were also "ranked." Speaking in tongues, making utterances in a "spirit language," was highly prized in the Hellenistic world as a mode of communication between divine and human realms. Oracles such as that at Delphi delivered divine messages in this mode, which were then translated for worshipers. Some members of the Corinthian community exercised this spiritual "gift," but it had apparently become yet another status marker, a boundary between spiritual adepts and the rest. Having confronted so many status distinctions within the group, Paul addresses the use of spiritual gifts as emblematic of all such divisions. Stressing that spiritual powers are all given "for the common good," he portrays the community as a single body whose members have different functions. Difference indicates neither rank nor division; no body part is better than another, nor can they function independently. On the contrary, says Paul, any gift exercised without the quality of *agape,* love for others, is meaningless.

Paul's extended discussion of spiritual gifts mirrors his treatment of the various social and moral problems in the community. All involve issues of status. The Corinthians live in a world where, even more than in our own, status existed to be exploited. Anything less would be weak, even dishonorable. Their new experience of spiritual power is something to enjoy, something in which to excel. The old social and moral codes have been transcended. The exceptional spiritual strength of the community allows them to justify everything from incest to communal meals in which some go hungry. The Corinthians enjoy all spiritual gifts except the one Paul says is required: a love that responds to the needs of others. Paul struggles to move the Corinthians out of the dominant value system and into one shaped by Jesus' crucifixion—the rejection of what is highest in this world in favor of what is lowest. Paul faces an uphill battle with his status-conscious Corinthian congregation; one almost wonders what they saw in one another in the first place.

The final controversy Paul addresses is by far the most confusing: some members of the congregation deny the reality of the resurrection. The problem stems from a clash in paradigms. Many forms of Greek philosophy taught that the soul was by nature immortal, awaiting liberation from the body that was, in the dictum cited by Plato, its prison. The spiritual world, being eternal, was the only "real" world. Salvation was often understood to include immortality, the continued life of the soul, *freed* from the prison of the body. Such an image of immortality, however, is essentially at odds with the Jewish idea of resurrection. In the biblical period, Jews did not consider souls immortal. Immortality was achieved through one's progeny and the memory of one's good deeds. Beyond those very embodied forms of immortality, dead was dead. Probably in the second century B.C.E., belief in the resurrection developed together with belief in a final judgment, a time when the righteous would be vindicated. In order to be vindicated, however, they had to be alive; hence the idea of resurrection. The concept of resurrection, however, is fundamentally different from the idea of an immortal soul. If souls are already immortal, resurrection is superfluous.

Some members of the Corinthian community, presumably those "strong" believers who were of higher status and a more sophisticated turn of mind, objected to the idea of dead bodies being revivified. They had signed up for immortality, not resurrection. What, then, did Christianity have to offer them? First, Christian worship provided an experience of spiritual power in this lifetime. Spiritual charismata, or gifts, were much-sought-after signs of divine presence and favor. And, like various mystery religions, Christianity did offer its adherents immortality following resurrection. But neither spiritual power now nor immortality later required that their bodies be revived after death. The Corinthians simply expected immortality on their terms. It may also be that some believers' denial of the resurrection was related to class divisions within the community. Although popular philosophy often affirmed the immortality of the soul, many among the uneducated would have believed that the dead either inhabited the underworld or simply ceased to exist altogether. Those who had no other hope might have found the idea of resurrection more appealing than those who saw it as a comedown from the already-immortal soul's liberation at death.

Paul sets about to (re)teach the Corinthians that Christ both died and was buried before being raised from the dead. He was really dead (not immortal) and was really raised. Why does this matter? First, because Christ died for their sins to create a new relationship with God. If Christ was not raised, "your faith is futile and you are still in your sins." Also, if Christ was not raised, then neither will they be. "Those also who have died in Christ have perished. If for this life only we have hoped in Christ, we are of all people most to be pitied" (15:18–19). A major problem with resurrection, of course, is how to imagine the resurrection of the body without picturing a lot of revived corpses—a universal night of the living dead. Paul argues that the resurrected body is not a physical but a "spiritual" body, though (perhaps wisely) he never

BAPTISM FOR THE DEAD

In 1 Cor. 15:29 Paul alludes to the fact that the Corinthians are baptizing people on behalf of the dead. To the chagrin of scholars over the centuries, Paul does not spell out just what the point of this baptism was. Since very early times some Christian groups have taken 1 Cor. 15:29 as authorizing vicarious baptism, in which the living are baptized on behalf of non-Christian dead, thereby giving them access to Christian salvation. The practice was prohibited by church councils as early as the fourth century but was continued by a minority. The Egyptian Copts have practiced the rite from ancient times to the present day. Apart from the Copts, the best-known Christian sect to practice baptism for the dead are the Latter-day Saints (Mormons).

attempts to describe one. Instead, he affirms that in Jesus' resurrection "death has been swallowed up in victory" (Isa. 25:8, LXX).

In affirming Christ's victory over death, Paul includes a striking description of the end time. Christ is only the "first fruits" of those to be resurrected, for, says Paul, "as all die in Adam [that is, in the normal of course of human life], so *all* will be made alive in Christ" (15:22). Paul describes Christ subjecting all his enemies, the last of which is death. Finally, Jesus hands over the kingdom to his Father. Paul's scenario differs significantly from later Christian depictions of the end time, most notably in his claim that "the Son himself will also be subjected" to God. Paul maintains a fully Jewish understanding of the messiah's ("Christ's") relationship to God: the messiah is God's servant, who will report back to his superior upon completing his mission. At a later point in Christian history Paul's position—subordinationism—will be declared heretical. His view of the end time is fully consistent with that held by many Jews of his era, but less easily reconciled with later beliefs regarding Jesus' divinity.

Throughout his letter Paul struggles to wean the Corinthians away from a status-centered value system and toward a system grounded in mutual care. The Corinthians, for their part, have been given extraordinary spiritual gifts and are in a mood to enjoy them. They have transcended mere physical reality, so what's the harm in sleeping around? It's only bodies, after all. As for idolatry, it's a meaningless category. What's wrong with eating with friends who happen to worship the gods? Paul is faced with trying to convince the Corinthians to give up what looks to be the best of both worlds. In seeking to combat their insistent recourse to pagan values, Paul offers his own Jewish norms. Paul seems to see the congregation as converts to a sectarian form of Judaism; hence, the laws of Deuteronomy were written "for us" and the exodus was experienced by "our ancestors." The community must shun the ways of "the Gentiles." The Corinthians, for their part, seem all too happy to live as Gentiles who have just been admitted to a very special club.

SECOND CORINTHIANS

WHEN WE LAST SAW OUR HERO, Paul was struggling valiantly with his wayward congregation at Corinth, trying to convince them that their expressions of freedom in Christ looked a great deal like old-fashioned fornication and idolatry, while their pursuit of spiritual exaltation had a suspicious air of status-seeking. He warned them lest they become like the Israelites in the wilderness who, despite enjoying the gifts of God, were led astray by fornication (Num. 25) and idolatry (Exod. 32) and ultimately perished.

Between the end of 1 Corinthians and the beginning of 2 Corinthians, much has transpired. Unfortunately, no one knows exactly *what* has transpired, and 2 Corinthians provides ambiguous guidance. The letter is extraordinarily disjointed, so much so that it is widely considered a composite. Piecing together the bits of information available, one can surmise the following: After writing the letter known as 1 Corinthians, Paul seems to have visited the congregation; if so, the visit did not go well. A group Paul ironically calls super-apostles has either arrived or made inroads with the congregation, causing a further decline in Paul's reputation and authority. Whatever the content of the super-apostles' message, Paul believes they have misled the Corinthians (11:20), proclaiming "another Jesus" and "a different gospel." Paul mentions an additional visit he had planned but did not make, fearing it would be another "painful visit" like the last one. Paul writes 2 Corinthians primarily to mend fences. The letter follows the form of the Hellenistic "letter of commendation," or recommendation letter. Sadly, it serves as Paul's self-commendation to those who formerly called him their father. Most of the letter sticks to familiar theological territory. Paul's suffering is a sign of his apostleship. Reconciliation is the heart of the gospel; hence he and they should be reconciled. This otherwise poignant and conciliatory letter also includes a midrash on Moses at Mount Sinai that stands as one of the New Testament's most damning—and enduring—images of the Jews.

Paul begins with an explanation of why he did not visit as intended, and with a defense against the accusation that he is "vacillating." His eagerness for reconciliation is balanced by his desire both to teach them and to affirm the validity of his apostleship. He thus points out that, far from his needing a letter of recommendation *to* them, they themselves should serve as a living recommendation *for* him. They are "a letter of Christ, prepared by us, written not with ink but with the Spirit of the living God, not on tablets of stone but on tablets of human hearts" (3:3). The image of Paul as a new Moses, mediating God's message "on the tablets of human hearts," will be developed into the book's central image. Paul combines the metaphor of himself as Christ's scribe and the community as Christ's message to the world with a metaphor borrowed from Jeremiah and Ezekiel, of God's law written on the human heart. It is this second image that Paul will develop in his midrash.

Both Jeremiah and Ezekiel, writing during the Babylonian exile, promise that God will one day not only restore the people, but re-create them with hearts willing and able to follow God's ways. In Jeremiah this re-creation takes the form of a new covenant to be established in the end time:

> The days are surely coming, says the Lord, when I will make a new covenant with the house of Israel and the house of Judah. It will not be like the covenant that I made with their ancestors

when I took them by the hand to bring them out of the land of Egypt. . . . But this is the covenant that I will make with the house of Israel after those days, says the Lord: I will put my law within them, and I will write it on their hearts; and I will be their God, and they shall be my people. (Jer. 31:31–33)

Ezekiel adapts Jeremiah's metaphor, saying that God will take away the people's hearts of stone, giving them hearts of flesh into which he will put his spirit (36:26–27). Combining Jeremiah's and Ezekiel's prophecies, Paul says that the message of Christ is "a new covenant," written "not on tablets of stone but on tablets of human hearts." Paul's work as a scribe, writing Christ's message onto human hearts (that is, his preaching), thus parallels Moses' work of transcribing the covenant onto tablets of stone.

In Paul's understanding, the divine word he transmits is in every way superior to that brought by Moses, since it conveys the living presence of the one who gave it. But as always Paul supports his beliefs, including his belief that Torah has been excelled, on the basis of Torah. And so he turns to a discussion of Moses at Sinai. Exodus 34 describes Moses' second reception of the tablets of the law. He had already received them once but, upon seeing the idolatry of the people, had thrown down and broken the original tablets. He therefore ascended Sinai a second time and inscribed a second set of "the words of the covenant." As he descended the mountain "the skin of his face shone because he had been talking with God" (Exod. 34:29), and the people were afraid to approach him. Moses spoke to the people, gave them the commandment of God, and *then* covered his face with a veil. Thereafter, "whenever Moses went in [to the tent of meeting] before the Lord to speak with him, he would take the veil off, until he came out; and when he came out and told the Israelites what he had been commanded, the Israelites would see the face of Moses, that the skin of his face was shining; and Moses would put the veil on his face again, until he went in to speak with [God]" (34:34–35).

The passage is clear in most respects but presents one problem that continues to baffle interpreters: Why, if the people are afraid to look at

Moses' shining face, does he wait to veil it until *after* he speaks with them? Conversely, if he speaks to the people with his shining face unveiled, why does he bother veiling it afterward? The text says that his face was shining "because he had been talking with God"; some of God's splendor seems to be reflected in Moses' face. Moses talks with God "face to face," and so it makes sense for him to unveil himself when he enters the divine presence. When he comes out, he leaves his shining face unveiled *just long enough* to communicate God's commands to the people before replacing the veil. It is as if, in communicating the divine message, Moses serves as a sort of stand-in for God, shining with reflected glory. But just as Moses sees God only when *receiving* the divine word, so the people look upon the reflected glory only when Moses is *conveying* God's word to them. Otherwise, the glorified Moses remains, like God, "hidden" from their sight.

Paul examines Exodus 34 and reaches a different conclusion: Moses hid his face neither to protect the people nor out of respect for the divine glory but because he had something to hide. He did not want the people to look upon "the *end* of the glory that was being set aside" (3:13). These are murky waters indeed. What "end" of the glory? Who says it was being set aside? To follow Paul's reasoning, one needs to understand his view (as worked out in Romans and Galatians) of the relationship between the Torah and the gospel. The Torah, for Paul, was and remained God's revelation to the Jews. It became relativized, however, with the coming of the messiah. Regardless of the Torah's continuing validity for the Jews, God's new self-revelation in the messiah now takes precedence over the Torah. Thus, "what once had glory [the Torah] has lost its glory because of the greater glory" (3:10), the glory of the gospel. In that respect, the Torah, especially in regard to the Gentiles, has been "put aside." Paul, however, says that Moses veiled his face "to keep the people of Israel from gazing at the *end* of the glory that was being set aside." How could the glory have ended even as it was being revealed on Sinai? The word *telos*, translated "end," allows for two options.

Telos can mean "end" in the sense of cessation, but more frequently it means "goal" or "completion." If the *telos* is the cessation of the glory, then Moses is simply being deceitful. His own face ceases to shine between his sessions with God, but he hides that fact from the Israelites. Similarly, he does not want the people to know that the law he brings them is less than permanent. This reading has much to recommend it, particularly given Paul's complaint that the Corinthians have been *deceived* by "super-apostles" who boast of their Jewish credentials (11:3–5, 20, 22–23). On the other hand, in Romans Paul speaks of Jesus as the *telos* of the law, using the more common meaning of "goal." If the messiah is the goal or completion of the law, then Moses is simply cutting off his disclosure of the divine glory "before the end," that is, before its full revelation. The Israelites were not allowed to peek at the "end" of the story.

Whether Paul considers the law to be abolished (*telos* as ending) by the messiah or completed (*telos* as goal), he believes his own ministry is superior to Moses', since he transmits a greater glory. So also the (gentile) Corinthians' *reception* of the divine message is superior to Israel's. "To this very day," he claims, "when they hear the reading of the old covenant, that same veil is still there. . . . [W]henever Moses is read, a veil lies over their minds" (3:14–15). The veil has moved from Moses' face to the Jews' minds. Paul believes that Jews who do not see Jesus as messiah are simply failing to understand the Torah. If they read Torah as he reads it, they would see the "goal" toward which it points. Only "when one turns to the Lord," that is, Jesus, however, is the veil removed. An encounter with Christ is the equivalent of Moses' face-to-face encounter with God. "All of us," says Paul, "with unveiled faces, seeing the glory of the Lord, . . . are being transformed into the same image from one degree of glory to another." Here is the most fundamental Pauline claim: God's spirit replicates the life of the messiah in the believer.

The midrash is at once brilliant and disturbing. Paul ingeniously exploits the question of why Moses covers his face only *after* having already spoken to the terrified Israelites; he veils it because the Torah is only part of the story. He takes his proof-text from Jeremiah's and Ezekiel's prophecies of a future covenant, written not on stone but on human hearts. His exegesis is impressive, its potential implications alarming:

- the Torah does not mediate God's spirit and is a "ministry of death" to its followers (3:7);
- the Torah has "lost its glory" (3:10);
- the Jewish people have a "veil over their minds" when they hear the reading of Torah, "the old covenant" (3:14–15).

Paul's explication of Moses has funded generations of Christian contempt for Jewish faith and practice. (Poor souls; if only their minds could be unveiled.) In context, Paul is not concerned with Judaism per se; he's fighting to prove that his own somewhat discredited ministry is still valid. Just as Moses was called to mediate the law written on tablets of stone, so Paul has been called to mediate the law written on the hearts of his congregation. The fact that the super-apostles seem to be pushing for a more traditionally Jewish version of the sect may also underlie Paul's disparagement of Jewish worship. Like any sectarian, he believes that his group has the only true grasp of reality. God promised Jeremiah to send a new covenant; if that covenant has arrived, it is superior even to Moses'. Paul, of course, sees this new covenant as one more sign of the end of the world. He is expecting the last judgment, not the rise of gentile Christianity. Taken out of context, however, and placed against the backdrop of Christian disputation with Judaism, Paul's analysis becomes a vicious slander, portraying Jewish devotion as willful blindness to the desires of God.

Pursuing his goal of "recommending" himself to the Corinthians, Paul continues to defend himself and attack his opponents. He is a "clay jar" that holds the "treasure" of God's light; he is Christ's "ambassador," sent to them on a reconciliation mission (4:7; 5:20). He fears that, like Eve, they have been seduced by the super-apostles, who proclaim "another Jesus." Paul gives no indication as to who or what this different Jesus might be; instead, he claims that the other missionaries are merely "disguised" as apostles of the messiah (11:15). Paul can match the super-apostles boast for boast. And, it seems, the super-apostles' first (or perhaps just their most galling) boast has to do with their qualifications as Jews:

Are they Hebrews? So am I. Are they Israelites? So am I. Are they descendants of Abraham? So am I. Are they ministers of [the messiah]? . . . I am a better one: with far greater labors, far more imprisonments, with countless floggings, and often near death. Five times I have received from the Jews the forty lashes minus one. Three times I was beaten with rods. Once I received a stoning. . . . [I was] in danger from rivers, danger from bandits, danger from my own people, danger from Gentiles, danger in the city, danger in the wilderness. (2 Cor. 11:22–26)

Paul's list of "accomplishments" provides a fascinating look at his experiences and, even more, at his complex religious identity. We can infer from Paul's defense that his opponents boasted of their Jewish credentials—though he does not suggest that those credentials consist in anything beyond the fact that they *are* "Hebrews," "Israelites," and "descendants of Abraham." Paul's own defensiveness may stem from his unwillingness to proselytize Gentiles into observance of Jewish law. He proudly asserts that he is Jewish in every sense of the word. His exemplary service of the messiah even includes floggings received "from the Jews" and danger "from my own people." Both his Jewish birthright *and* his censure by the Jewish community serve Paul as apostolic credentials. To be punished for his beliefs is a badge of honor. Paul's "boast" to the Gentiles highlights his isolation as a Jew rejected by Jews, mistrusted by Gentiles, and opposed even by Jewish members of his own sect.

Paul's final self-defense involves claims to mystical experience. Although he had already claimed in 1 Corinthians that he spoke in tongues "more than all of [them]," he seems, in the face of the super-apostle challenge, to feel a need to elaborate his mystical résumé. The super-apostles, who, as "apostles of Christ," are clearly believers, seem to have been Jewish Christians with a mystical background. Not to be outdone, Paul "boasts" to the Corinthians about "a certain man" (whom he modestly refrains from naming) who "was caught up to the third heaven . . . into Paradise and heard things that are not to be told, that no mortal is permitted to repeat" (12:2, 4). Moreover, having himself performed "signs and wonders and mighty works," he has proved that he is "not at all inferior to these super-apostles." Finally, after his long concatenation of pleas, boasts, and arguments, Paul concludes by moving in the direction of threats. Fearing that when he comes to them "there may perhaps be quarreling, jealousy, anger, selfishness, slander, gossip, conceit, and disorder," he warns that he "will not be lenient" on his next visit. If they continue to demand "proof that Christ is speaking in me," they may not like what they hear! "I write these things," he says, "so that when I come, I may not have to be severe in using the authority that the Lord has given me" (13:10).

Paul's oscillation between pleading, cajoling, and threatening his readers makes 2 Corinthians a bit of an emotional workout. It also displays the ambiguities of Paul's Jewish identity. The touchstone of Paul's authority remains the Torah, but Paul validates his ministry on the grounds that he is the mediator of the promised "law written on human hearts." His ministry to the Gentiles is thus superior even to that of Moses. Paul is a man who prides himself on his Jewishness but is equally proud to have Jews punish and reject him. He seems a Jew in comparison to Gentiles and a Gentile in comparison to Jews. As God's "apostle to the Gentiles" he affirms his Jewish beliefs by treating unconverted Gentiles as Jews. Such a position would become increasingly difficult to negotiate as the generations passed.

GALATIANS

Paul's letter to the Galatians, gentile believers in northern Asia Minor, starkly illumines the problems created as the Jesus sect moved from a Jewish into a gentile milieu. Attempting to dissuade Gentiles from full conversion to Judaism through circumcision, in Galatians Paul brutally disparages *Jewish* adherence to the Torah. Sometimes called "the charter of Christian freedom," Galatians champions freedom from "the law," here called "the *curse* of the Torah." Galatians is less than friendly territory for a Jewish reader.

Little is known about the churches of Galatia except what we learn from Paul's letter. The Roman province of Galatia in central Asia Minor comprised a southern section with several prominent cities and a northern section inhabited by the "Galatians" proper, Celtic people who had by and large not assimilated into the culture of the Roman empire. Although Paul worked in the cities of southern Galatia, his use of the ethnic designation "Galatians," together with the note that he founded the congregation only because he fell ill while journeying through their territory (4:13), suggests that Paul's Galatians are the Celts of northern Asia Minor. The letter's date is unknown (sometime in the mid- or late 50s), but its occasion is clear. Competing missionaries, probably other Jewish Christians, have arrived and convinced members of the community to become circumcised. The Galatians' interest in circumcision may in part stem from contact with the indigenous cult of the goddess Cybele, whose devotees sometimes engaged in self-castration. Paul, however, is furious and informs the congregation that in becoming circumcised they have "cut themselves off" from Christ.

Paul's outrage over the Galatians' circumcision is puzzling. Why *shouldn't* they get circumcised? The Jerusalem Council (Acts 15) freed Gentiles from the requirement of circumcision, but it hardly outlawed the practice. Paul, however, assigns circumcision a significance that turns obedience to Torah into rebellion against God. Paul identifies two problems with the Galatians' eagerness to undergo the ritual. First, as a sign of the covenant, circumcision constitutes a quasi-legal agreement to keep the Torah. Paul warns that the covenant carries not only blessings but also obligations and, if the obligations are not met, a curse. Second, the Galatians' circumcision can enhance their religious experience only if their current religious experience is incomplete. For Paul, gentile circumcision effectively negates the affirmation that "God makes no distinction" between Jew and Gentile, that is, between circumcised and uncircumcised. If God makes no distinction, then gentile circumcision signifies not *greater* faith, but a lack of faith in God's gift of acceptance. Furious at any suggestion that the Gentiles' faith is inherently less than the Jews', Paul rages, "I wish those who unsettle you would castrate themselves!" (5:12).

Despite Paul's extravagant language, the theological premises of his letter are the same as those described in the Jerusalem Council of Acts 15: Gentiles can join the movement without observing Jewish law. In constructing his argument against other Jewish messianists, however, Paul draws a damning—and enduring—contrast between Torah and gospel as a choice between flesh and spirit, curse and blessing, slavery and freedom. Paul seeks to demonstrate that gentile adherence to Jewish law is not only misguided but faithless, a fundamental preference for "worldly"—human or material—standards over spiritual ones.

Opening his letter with a standard greeting, he abruptly lashes out, "I am *astonished* that you are so quickly deserting the one [God] who called you!" (1:6). The Galatians must have been equally astonished at

Paul's rebuke. Far from deserting, they have deepened their commitment through circumcision; they might have been expecting warm congratulations from their teacher. Paul ignores their intentions and instead pronounces a curse upon whoever has taught them this "different gospel." He moves directly from this castigation into a review of his own "earlier life in Judaism," the days when he was "violently persecuting the church . . . and trying to destroy it." "I had advanced," he claims, "beyond many among my people of the same age, for I was far more zealous for the traditions of my ancestors" (1:14). Strange as it may seem for Paul to switch from condemning the Galatians' observance to bragging about his own, Paul does so to make a point: precisely when he was most zealous for the "traditions," he was most hostile to the church. Observance of Torah pitted him against the will of God. Paul describes his conversion but emphasizes that at every turn his apostleship came directly from God. He was dependent upon no human being, least of all the leaders of the Jerusalem church. Why does this matter? Because some of the Jerusalem leaders oppose his "circumcision-free" mission to Gentiles. Paul must prove that he is not subordinate to the apostles in Jerusalem. As in Acts 15, so also in Galatians, the Jerusalem Council is invoked as affirming that "God shows no partiality" and that Paul has been "entrusted [by God] with the gospel for the uncircumcised" (2:6–7).

Attempting to discredit the entire enterprise of circumcising converts, Paul accuses more traditional Jewish missionaries, including Peter (Paul uses the Aramaic form, Cephas), of hypocrisy. According to Paul, Peter had chosen to share meals with uncircumcised gentile believers in the city of Antioch until "certain people came from James"—Jesus' brother who apparently favored circumcising gentile converts. Only then did Peter draw back "for fear of the circumcision faction" (2:12). The halakic (Jewish legal) dynamics of the situation are not clear, since Paul assumes (as does Acts 10) a level of separation between Jew and Gentile that was far from universal in the first century. The question of who may eat with whom, however, seems not to center on kashrut (food laws), a problem that could be resolved by holding meals in a Jewish home or having Jews bring their own food to a gentile home. Peter does not withdraw from the community's meals for fear of a "kashrut party"; he fears "the circumcision party."

Paul's account reveals a side of the early church that is generally suppressed in the New Testament as well as in the Christian imagination: many of the movement's most prominent leaders opposed the inclusion of unconverted Gentiles. Paul, however, will argue, as he will do again in his letter to the Romans, that no one, Jew or Gentile, is saved by "the works of the Torah," including circumcision. All are saved by "the faith of the messiah" (see textbox, page 189). As he discusses in 3:10–14, by being crucified, Jesus has allowed himself to become "cursed" under Jewish law: "Cursed is everyone who hangs on a tree" (3:13; Deut. 21:23). If the messiah himself became cursed, and so "outside the law," his resurrection must mean that God has decided to ignore the law, thus vindicating Jesus and, by extension, those who follow him. Gentiles who undertake to *keep* the law thus not only take a considerable risk (given, as Paul understands it, the penalties for failing to keep the entire Torah); they are in effect rejecting the gift God has given by accepting them "outside the Torah."

To illustrate the status of the Torah, Paul undertakes a lengthy midrash on the figure of Abraham. His choice to focus on Abraham is probably a response to the circumcisers. Abraham, after all, had confirmed his faith by undergoing circumcision (in Gen. 17). Nor was his circumcision optional: "Any uncircumcised male . . . shall be cut off from his people," says God; "he has broken my covenant" (Gen. 17:14). If Paul's opponents have appealed to Abraham in making their case for circumcision, Paul has no choice but to respond. He begins by pointing out that the Galatians' experience of God's spirit came as a result of their belief, not of "works of the law," that is, of circumcision. He then compares the Galatians to Abraham, who "believed God, and it was reckoned to him as righteousness." In relating to God "by faith," they become descendants of Abraham. Indeed, God foretold their inclusion by promising Abraham that the Gentiles would be blessed through him (3:8; see Gen. 12:3). God's promise was made to Abraham's "offspring" (*sperma,* or seed). Exploiting the potential of the collective noun *offspring,* Paul claims that the promise was not made to many—to "offsprings"—but to one, namely, the messiah. If the promise passes, in effect, directly from Abraham to the messiah, what was the point of the Torah? Well, says Paul, the Torah was an addition after the fact, intended to keep people in line until the messiah came. Paul's view of Torah as an interim measure would have been shocking to many first-century Jews, who affirmed the "preexistence" of Torah from before the beginning of the world (cf. Sirach 1:4).

Even more shocking, however, was his stand on social relations in the messianic age: "There is no longer Jew or Greek, there is no longer slave or free, there is no longer male and female; for all of you are one in Christ Jesus" (3:28). Paul's proclamation epitomizes the "freedom" he has been preaching. In granting eternal life to *all* who trust the gospel, God has erased the significance of earthly status markers, including those separating Jew and Gentile. In the Roman world, social status was far more determinative and less mutable than in our own; the elimination of such basic status markers as slave and free or male and female was almost inconceivable. Even today, many Christians are uncomfortable eliminating distinctions between men and women in the church. This, says Paul, is the extent of the freedom God has offered. But this is precisely the treasure the Galatians will lose by reverting to the "status marker" of circumcision.

Paul returns to his analogy of Abraham, developing a convoluted allegory about Abraham's two sons, Ishmael by a slave woman (Hagar) and Isaac by a free woman (4:21–31). Here he abandons his usual rabbinic-style midrash in favor of an explicitly allegorical approach of the kind used by other Jewish interpreters such as Philo. The two women, says Paul, represent two covenants. Hagar, the Egyptian, is from Mount Sinai, which Paul claims is "in Arabia." Confounding his already shaky geography, he asserts that Hagar/Sinai corresponds to Jerusalem. Why? Because, like Hagar, Jerusalem is "in slavery" with her children, that is, enslaved to the Romans. Geographical plausibility aside, Paul argues that both Jerusalem and Mount Sinai correspond to Hagar, "bearing children for slavery." Sarah, on the other hand, is free, and bears the child of the promise. Therefore, says Paul, Sarah corresponds not to the earthly Jerusalem, which is enslaved, but to the "Jerusalem above," in heaven.

Paul has set up his premises for a spectacular sleight of hand. The Galatians, says Paul, are "children of the promise, like Isaac." As Gentiles, they are Abraham's heirs in a spiritual, not in a biological sense. Jerusalem, home of Abraham's biological heirs (and, not coincidentally, of those pesky, circumcising Jewish Christians), remains in slavery to Rome. And "just as at that time the child who was born according to the flesh [Ishmael] persecuted the child who was born according to the Spirit [Isaac], so it is now also" (4:29). Paul has created a thoroughly astonishing scenario. First, and most remarkably, he claims that Jews are descendants of Hagar and Gentiles descendants of Sarah. This dizzying premise allows him to compare the Jewish believers' persecution of the uncircumcised Galatians to Ishmael's persecution of Isaac. The obvious solution? As the scripture says, "Drive out the slave and her child" (4:30; Gen. 21:10). Indeed, "the child of the slave *will not share the inheritance* with the child of the free woman." Gentiles are the heirs to God's promise; Jews need not apply.

What is going on here? What can Paul, who prides himself on his Jewish identity, possibly have in mind? Paul's argument that the Gentiles, having been accepted on the basis of their faith, are the "true" heirs of Abraham is similar to one he will later use in his letter to the Romans. Here, however, Paul's goal is not only to establish the legitimacy of the Gentiles' claim as "heirs," but to prove their claim *superior* to that of the Jews. He takes this approach because of his opponents: Jewish-born Christians (the so-called circumcision party) are using their status, both as Jews and as representatives of Jesus' original disciples in Jerusalem, to argue that the Galatians must convert in order to inherit God's promise. Paul construes this theological pressure as "persecution." Should the Gentiles, children of the promise, submit to persecution? Of course not. On the contrary, "casting out the slave woman and her son," they need to get rid of Paul's Jewish-Christian opponents.

Having refuted his opponents' position, Paul alludes, almost in passing, to an additional factor in the debate over circumcision: the opponents' own fear of persecution. Those, says Paul, "that try to compel you to be circumcised" do so "only that *they* may not be persecuted for the cross of Christ." In fact, Paul claims that he himself faces persecution he could avoid by "preaching circumcision." How does circumcising one's associates ward off persecution? Is Paul referring only to pressure from within the church (such as that levered by James's associates on Peter)? Or do local missionaries face more aggressive coercion from the Jewish community (such as Paul's own vigilantism, back when he was "zealous" for the Torah)? Is the movement creating trouble for the local Jewish community by causing Gentiles to abandon their religious duties? In any case Paul urges the Galatians not to allow their bodies to be used as trophies by his opponents.

We do not know how Paul's angry epistle was received. Did the Galatian churches "drive out" the other missionaries and leave off circumcision? We have no data on which to base even a guess. The choice made by the Galatians themselves, however, means little compared with the impact of Paul's words on subsequent generations of readers. Paul's impassioned letter once sought to free devout Gentiles from a false sense of obligation to Torah. Since then, Gentiles with no interest in keeping Jewish law have internalized Paul's argument as a wholesale condemnation of Jewish ritual observance as practiced by *Jews*.

The difficulty of interpreting Galatians fairly is compounded by Paul's own extreme views on Judaism, both before and after his messianic conversion: both as a Jew and as a Jewish Christian, Paul was far from typical of Jewish belief and practice. In what he calls his "earlier life in Judaism" he was fanatical, to the point of "trying to destroy" the Jesus movement, people he perceived as enemies to the Torah. Now, despite having renounced his former fanaticism, he continues to believe that as a fanatic he was a model Jew. Once assiduously Torah-observant, he now takes his own past as the measure of what law-observant Judaism has to offer. Never does he consider that a less-strict version of observance might be acceptable to God. On the contrary, "Cursed is everyone who does not observe and obey *all* the things written in the book of the law" (Deut. 27:26 LXX). Any abrogation of any law brings God's curse. Ironically, the insistence on keeping "all" the laws appears only in the Greek translation (the Septuagint) of Deuteronomy; Paul's standard for legal observance actually exceeds that stated in the (Hebrew) Torah. Even leaders like James and Peter, who favored—perhaps insisted on—the full conversion of Gentiles, probably defined Jewishness in less rigid terms than Paul did. For Paul, the covenant was an all-or-nothing affair.

Judged by the existing first-century evidence, Paul's understanding of Jewish law, like that of the Qumran sectarians, was anomalous in its stringency. And, like the beliefs of other sectarians, Paul's views might have remained a theological curiosity if it were not that generations of Christians have taken him at his word, believing that Judaism requires perfect adherence to Torah. Finding no reason to doubt Paul's self-presentation as a model Jew, Christians have tended to credit his extremist views as normative. It sounds all too attractive (from a Christian perspective) that Christianity represents freedom and Judaism slavery, Christianity the spirit and Judaism the law. Galatians has gifted the church with a legacy of freedom but has burdened it with a legacy of misunderstanding. Paul fought bitterly against those who taught that one must become Jewish to be saved. Paul's anger at his fellow Jewish *Christians,* however, has since been read as his righteous anger against the *Jews.*

PHILIPPIANS

Paul's congregation at Philippi was a gentile community. Named by Philip of Macedon for himself in 356 B.C.E., Philippi became a Roman military colony in 42 B.C.E. The city was home to many retired soldiers, and devotion to the imperial cult was strong. Paul writes to his Philippian followers from prison—which imprisonment, we do not know—probably late in his life, about 60 C.E.

Paul begins with a standard greeting, followed by an extended and enthusiastic thanksgiving. First expressing his own joy over the community, he repeatedly calls for them also to rejoice: "Rejoice in the Lord always; again I will say, Rejoice." This ever-present refrain lends a buoyant tone to the letter but also raises a question: why must Paul so constantly urge these people to rejoice? Are they excessively dreary? In the midst of his congratulations, Paul hints at trouble; he hopes to hear that they are "in no way intimidated by [their] opponents." What form of intimidation did the Philippian community face, and from what opponents?

The Philippian Christians lived in an environment defined by its identity as a military outpost. The city had been granted special legal status, *ius italicum,* in recognition of its service to the empire. This was a "company town," and the Roman army was the company. The Christians, for their part, extolled a man crucified for sedition against the empire. Given the awkwardness of the situation, one wonders how anyone in Philippi found Paul's message attractive in the first place. The congregation would certainly have been subject to intimidation by neighbors, associates, and even (or perhaps especially) families. First, they glorified a criminal. Worse, loyalty to this seditionist required them to abandon religious duties to the city and the empire. Offending both the emperor and the gods, they constituted a serious liability to the community. For Paul's followers, the choice to accept voluntary separation from community activities, rituals, and identity must have been excruciating. Paul writes to acknowledge the group's freely chosen hardships, and to exhort them to joy in the midst of suffering.

Throughout the Roman world, religious associations served to establish a sense of belonging for their adherents. Burial societies, mystery religions, philosophical brotherhoods, all provided a sense of place in the status-conscious but often disorienting social and ethnic mix that was the empire. The brotherhood of the Christians spread partly because, like other religious groups, it created a home for those who found themselves socially, emotionally, or geographically dislocated by the empire. Christianity, however, was something of an anomaly since, at the same time that it provided a sense of place, status, and identity to its adherents, it required that they take on "outsider" status within the larger culture. Unlike cults whose adherents could separate themselves during cultic rituals and then return to their normal life within the society, Christians, both Jewish and gentile, placed themselves in opposition to their normal social networks. For Jews, membership in the movement meant punishment within or perhaps even exclusion from the local synagogue. For Gentiles, membership meant alienation from family, social, and business associations. Even in the absence of overt persecution, the costs of affiliation were high.

Paul's letter to the Philippians addresses the congregation's crisis of belonging. Paul's constant concern is that the community accept loss of status and rejoice in communion with one another and with God. This joy and fellowship must counterbalance their all too evident grief and loneliness. "If . . . there is any encouragement in Christ, any consolation from love, any sharing in the Spirit, any compassion and sympathy, make my joy complete," writes Paul, by being "of the same mind, having the same love, being in full accord and of one mind" (2:1–2). This call to mutuality is reinforced by one of the best-known passages in the New Testament: "Let the same mind be in you that was in Christ Jesus, who, though he was in the form of God, did not regard equality with God as something to be exploited, but emptied himself, taking the form of a slave, being born in human likeness. And being found in human form, he humbled himself and became obedient to the point of death—even death on a cross" (2:5–8).

The Philippian community must find in Jesus' experience a model for their own. This model, however, is far from attractive, as it requires voluntary acceptance of shame. Shame, in Roman culture, was to be avoided at all costs, and Jesus' extreme humiliation rendered Christian belief not only puzzling but repugnant within the dominant value system. Paul addresses that scandal head-on. Jesus, says Paul, willingly gave up existence "in the form of God" to take on first "the form of a slave" and finally the even more shameful form of a crucified criminal. Paul's statement is strong on shock value—the assertion that Jesus accepted such extreme shame being every bit as startling as the claim that he once shared the form of God.

The belief that before his birth Jesus had the form of God is not without precedent in either the Roman or the Jewish world. In Roman mythology, human beings could share in divinity in a number of ways and to varying degrees. In Jewish thought, Daniel's "Son of Man" arrives on earth from a heavenly realm, and in some circles Moses was understood to have been partially divinized after his death. Even Adam was thought of by Philo and others as having originally shared the form of God, since he was made in God's "image." Still, the claim that Jesus began life as something other than an ordinary human being is not common in Paul's writings. Here he employs the paradigm of the "man from heaven" to make a crucial point about status. Despite having the form (*morphe*) of God, Jesus chose not to "grab" equality with God. Instead, he "emptied himself," taking the form of a slave, that is, a slave to God: a human being. Having accepted this first status deprivation (a gesture that in the Roman world might be mistaken for the sort of god-in-human-guise jaunt that gods were wont to take), Jesus goes still further, accepting the most horrifying and terrifying death. Why? Why would *anyone* choose crucifixion, let alone exchange divine status for such a fate? Paul gives no motivation except that Jesus was "obedient" to God, the one in authority over him. At this point Jesus seems a particularly unattractive role model.

Paul's point, however, is not Jesus' abasement but his subsequent exaltation. "Therefore," he says, "God also highly exalted him and gave him the name that is above every name, so that at the name of Jesus every knee should bend, in heaven and on earth and under the earth." Humiliation and loss of status turn out to have been but moments along the way; Jesus' end is triumph. In fact, it is not only triumph but dominion: every knee shall bow to him as "Lord." By encouraging the Philippians to share in "the same mind" as Jesus, Paul is not only acknowledging—even encouraging—their debasement; he is also promising their glorification.

Paul's language, which sounds so heavily theological to the modern ear, is also, in context, highly political. Jesus, he says, had the form of God, but not full equality with God (*iso theos*). In Greco-Roman traditions, heroes like Heracles underwent *apotheosis*, or transformation to divine status, but it was the emperor who specifically claimed *iso theos*, equality with the gods. Paul draws an explicit contrast between Jesus' divine claims and the emperor's. Unlike a human ruler, Jesus did not despoil what by right belonged to God, but chose service to God over equality with God. God has now freely given Jesus the very status he refused to plunder; he, not the emperor, is *soter* and *kyrios*, savior and lord, before whom every resident of heaven, as well as of earth, must bow. But why bother drawing this emphatic contrast between Jesus and the emperor? Here we may begin to understand the nature of the Philippians' "opponents."

Faced with intimidation from the surrounding gentile society, the Philippian Christians did have one available source of refuge: Judaism. Unlike Judaism, the Jesus movement was a *religio ilicita,* an illicit association in the eyes of Rome, and as such its members were subject to investigation and varying degrees of punishment. But if those who followed Jesus were the "true Israel," why shouldn't they enjoy the protections afforded Jews under Roman law? The answer was straightforward: circumcision. Romans knew that Jews were circumcised, and that circumcision formed the boundary between gentile sympathizers and gentile converts to Judaism. These uncircumcised Christ-followers had withdrawn from pagan worship, but they enjoyed no recognition as converts to Judaism. This meant that, unlike traditional God-fearers, who might participate in both synagogue and gentile civic life, in some circumstances gentile Christians had a great deal to gain from undergoing circumcision. Allying them with a licit religion, circumcision would provide the Philippians with both a recognized social identity (as Jews) and legal protection. This was not a choice Paul condoned.

On the contrary, Paul uses circumcised Christians (whether they are ethnically Jewish or circumcised gentile converts is unclear) as the specific counterexample the Philippians should avoid. "Observe" (3:2; NRSV, "beware of"), he says, "the dogs," "the evil workers," and "the mutilators." The terms are all derogatory references either to Jewish Christians or to circumcised gentile Christians. "Dog" is a derogatory term sometimes used by Jews to denote Gentiles; "evil workers" plays on Paul's designation of fellow missionaries as "co-workers"; and "mutilators" is a crude reference to circumcision. Somebody is advocating circumcision as a "way out" for the beleaguered congregation. Paul contrasts his followers with these "evil" workers, claiming that "it is we who are the circumcision," that is, the circumcised ones. In what sense are they circumcised? They "worship in the Spirit of God . . . and have no confidence in the flesh." In effect, Paul claims that they are, in the words of Deut. 30:6, circumcised in the heart rather than the flesh.

Never one to underestimate his own qualifications, however, Paul goes on to say that personally, of course, he *could* boast in the flesh if he wanted to. Not only was he circumcised, but on the eighth day—that is, as a born Jew rather than as a convert. Flaunting his tribal lineage (Benjamin) and his former Pharisaic affiliation, Paul pulls rank. *They* want to be Jewish? *He'll* show them being Jewish! But, says he, whatever "gain" his Jewish credentials might have earned him, he now regards as "loss."

Why? Because, emulating Jesus, he now loses status in the hope of gaining eternal life. This is the model he urges on his Philippian congregation. Some may be willing to use circumcision as a means of social protection, "but *our* citizenship is in heaven" (3:20). Paul's word choice is instructive. The word translated in the NRSV as "citizenship" is *politeuma,* the legal designation for a minority group living with independent rights and customs within the larger society—the status of the Jews, which the Philippians could gain through circumcision. But we, says Paul, are not citizens of the empire, nor is this our home. Our *politeuma* is in heaven, whence we await a "savior" far superior to the emperor who also makes use of that name. The Philippians' humiliation will, like Jesus' own, be transformed to glory as part of Jesus' universal reign. They accept social homelessness in this world in order to gain citizenship in the world to come.

Philippians is often referred to as a "joyful" letter, in light of Paul's many references to his own joy and his calls for his readers to rejoice. Underlying Paul's rejoicing, however, one detects the sadness of those who have lost family and friends, have set themselves dangerously outside the social matrix, and have forfeited whatever status they might once have had. Even circumcision looks attractive as a means of gaining both legal protection and a known social niche. Paul, however, designates humiliation as the emblem of their unity with the one who "did not count equality with God as something to be grasped, but emptied himself, taking the form of a slave." Paul redirects their attention to Jesus and to the communal aspect of their Christian life—they are fellow workers, fellow strugglers, fellow sufferers with Christ, sharing one mind; in short, he emphasizes the community they have gained rather than the one they have lost. Certainly Paul's letter is infused with a profound sense of joy, but the letter also provides an all too rare glimpse into the poignancy of the gentile Christian experience. For Gentiles, this not-quite-Jewish identity came at a cost. Like Jewish members of the movement, so Gentiles also soon found that they could not embrace their new community without letting go of the old.

PHILEMON

T HE BRIEF LETTER FROM Paul to Philemon has no direct relevance to the Jewishness of earliest Christianity. Instead, the letter provides a rare and amusing glimpse into the tensions created by the competing power and authority systems of Rome and the Christian movement. The "plot" of Philemon involves Philemon's slave, Onesimus. Paul writes from prison (which imprisonment is unknown), where Onesimus has sought him out for help. Onesimus has traditionally been understood as a runaway slave, but far more likely is that, in light of some trouble with his owner, he has taken advantage of a law allowing slaves to appeal to an *amicus domini,* literally a friend of the master, who will mediate with the slave owner to resolve the problem. Ideally, a slave would "run upward," that is, seek out a friend of higher status than the owner. Because the friend is of higher status, the owner can accept his direction without losing face. Paul, an itinerant preacher and now a prisoner, does not count as a highly placed friend in the ordinary sense, but it is Paul's struggle to pull spiritual rank while acknowledging Philemon's social rank that gives the letter its distinctive flavor. Paul deftly manipulates Philemon's honor in order to "shame" him into complying with his wishes.

Philemon is the only personal letter in the New Testament, and even it is not so private as it might appear. The letter begins with a greeting to Philemon, the head of a house church in Colossae in western Asia Minor, as well as to Apphia and Archippus, presumably members of Philemon's household. Paul continues, however, with a greeting "to the church in your house." With these few words Paul signals that the letter is not strictly private. On the contrary, by bringing the entire church into the picture Paul has created a backdrop of public opinion, people who will approve or disapprove of Philemon's actions. Paul begins by flattering his "beloved" Philemon, acknowledging his love for "the saints" whose hearts he has "refreshed," a reference to Philemon's financial support and hospitality. Having recognized Philemon's status as his patron, Paul immediately turns the tables. "I am bold enough in Christ," he says (pulling out the heavy artillery), "to command you to do your duty." Ouch. Poor Philemon doesn't know whether he is being courted or court-martialed, and Paul quickly retreats to a more conciliatory tone: rather than command, he will appeal on the basis of love. "I, Paul, do this as an old man, and now also as a prisoner of Christ Jesus."

Paul gets to the point in verse 10: "I am appealing to you for my child, Onesimus." Onesimus, it seems, has become Paul's child by virtue of having undergone a conversion while visiting Paul. This changes the picture considerably, since the out-of-favor slave has now become Philemon's Christian "brother," and a "child" to Philemon's spiritual father, Paul. Paul jokes to the effect that Onesimus, whose name means "helpful" or "useful" (a popular name for Roman slaves), has gone from having been "useless" (*achrestos*) to being very useful (*euchrestos*) to Paul as well as to Philemon. The joke is a double pun, since the words *a-chrestos* and *eu-chrestos* allow Paul to emphasize that "Mr. Useful" has gone from useless to useful precisely by going from being "unchristian" to becoming "a good Christian."

Paul says he is sending Onesimus back to Philemon, but his announcement includes a number of barbs. He is reluctant to send Onesimus ("my own heart"), who could otherwise be of service "in your place" during Paul's imprisonment. Prisoners in the Roman empire were not fed and clothed by the state but by their own friends and family. Paul is suggesting that if Philemon is not going to come himself, the *least* he could do would be to send a useful slave! But no, Paul does not want to impinge on Philemon's authority; he will leave it to Philemon to do his good deed on a voluntary basis. Meanwhile, Philemon should welcome back Onesimus "as you would welcome me." Poor Philemon hears that although he *should* allow Onesimus to stay with Paul, he must at any rate welcome him as if he were a church leader. And, Paul adds, if Onesimus should happen to owe you anything (probably a reference to the underlying conflict between master and slave), he, Paul, will repay it. "I say nothing," he hastens to add, "about *your* owing *me* even your own self" (v. 19). Paul was evidently instrumental in Philemon's conversion; hence Paul is *his* patron, and Philemon is forever in his debt. But Paul would never draw attention to the fact.

Paul has ever so deferentially browbeaten Philemon to the point where he must accede to Paul's request or dishonor himself before his own church by disobeying the venerable old apostle, abandoning their spiritual father in his prison cell. Paul makes his request, but does so with such delicacy that to this day scholars argue over exactly what Paul wants. Recalling Philemon's previous philanthropy, he calls upon him to "refresh my heart." In this, Paul says he is "confident . . . that you will do even *more* than I say" (v. 21). But what *does* he say? Is Paul requesting only Onesimus's restoration into Philemon's household? Or that Philemon grant Onesimus his freedom? Or does Paul ask that Onesimus be sent back again to be "useful" to Paul, whether as slave or as freedman? Ironically, while scholars are divided as to what Philemon is asked to do, they are universally agreed that, in light of Paul's elegantly applied pressure, he probably did it.

Philemon's charm can easily mask the fact that it is a letter about power. The slave Onesimus employs Roman law to seek help from one he considers more powerful than his owner. Paul's own power, however, is ambiguous, and he must balance deference to Philemon's greater status with the assertion of an alternative power structure, that of God's household. In the Roman household Onesimus is a "useless" and out-of-favor slave; in God's household he is a beloved (and useful) son.

Which rules will apply? In its twenty-five verses, Philemon demonstrates the tenuous position of the early church as a social and political anomaly. Paul seeks to assert the priority of the church's hierarchy—his own authority as "father" and patron, and Onesimus' status as "son"—but must do so without offending against the Roman patronage system. So Paul is both prisoner and patron, Philemon is both benefactor and debtor, and Onesimus is both slave and brother, depending on which criteria are applied. Paul does not challenge the power structures of Roman society; the institution of slavery, for example, goes unquestioned. Neither does he challenge Philemon's rights as either patron or master. Rather, Paul attempts to negotiate a position for "the household of God" within the terms of Roman social norms. In the end, then, though adopted as a "good Christian" by Paul and by God, Onesimus must depend on Philemon to decide his fate.

COLOSSIANS

T HE LETTER TO THE CHURCH at Colossae is one of the less-read
writings of the New Testament. Consisting largely of abstract theological descriptions of Christ as a cosmic power, it makes for a rather
dull read. While less engaging than most of the New Testament, Colossians emerges out of an extraordinary circumstance: the encounter between a mystical-apocalyptic Judaism similar to that practiced at
Qumran and another apocalyptic sect called Christians. Members of
the church at Colossae, in southwestern Asia Minor, are being encouraged to seek union with the angels by means of ascetic mysticism. The
author writes to bring them, as it were, back to earth, to the Pauline
ideal of manifesting spiritual maturity through the exercise of mutual
love within the community.

The question of the letter's authenticity (whether or not it was written by Paul) is a weary one: most conservative scholars argue for the
book's authenticity; most liberals, for its pseudonymity. Colossians's
image of a cosmic Christ leads many to conclude that it reflects late-
first-century or even second-century developments in Christian
thought. The problems with considering Colossians to be pseudonymous are, however, substantial. The most important is the way the
letter either reflects or feigns details of Pauline authorship. The author,

for example, concludes with "I, Paul, write this greeting with my own hand" (4:18). Claiming to be writing from prison, "Paul" sends greetings from co-workers whose names are known from the undisputed letters. Such attempts at verisimilitude would be unusual in ancient pseudonymous literature. Pseudonymity was ordinarily a transparent fiction; the point was not to fool the readers but to inform them of the "family tree" with which the author wished to be associated. So the very touches of authenticity that have been read as evidence of artifice can also be taken as signs of authenticity. The strongest argument against Pauline authorship is the dubious claim that Paul "could not" have thought in certain ways. Here, the letter will be treated as a document produced either by Paul himself or under Pauline sponsorship.

The congregation at Colossae was one of at least three in the Lycus Valley in southwestern Anatolia. Although the valley's population included a large number of Jews (originally settled there by Antiochus III around 200 B.C.E.), the Colossian church seems to have been made up of Gentiles. None of the Lycus Valley churches was founded by Paul, and it is unclear whether he ever visited them. The stated occasion for his writing is that while in prison (the same imprisonment mentioned in Philemon) he has become acquainted with Epaphras, a fellow prisoner and the founder of the Colossian congregation. Paul (or possibly Epaphras himself, writing in Paul's name) writes a letter of instruction to the congregation. The Colossian letter bears many similarities to the one addressed to the Ephesians, and it is possible that the two were composed by the same author at the same time.

Colossians presents the reader with a seemingly endless string of impressive but vague claims concerning both Christ and the Colossians themselves. Christ is "all in all . . . before all things, . . . the image of the invisible God." The Colossians have "died" but now have a life "hidden with Christ in God." What, exactly, does any of this *mean?* The misty language of Colossians, it turns out, is directly related to the letter's purpose. Writing to a congregation who seek ever higher mystical experience, Paul will attempt to convince them that their own experience is as good as it gets. He employs three techniques: he portrays Christ as the embodiment of cosmic wisdom, he argues that the

Colossians already participate fully in Christ's glory, and he discredits the opposition.

Paul begins and ends the letter emphasizing his support of Epaphras (1:7; 4:12–13), whose status has apparently been compromised. Certifying that the Colossians are already "qualified [to] share in the inheritance of the saints in the light," he assures them that, whatever it is that saints inherit, they will inherit it also. Spiritually speaking, they've made it. Paul now begins a lengthy description of Christ in terms of divine wisdom. The "image of the invisible God," Christ resembles divine wisdom, which is portrayed as the "reflection of eternal light, a spotless mirror . . . and an image of his goodness" in Wisd. of Sol. 7:26. Paul's homage to the "firstborn of all creation" through whom "all things in heaven and on earth were created" (1:15–16) echoes Proverbs's description of wisdom as God's firstborn assistant in the creation of the world (Prov. 8:22, 27, 29). The messiah (Christ), however, is not only the foundation of the world; he is also its ruler: "Things visible and invisible, whether thrones or dominions or rulers or powers—all things have been created through him and for him" (1:16). The thrones, rulers, and powers over which the messiah rules are not human powers but the celestial powers who populate Jewish mystical literature of the period. Just as 1 Enoch claims the messiah was "concealed in the presence of [the Lord] prior to the creation of the world" but has now "revealed the wisdom of the Lord" to the righteous (1 Enoch 48:6–7), so also Paul's messiah has been "hidden throughout the ages and generations but has now been revealed to his saints." The mystical language of Colossians comes directly from Jewish apocalyptic mysticism of the period.

Why would the author afford such prominence to the language of mystical speculation? Here we begin to see the letter's purpose. Paul informs his audience that Christ has reconciled them with God, *provided they continue* "established," "steadfast," and "without shifting." The congregation, it seems, has begun to wander. Paul states and restates that the Colossians share in the "riches," the "hope of glory," the "treasures of wisdom," and the "mystery" that are hidden in Christ. Like so much buried treasure, the good stuff, spiritually speaking, is hidden. Why do the Colossians need this mystical pep talk? "So that no one may deceive you" by teaching "according to the elemental spirits of the universe" (2:8). A competing mystical system beckons.

The precise nature of Paul's competition is unclear. The "elemental spirits" (*stoicheia*) to which he objects should probably be understood as angelic or spiritual cosmic forces mentioned in both Jewish and pagan sources. Although the interest in allying oneself with cosmic forces and participating in divine wisdom was common to both Jewish and non-Jewish arcane speculation, here the worship of elemental powers is connected specifically with Jewish ritual observance. The issue, however, seems not (as, for example, in Galatia) to be a simple "to circumcise or not to circumcise," but the possibility that by means of ascetic self-discipline the Colossians can reach a plane of spiritual existence higher than the one they currently inhabit.

Like other gentile converts to Christianity, the Colossians would have undergone an initiatory baptism, but not circumcision. They neither completed the requirements for full conversion to Judaism nor undertook Jewish dietary and sabbath observance. Such converts, like those at Galatia, might well be open to the idea that they had only *begun* their conversion, that their spiritual education was incomplete. Now, perhaps in the absence of the group's founder, Epaphras, someone has offered to supply the needed spiritual enhancement. In 2:16 Paul warns the Colossians not to let anyone "condemn [them] in matters of food and drink or of observing festivals, new moons, or sabbaths." The mention of sabbaths moves the discussion into a strictly Jewish context, but we soon see that observance versus nonobservance is not at issue here. Instead, the spiritual teachers are "insisting on self-abasement and worship of angels." Self-abasement (asceticism) seems an unlikely characterization of Jewish observance, but combined with the worship of angels it evokes the mystical-apocalyptic Judaism of the Dead Sea Scrolls, 1 Enoch, and other Jewish apocalyptic texts. The Qumran (Dead Sea Scroll) sectarians, for example, practiced ascetic discipline as a means of progressing to higher planes of spiritual purity. The Dead Sea Scrolls not only describe angelic worship in the various levels of heaven but provide the texts of the angels' hymns, presumably so that spiritual adepts could sing along. First Enoch 61:10–12 similarly describes the elect joining in chorus with heavenly powers. The Colossian Christians are thus not so much concerned that they aren't "real Jews," but that they are missing out on advanced forms of Jewish mystical experience.

It is not known who was offering this enhanced spiritual program to the Colossian community. Although not impossible, it seems highly unlikely that local synagogues practiced such an esoteric brand of Judaism. It is reasonable to imagine a Jewish branch of the Jesus movement that advocated a spiritually "advanced" form of ritual practice. The Jesus movement may well have attracted Jews who had already undergone spiritual training in other mystical-apocalyptic groups (perhaps pagan as well as Jewish); such spiritual experts would naturally want to share their knowledge with the Colossian neophytes.

Paul's advice—not to submit to self-abasement for the purpose of obtaining visions or worshiping with angels—suggests that he, at least, understood Christian experience to be fundamentally different from the pursuit of spiritual illumination. To make his point, he must both validate the Colossians' current experience and invalidate the experience they seek. Those who pursue spiritual experience through self-denial, he says, are engaged in a fundamentally selfish and, ironically, self-indulgent enterprise. If the spiritual "advancement" sought by the Colossian mystics is similar to that practiced at Qumran, then it is in fact a matter of attaining status through successive initiations into higher planes of the spiritual realm. Paul condemns such pursuit of spiritual attainment as self-aggrandizement.

What the Colossians already have, Paul argues, *surpasses* the spiritual advancement they seek. It is here that Paul's description of the cosmic Christ gains its relevance. Through baptism, Paul argues, the Colossian Christians are "circumcised with a circumcision not made with hands" (2:11; see NRSV note), presumably a reference to the "circumcision of the heart" advocated in Deut. 30:6 and Jer. 4:4. They are better off than those whose circumcision is merely physical. And, participating through baptism in Christ's death (see Rom. 6), they now participate in his resurrection. This superior form of spiritual existence is, of course, "hidden" for the time being, but "when Christ who is your life is revealed, then

you also will be revealed with him in glory" (3:4). Christ, after all, is superior to the various powers and authorities who inhabit the heavens,
the powers the spiritual adepts seek to join in their worship. If they can
be at the top with Christ, why settle for less? There is a certain irony in
appealing to the Colossians' self-interest in order to steer them *away*
from spiritual athleticism, but Paul is clearly sincere in his belief that
the experience of Christ is transformative in ways that mystical asceticism is not.

Having argued that the Colossians must continue to grow in the
gospel as they have been taught it, Paul instructs them as to the kind of
"spiritual discipline" they must undertake. With the esoteric side of
their transformation already assured, they must now cultivate the
virtues of "compassion, kindness, humility, meekness, and patience."
The task is less glamorous than ascetic self-denial, but it is at least as
difficult. Moreover, says Paul, it more accurately reflects their inner
transformation. Paul concludes with an even more pedestrian list of
"household virtues" for the Colossians to practice: "Wives, be subject
to your husbands. . . . Husbands, love your wives and never treat them
harshly. Children, obey your parents in everything, for this is your acceptable duty in the Lord" (3:18–20). And so on. Have we really moved
from angelic worship to this? We cannot know, of course, what specific
concerns prompted the inclusion of such banal law-and-order instructions. Perhaps basic social structures needed support at Colossae. Regardless of the circumstances, however, the *haustafel,* or table of
household rules, is not inconsistent with the rest of the letter.

From the beginning Paul has tried to tell the congregation that their
hope is "laid up" for them in heaven. The divine side is already taken
care of. Now this spiritual reality must "bear fruit" among them, not
through their increasingly esoteric spiritual advancement but through
concrete manifestations of their new spiritual life. Thus, they are first
instructed to treat one another individually with kindness and humility; next they are told to conform to established social patterns of de-
cency. Or rather, they are told to conform those patterns to the reality
of their new spiritual life. The relationships Paul outlines—wife/hus-
band, child/parent, slave/master—were the basic power relations on

which Roman society was built. The ontological reality of these hierarchical categories was part of the fabric of the universe. Nor has this fabric disintegrated in light of the messiah's advent. It has, however, been altered. In 3:11 Paul tells the Colossians (just as he told the Galatians) that in Christ, the hierarchical divisions of society have become meaningless: "there is no longer Greek and Jew, circumcised and uncircumcised, barbarian, Scythian, slave and free." Paul asserts the radical dissolution of boundaries as a spiritual reality, but he is not prepared to advocate it as social reality. Instead, he provides a picture of household structure in which the immutable divisions are tempered by the knowledge of their penultimate character. Of course wives are to be subject to their husbands, but husbands are not to treat their wives harshly. (This sounds minimal to modern ears, but by ancient standards any limitation on the rights of a paterfamilias was revolutionary.) Slaves must obey their "earthly" masters wholeheartedly, but masters are reminded that they too have "a master in heaven" and should therefore treat their slaves justly. Having been invited to the pursuit of glorious transcendence, the Colossians must, alas, direct their spiritual gifts into more humble but useful channels.

EPHESIANS

THE LETTER TO THE EPHESIANS, perhaps more than any other New Testament writing, embodies the early Christians' desire to integrate Gentiles into a community still conceived of as Jewish. The usual Christian reading sees in Ephesians an absolute rejection of Israel and its religion as things of the past, but this reading, rooted in centuries of Christian anti-Judaism, fundamentally mistakes the author's project. Writing as a Jew, the author explicitly addresses his readers as Gentiles, who by birth are "aliens from the commonwealth of Israel" (2:12). They are outsiders. By virtue of God's gift, however, these Gentiles have been "adopted" and so allowed to live as "members of the household of God." Jew and Gentile are united in the messianic community, but the community's norms and expectations are those of first-century Jewish messianism.

Ephesians enjoys the dubious distinction of having not only a disputed author but disputed recipients as well. Although every modern translation of Ephesians names the addressees as "the saints who are in Ephesus," many of the best and oldest manuscripts leave the recipients unnamed. These manuscripts are awkwardly addressed to "the saints who are and who are faithful." This rather messy grammatical situation turns out to be a boon to scholars, because the designation "to the Ephesians" makes, in its own way, even less sense than the garbled alternative. The letter, which purports to come from Paul to the church at Ephesus, is virtually a form letter. He claims only to have "heard of" the congregation's faith, and he sends no personal greetings. But the church at Ephesus was founded by Paul, and according to Acts he stayed with them for more than two years! Why would even a pseudepigrapher portray Paul writing to his own congregation as if they were strangers to him? The letter is better understood as addressed to an unknown group of gentile Christians than to the congregation at Ephesus. The most popular hypothesis for the letter's origin and destination is that it was composed as a circular epistle to be read by the churches of the Lycus Valley (at Colossae, Hierapolis, and Laodicea in the southwest of modern Turkey). The Lycus Valley connection is suggested by the letter's mention of Tychicus, who also appears in the letter to the Colossians, apparently as the emissary bearing the letter. The Colossians are told (Col. 4:16) to exchange letters with the church at Laodicea, and it is possible that the letter now known as Ephesians is in fact the lost letter to Laodicea, a congregation not founded by (and perhaps not personally known to) Paul. The word-for-word correspondence between parts of Colossians and parts of Ephesians confirms a connection between the two.

Like Colossians, Ephesians purports to have been written by Paul from prison. As with Colossians, however, so also with Ephesians: both style and content show some differences from Paul's "undisputed" letters. Ephesians employs an overblown, grandiloquent prose style; the benediction in 1:3–14, which comprises six rather complex sentences in the NRSV, is in the Greek a single, seemingly unending sentence. Moreover, the author of Ephesians claims that Christ "has abolished the law" (2:15), a statement not easily reconciled with Paul's assertion in Rom. 3:13 that the law has "by no means" been abolished. If the author of Ephesians was not Paul, however, who was it? If one expands the notion of authorship to include sponsorship, then it becomes easy to imagine Ephesians as a companion piece to Colossians—a letter of general exhortation to the Lycus Valley congregations. According to Colossians, while in prison Paul has become acquainted with his fellow prisoner,

Epaphras, the founder of the Colossian congregation. It seems that Epaphras has been bending Paul's ear about conditions in his region, and the senior apostle has decided to fire off a letter or two. Alternatively, Epaphras himself could have composed the letters and sent them bearing the signature and authority of Paul. Such a solution is plausible, but by no means certain. As it turns out, however, Ephesians is so general, so short on specifics, that its overall thrust is clear even without a positive identification of its author or date of composition. Here we have no raging conflict between Paul and his opponents; Ephesians presents a generic letter from a Jewish-Christian teacher to a community (or communities) of gentile Christians. For the sake of convenience I will refer to the author by his self-designation (whether fictional or genuine) as Paul. The letter's contents are easily summarized: first, Gentiles are now eligible for inclusion in the "household of God"; and second, being so included, they should live accordingly.

After the initial greeting, Ephesians opens with an extended prayer of blessing. This blessing deserves our attention because it takes the form of a *beraka,* the dominant form of Jewish liturgical prayer. The prayer begins by blessing God, goes on to describe God's previous acts on behalf of the community, and concludes with further praises of God. In addition to following the structure of a *beraka,* the prayer employs vocabulary common to several of the most important Jewish prayers. If we omit its extended references to Christ, the blessing goes: "*Blessed* be the God and Father of our *Lord* Jesus Christ, who has blessed us . . . [who] *chose us* in Christ before the foundation of the world *to be sanctified* and blameless before him *in love* . . . according to *the delight of his will.* . . . In him we have been redeemed . . . [and] have also obtained an *inheritance* . . . so that we . . . might live for the praise of his glory. . . . This is the promise of our *inheritance,* toward redemption as God's own people, to the praise of his glory" (1:3–14). This skeletal version of the Ephesians blessing may not appear distinctively Jewish at first glance, but compare it with the kiddush, the blessing over the sabbath wine: "*Blessed* are you, *Lord* our God, ruler of the universe, *who sanctifies us* with your commandments and *takes delight in us. In love* and *delight* you have given us your holy sabbath as *an inheritance,* a reminder of your work in creation. It is a day of . . . remembrance of our coming forth from Egypt. . . . For *you have chosen us* and *sanctified us* out of all other peoples, and *in love* and *delight* have given us the sabbath as a sacred *inheritance. Blessed* are you, *Lord,* who *sanctify* the sabbath."

In addition to their substantial overlap in vocabulary, both prayers focus on the community's redemption—in Ephesians, a promise of "redemption as God's own people"; in the kiddush, the redemption from slavery in Egypt. Both prayers highlight the community's status as God's distinctive people. Not surprisingly, where the kiddush rejoices that God has chosen and sanctified Israel out of (or "more than") all people, Ephesians's gentile *beraka* claims only that they have now become "God's own people." In fact, the Ephesians blessing seeks to explain the Gentiles' unexpected claim to this status: "He chose us in Christ before the foundation of the world. . . . He destined us for *adoption* as his children through Jesus Christ." The tension is striking. Chosen before the very foundation of the world, the Gentiles nonetheless enjoy their status only through adoption. This profound contradiction runs like a unifying thread throughout the New Testament writings. Gentiles, people defined precisely by their status as not-Israel, suddenly *are* Israel, the chosen people to whom God has promised an inheritance. The contradiction is absolute. These are, so to speak, Jewish goyim. Not converts, not circumcised, but Jewish goyim.

The blessing that opens the book of Ephesians epitomizes the early church's self-understanding as the eschatological people of God. By their presence in the congregation of Israel, they achieve the day when "many peoples shall come and say, 'Come, let us go up to the mountain of the Lord, to the house of the God of Jacob; that he may teach us his ways and that we may walk in his paths' " (Isa. 2:3). The author of Ephesians has created a sort of eschatological blessing of the Gentiles. If the letter's opening welcomes the Gentiles into a new identity as the people of God, its remainder is devoted to explaining how they came to have this status, and the consequences of their new identity.

"I have heard," writes Paul, "of your faith in the Lord Jesus and your love toward all the saints" (1:15). The sentence duplicates Col. 1:4. Paul goes on to pray that his readers will enjoy wisdom, enlightenment, and the "riches of [God's] glorious inheritance among the saints" through Christ, who has been seated at the right hand of God. The wisdom terminology, the promise of hidden riches, and the triumph over inimical spiritual powers all echo Colossians. But whereas in Colossians the issue was the opponents' attempt to "disqualify" the community because they did not pursue mystical experiences, Ephesians turns to a more general discussion of the relationship between gentile believers and the heritage of Israel.

Paul bluntly addresses his readers as "you Gentiles in the flesh," those "called 'the uncircumcision' by those who are called 'the circumcision' " (2:11). After drawing attention to his readers' outsider status vis-à-vis those who are circumcised, he then disparages circumcision as merely "a physical circumcision made in the flesh by human hands." So the Gentiles are excluded because they are not Jews, but the Jews are belittled because their circumcision is "physical." What is going on here? The idea of spiritual circumcision derives from Deut. 30:6 and Jer. 4:4, in which Israel is urged, "Circumcise the foreskins of your hearts." It's hard to imagine that the average gentile listener would have caught the allusion, but the basic message—what you've got is better than a mere cut on your body—would be clear enough.

Paul impresses on his readers that although by birth they were "without Christ, being aliens from the commonwealth of Israel, and strangers to the covenants of promise," those who were once "far off" have now been "brought near" (2:12–13). The language of drawing or being brought near is typically used in rabbinic sources to describe gentile converts. Here, however, the Gentiles have been brought near "in Christ Jesus." Paul establishes an implicit syllogism: when they were without the messiah they were strangers to Israel; now they are "in the messiah" and have thus been "brought near," that is, accepted as converts into Israel. Acceptance of Israel's messiah constitutes membership in Israel. The problem, of course, is that these "converts" have not, in fact, undergone conversion, and so, as both Paul and his reader know, they are not technically part of Israel. This problem, *the* problem posed by the existence of uncircumcised gentile Christians (those Jewish goyim), is precisely the difficulty Paul believes God has removed through the cross.

"Christ," says Paul, "is our peace," who by his blood on the cross has "broken down the dividing wall, that is, the hostility" between Jew and Gentile (2:14). Here Paul addresses, as in Romans, the meaning of Jesus' death "outside the Torah." Now, however, he emphasizes the role of Torah in "making a distinction," and so dividing Jew from Gentile. If the messiah himself could die a death that rendered him "cursed" according to Torah, then the force of that curse was effectively nullified. Therefore Paul says that the messiah (Christ) has "abolished the law with its commandments and ordinances, that he might create in himself one new humanity in place of the two, thus making peace." Those who keep the law as well as those outside the law can now be equally included in the "commonwealth" of Israel; they are, in effect, one people.

Paul's claim is radical, though not nearly so radical as it has been taken to be. Speculation about the messianic age was widespread in the Judaism of this period, and in many circles that age was expected momentarily. Messianic conjecture frequently included consideration of the fate of the Gentiles, and while some communities (cf. Jub. 22:21–22) considered the Gentiles to be doomed, others focused on scriptural passages that promised the inclusion of the nations "on that day." Whether for blessing or for curse, apocalyptic Jews expected the work of the messiah to result in dramatic changes for Gentiles as well as for Israel. For Paul, the messiah has not abolished the Torah per se but has eliminated only its function of creating a "dividing wall" between Jew and Gentile. After all, in Eph. 6:2 he commands his gentile congregation, "Honor your father and mother" (Exod. 20:12). Paul is simply articulating the claim on which the entire mission to the Gentiles was founded: that the Torah's prescribed "wall" between Jew and Gentile no longer stands.

Even though the image of the Torah as a wall between Israel and the nations was used as early as the second century B.C.E. (see Aristeas, 139, 142), Paul may have envisioned a physical wall as well. The Jerusalem temple was surrounded by a series of walls controlling access to the temple building itself. Only priests were allowed to approach the temple building and main sacrifice altar. Jewish males were allowed into the central courtyard in which the temple and altar stood, and Jewish women worshiped in the next courtyard, outside the "court of the [male] Israelites." Gentiles were permitted only in the most peripheral enclosure. A sign recovered by archaeologists in the twentieth century warned that Gentiles trespassing beyond the wall would be punished by death. The "dividing walls" of the temple complex, intended to ensure the ritual purity of the sanctuary, created a physical manifestation of the division between Jew and Gentile. Whether or not a Gentile of Anatolia would have been familiar with the layout of the temple complex, anyone who had participated in local synagogue worship would have experienced similar physical, as well as ritual, boundaries.

Paul construes the dividing wall between Jew and Gentile as an expression of primordial hostility, a rupture in the fabric of humanity. By removing the division, Christ has allowed the reunification of humanity into a single people. This healing of the human family not only establishes "peace" but permits those who had been "aliens" to have full access to God and to live as both citizens and members of the "household" of God. The language of peace, access, citizenship, and household membership had strong resonances for people of the Roman empire. Rome had established "peace," but citizenship and access to power and status were rigidly controlled. Within Rome's hierarchy the Jews had the status of a *politeuma,* a commonwealth with rights to live (to some extent) by ancestral rules. Paul's announcement that those who were once "aliens from the commonwealth of Israel" are now "citizens" is a concrete and politically provocative claim, extending Jewish legal status to non-Jews. Paul thus claims that, having been "brought near" (converted), these Gentiles are now included in the legally constituted Jewish people. "In Christ" they have become what they manifestly are not.

On the one hand, Paul declares that "one new humanity" has replaced both Jew and Gentile; on the other, he claims a distinctly Jewish identity for the resulting group. Nor is this paradox surprising. Although Christian commentators commonly argue that in Ephesians Judaism is a thing of the past, the opposite is true. Just as the biblical prophets foresaw the inclusion of Gentiles into Israel as part of the messianic age, so Paul depicts a world in which the end of Jewish-

Gentile separation means that both can enter the temple; both can, in effect, be Jewish. Membership in the *politeuma* of Israel, not just the political and social *politeuma,* but the eschatological community, has been made available to Gentiles.

Paul concludes his consideration of the Gentiles' new life in Christ by emphasizing (in lots of Colossians-like language) the "mystery" of God's work among them and their newfound access to spiritual "riches," "glory," and "the fullness of God." Having spent three chapters explicating the nature of the Gentiles' new life, Paul goes on in the next three chapters to spell out its consequences. "Therefore," he says, "I, the prisoner in the Lord, beg you to lead a life worthy of the calling to which you have been called" (4:1). All those spiritual rights entail a few responsibilities. The readers must exhibit humility, gentleness, and patience—in short, "making every effort to maintain the unity" that Christ has created. The unifying work of Christ can only be embodied by peaceful unity within the church.

As is so often the case, Paul follows up his glorious affirmations of the congregation's spiritual transformation with an all-too-mundane picture of how they must actually behave from day to day. In doing so, he falls back on Jewish stereotypes about pagan morality: "Now this I affirm and *insist* on in the Lord: you must no longer live as the Gentiles live! . . . They are darkened in their understanding, alienated from the life of God because of their ignorance and hardness of heart. They have lost all sensitivity and have abandoned themselves to licentiousness, greedy to practice every kind of impurity" (4:17–19). Ideally, the "new humanity" transcends distinctions between Jew and Gentile; in practice, gentile morality is out. Inclusion in the community of Israel includes the adoption of Jewish moral norms. The spiritual rewards of celestial riches, power, and mystical sharing in the life of Christ are countered by "the wrath of God [that] comes on those who are disobedient." Now that they're in the household, they have to abide by its rules. Paul concludes with a literal list of household virtues, a common device for moral instruction in Roman antiquity. As in the letter to the Colossians, so also here he modifies the expected standards by requiring that husbands, fathers, and slave owners—the three roles of the *paterfamilias*—temper their treatment of their (Christian) subordinates. This relative mutuality within the household is as contrary to social expectations of the day as is unity between Jew and Gentile, and demonstrates the extent to which Paul expects a genuinely, if not entirely, new social order to emerge from his congregants' spiritual transformation.

Regardless of its original recipient or author, the letter to "the Ephesians" illustrates the conceptual and social challenges facing the new gentile Christianity and its Jewish teachers. Jewish liturgical forms and Jewish moral teachings provided a symbolic "home" for Gentiles promised a part in the inheritance of Israel. But as much as sect members saw the inclusion of Gentiles as the realization of the ideal Jewish community of the last days, most Jews saw their inclusion as evidence that the community was simply no longer Jewish. And so the messianists sought to affirm a third way, a "new humanity" neither Jewish nor gentile, but still conceived of in exclusively Jewish terms. It is no wonder that gentile Christians soon reduced this paradox to a claim that Judaism had itself been abolished. The prophetic vision of Gentiles' inclusion *as Gentiles* into Israel, had, after all, been a vision for the end of the world. No one had considered working out such an arrangement for the long run.

ROMANS

Paul's letter to the Romans is a complex and often ambiguous letter, one of the most difficult of all New Testament books. The book was, however, a favorite of both Saint Augustine and Martin Luther, whose readings of Romans changed the face of Christian theology. Romans is the source of the central Christian views on faith and salvation; it has also shaped Christian attitudes—both positive and negative—toward Judaism and Jews. It is here that Paul expands upon his claim (made earlier in Galatians) that Christians are justified "by faith" and here also that he undertakes to redefine the status of both the Torah ("the law") and the Jews for the messianic age.

The origins of the Christian congregation in Rome are not known. The historian Suetonius, however, notes that Claudius expelled the Jews from Rome, probably in 49 C.E., because of controversies over someone named "Chrestus." If Chrestus is Christ, then the Roman Jewish community was already divided over the claims of Jesus' followers by the 40s. Rome rather routinely expelled unruly groups, and the Jews had already been expelled at least once before, in 19 C.E. The later expulsion, however, would have had a particular impact on the young church. The Roman congregation would almost certainly have been founded by Jews, people like Paul who depended on synagogue worship to provide an opportunity for proselytizing. Much if not all of the early leadership in this Jewish-gentile group would have come from Jews. If, however, during the church's early years in Rome, its Jewish members were expelled, the church would have faced the daunting task of reinventing itself as a de facto gentile institution. After the death of Claudius in 54 C.E., the new emperor Nero allowed the Jews to return. The return of the Jewish Christians, including the former leaders of the Roman church, must have made for a bittersweet reunion with the now gentile Christian congregation. Conflict over the status of Gentiles within Christianity—the subject that, according to Acts, caused the first major division within the church—would have taken on a special urgency in Rome. The question of "how Jewish" Christian belief and practice should be would have arisen in new and painful ways.

From Paul's perspective, the impetus behind his letter was not primarily theological, but practical. Probably in 57 or 58 C.E., he was preparing to undertake a new missionary journey, this time as far west as Spain. A mission to the western end of the empire would require a base of operations considerably farther west than Antioch or Ephesus, so Paul writes to the congregation at Rome, informing them of his upcoming visit and of his hope that they will sponsor his new missionary venture. Paul cannot address this church as he does others, with the authority of a founder; with the exception of a few individuals, he has never even met the Roman Christians. His letter, then, is his self-introduction, a sort of expanded résumé in which he spells out his apostolic credentials as well as his theological stance. Paul takes the occasion of a letter to Rome to present his thoughts on a question of special urgency both to him and to the Roman Christians: the relationship between Jew and Gentile in the church.

Paul opens with a standard greeting, then introduces his primary theme, obedience to God as the appropriate demonstration of one's fidelity, and finally a subsidiary (but, for him, quite important) theme, his eagerness to come and reap a "harvest," that is, financial support, among the community. The letter is a diatribe, which in antiquity was not a vituperative tirade but a rhetorical form in which a thesis was proposed, tested by means of several antitheses, and then reasserted. Paul's thesis is presented in 1:16–17: the gospel represents "the power of God for salvation to everyone who is faithful, to the Jew first and also to the Greek." The elements of this claim are as follows: divine power has become available, equally so for Jews and "Greeks" (in this context a term equivalent to "Gentiles"); one benefits from this power on the basis of one's fidelity ("faith"); the results of the power are "salvation" and "righteousness." Much ink has been spilled over the meanings of "faith" (*pistis*) and "righteousness" (*dikaiosyne;* also translated "justification") and the relationship between the two. Paul will return to the topic at greater length in chapter 3. Here he simply sets forth his thesis, that the gospel, by which Paul means the reality that Jesus is both messiah and risen Lord, represents the power to obtain salvation on the basis of fidelity.

Paul next undertakes a lengthy refutation of the possibility that either Jew or Gentile might attain righteousness on any basis other than faith, or faithfulness. To prove that no one actually *deserves* God's favor, Paul condemns first the Gentiles (1:18–32) and then the Jews (2:17–3:20). The Gentiles, says Paul, have known God as displayed in nature "ever since the creation of the world." Paul's perspective on gentile morality is similar to that expressed in other Jewish literature of the period (cf. Wisd. of Sol. 13:1–19; Jub. 7:20ff.). Having a rough knowledge of good and evil, the Gentiles have no excuse for idolatry and immorality. Paul sees the self-serving attitude underlying idolatry (I give offerings to a god in exchange for the god's services to me) as the opposite of the "obedience" he considers the hallmark of faithfulness.

In 2:17–3:8 Paul turns to criticizing the Jews. Here he addresses an imaginary Jewish reader, presumably a Jewish member of the Jesus sect (a fact frequently overlooked by commentators). The Jew, he claims, brags about knowing God's Torah despite failing fully to observe its teachings. Paul concludes that "all, both Jews and Greeks, are under the power of sin." The universal human tendency to do wrong is not a matter of insufficient moral knowledge; for Paul, sin is a *power* that must be countered by divine power.

Paul's argument includes a carefully balanced presentation of Jewish and gentile vices as he understands them. At the midpoint of his argument, between his castigation of Gentiles and of Jews, he steps back from his equal-opportunity condemnations to observe that in light of universal human moral failure, no one (or no group) has a right to condemn another (2:1–16). Each group is likely to have committed the very acts it condemns. Paul's plea for interethnic tolerance is remarkable, all the more so as it appears immediately before a passage often read as a wholesale condemnation of the Jews.

Even more striking than Paul's call for mutual forbearance, however, is his statement on how God judges the individual. God, says Paul, repays people "according to each one's *deeds*" (v. 6; cf. Ps. 62:12). Many interpreters simply ignore this passage. Why? Because, as everyone knows, Romans is Paul's definitive statement that Christians are "justified by faith," or even "by faith alone." So how can they be judged according to their deeds one minute and according to their faith the next? As we will see below, most of the confusion comes from a misunderstanding of Paul's use of the word *faith* (*pistis*). Paul's point here is simply that *knowing* the good is irrelevant to the question of whether one *does* the good. Jew and Gentile alike, says Paul (vv. 9–11), will be judged on the basis of their deeds: God shows no partiality.

In 3:21–27 Paul restates his thesis in a text that forms the core of Christian teachings on justification by faith. The passage's meaning is ambiguous, however, and it is probable that centuries of Christian teaching and preaching have been based on misleading translations of the phrase *pistis iesou,* commonly rendered "faith in Jesus" rather than "faithfulness of Jesus" (see textbox, p. 189). This is the densest part of Paul's argument. He begins with his thesis: the "righteousness of God" has been disclosed "apart from the Torah" (3:21). This righteousness, argues Paul, although established apart from the Torah, has nonetheless been foretold in "the Torah and the prophets." What can Paul possibly mean by such a convoluted assertion? His claim that God's righteousness has been established apart from the Torah alludes to a problem he addressed more fully in Galatians: Jesus' death by crucifixion has rendered him cursed according to Deut. 21:23, "Anyone hung on a tree is under God's curse." According to the stipulation of Torah, the person Paul considers the messiah is cursed; hence, any divine affirmation of

JUSTIFICATION THROUGH FAITH *IN* JESUS, OR THROUGH THE FAITHFULNESS *OF* JESUS?

According to Rom. 3:22 as translated in the NRSV, the righteousness of God has been disclosed "through faith in Jesus Christ for all who believe." God's action, according to verse 26, was taken to prove "that he himself is righteous and that he justifies the one who has faith in Jesus." Most Christian understandings of justification, and so also of salvation, have hinged on this passage at least since the time of Augustine. Martin Luther, depending heavily on Augustine's reading, made "justification by faith alone" a core tenet of the Reformation. Remarkably, the translation reflected in the NRSV (and all other modern translations), as well as in most of the history of Christianity, is almost certainly incorrect. While it is possible to translate the Greek *pistis iesou* as "faith in Jesus," it is grammatically awkward to do so. Scholarly consensus has moved steadily toward accepting the translation "faith *of* Jesus," with faith understood as faithfulness or fidelity. (Most Bibles now include this at the bottom of the page as an optional translation.) The choice of translation is crucial; at stake is whether one is saved by Jesus' faith or one's own. This quirk in the history of translation means that, to understand Paul's argument in Romans accurately, one should read "the faithfulness *of* Jesus." To understand how the passage has been and for the most part continues to be interpreted in Christian circles, however, one must read "faith *in* Jesus."

Jesus must take place "apart from the Torah." Having been scrupulous in his own observance of Torah, Paul is deeply concerned with the disjunction between his *experience* that God has resurrected and thereby vindicated Jesus, and the clear dictum of Torah, according to which Jesus is accursed. Paul has no doubt that Jesus has been "justified" by

God, but this divine approval has taken place outside the boundaries set by the Torah. If God is abandoning the norms of Torah, however, *God's* righteousness becomes suspect. Hence Paul's need to establish "the righteousness of God," as well as of Jesus.

At this point readers may have difficulty identifying with Paul's dilemma. After all, isn't this just an issue of semantics? Either Jesus was resurrected or he wasn't. Why would someone who firmly believed that Jesus had been resurrected be so worried about a law that says crucifixion makes one cursed? To put it simply, Paul is worried about this because he's an exceptionally strict and well-educated Pharisee, and Pharisees were educated above all in the observance and interpretation of the law. A famous story from the Babylonian Talmud illuminates the status accorded the Torah in Pharisaic/rabbinic thought. In this passage Rabbi Eliezer and his colleagues have been disputing a point of law:

> R. Eliezer used every argument to substantiate his opinion, but they would not accept them. He said, "If the law is as I have argued, may this carob tree argue for me." The carob tree uprooted itself and moved a hundred cubits from its place. . . . They said, "From a tree no proof can be brought." Then he said, "May the canal prove it." The water of the canal flowed backwards. They said, "From a canal no proof may be brought." Then he said, "May the walls of this House of Study prove it." Then the walls of the house bent inwards, as if they were about to fall. R. Joshua rebuked the walls, and said to them, "If the learned dispute about the law, what has that to do with you?" So, to honor R. Joshua, the walls did not fall down, but to honor R. Eliezer, they did not become straight again. Then R. Eliezer said, "If I am right, may the heavens prove it." Then a heavenly voice said, "What have you against R. Eliezer? The law is always with him." Then R. Joshua got up and said, "It is not in heaven (Deut 30:12)." What did he mean by this? R. Jeremiah said, "The Torah was given to us at Sinai. We do not attend to this heavenly voice." (*b. Baba Metzia* 59b)

The dispute between Rabbi Eliezer and the other rabbis illustrates the remarkable authority granted the Torah and rabbinic interpretation of the Torah. Miracles are irrelevant; even the voice from on high must yield to the authority of the Torah. It is the rabbis' task to work out the meaning and application of Torah. Paul is trained in this mode of reasoning. He has not ceased to be a Jew and "become" a Christian; he is an observant Pharisee who believes that the messiah has come. Yes, a heavenly voice spoke to him on the Damascus road (Acts 9), but the Torah still stands and must be addressed. How, then, can he dispute Torah's direct condemnation of "anyone who is hung on a tree"? Only by means of other passages from Torah.

In Romans 4–8 Paul will construct an elaborate argument to demonstrate that Jesus' status, while extraordinary, is neither anomalous nor counter to the teachings of Torah. How, then, was Jesus vindicated? God has accepted Jesus' "faith," that is, his faithful obedience, as righteousness. This model of righteousness, says Paul, is available "for all who are faithful" (1:16; NRSV, "all who have faith"). "All who are faithful," of course, includes Gentiles as well as Jews. If Jesus was accepted by God "apart from the Torah" (because he was cursed), then no distinction remains between Jew and Gentile.

In verse 25 Paul introduces a new theme, that in his faithful death Jesus became a sacrificial offering whose blood removes the effects of sin. The idea here is that because an appropriate sacrifice has been offered, God can accept as "righteous" both the accursed Jesus and those who follow him, without thereby compromising God's own righteousness. The image is striking, particularly because Paul was writing when the temple and its sacrificial system were still intact. Jesus' sacrifice, says Paul, is effective both through blood (as J. Milgrom has dubbed it, the "ritual detergent" of ancient Israel) and "through faith" (that is, because of Jesus' fidelity). The notion that the blood of martyrs can atone for the people may seem more Christian than Jewish, but in fact it appears in literature addressing the Seleucid persecutions of the second century B.C.E. In 4 Macc. 17:21–22, for example (and cf. 4 Macc. 6:28–29), the blood of the seven brothers serves to wash away the people's sins. Jesus' willingness to offer himself as a sacrifice also evokes the even earlier image of Isaac in Genesis 22, and it is probably no coincidence that Paul next turns to consideration of Abraham as a model.

Paul concludes the restatement of his thesis in 3:21–31 with the claim that although one is accepted as righteous "apart from the Torah," the Torah is not thereby nullified, because Jesus' form of righteousness "upholds" or is consistent with Torah. In chapter 4 Paul undertakes his first proof of this claim, based on the example of Abraham. According to Gen. 15:6, "Abraham believed God, and it was reckoned to him as righteousness." That is, Abraham was considered righteous not because of his works but because of his faith, his willing-

ORIGINAL SIN

Paul's discussion in Romans 5 of Jesus as counterpart to Adam played an interesting role in the development of the Christian doctrine of original sin. In Rom. 5:12 Paul comments that sin and death came into the world through "one man" (Adam) and then spread to all, in that (NRSV, "because") all have, like Adam, sinned. After some asides, Paul returns to this thought in verse 18, concluding that "just as one man's trespass led to condemnation for all, so one man's (Jesus') act of righteousness leads to justification and life for all." Paul's analogy is straightforward enough on the face of it, but it underwent a slight change when it was translated from Greek into Latin. In verse 12, the Greek *ep 'o*, "in that," was translated into Latin as *en quo*, which can mean either "in that" or "in whom." Augustine, working from the Latin, understood Paul to mean that all had sinned already *in Adam*. Augustine's reading formed the basis for the doctrine in the Western church (a doctrine not found in Eastern Christianity) that Adam's sin contaminated his sperm, and that the germs (as it were) of sin were then communicated through his sperm to all subsequent human beings.

ness to believe God's promises. Moreover, says Paul, Abraham was considered righteous while still *outside* the covenant because he was still uncircumcised (v. 10). Justified "by faith" and while outside the covenant, Abraham thus serves as the ancestor, not only of the Jews, but especially of "all who believe without being circumcised" (v. 11), that is, gentile believers. The Gentiles' symbolic descent from Abraham also fulfills God's promise that Abraham would become the father of "many nations" (vv. 16–17). The audacity of Paul's move—depicting the father of the Jewish people as the father of the *un*circumcised (of "many goyim")—can hardly be overstated. By the time the Talmud was written, the rabbis were arguing that as the father of the Jews, Abraham had kept the entire Torah (despite the fact that it hadn't yet been revealed). Paul, however, removes Abraham from his connection to either the Torah or the Jewish people. Because Abraham was considered righteous before circumcision and on the basis of "belief," Abraham can be claimed as the father of those who believe "apart from Torah." Not surprisingly, Paul's daring appropriation of Abraham has allowed Christians for centuries to have confidence that they, not the Jews, are Abraham's true heirs. Paul himself was trying to argue a different case, namely that *not only* Jews but also Gentiles could be accepted as righteous by God.

Paul now introduces a new analogy, between the "one man" Adam and the "one man" Jesus (cf. 1 Cor. 15:20–29, 42–49). Just as both sin and death were introduced into the world by one person's—Adam's—faithless disobedience toward God, so also "justification and life" have become available through the faithful obedience of one person—Jesus. Paul supports his claim by asserting that the disobedient Adam was the "type" or prefiguration of Jesus, "the one who was to come." Jesus' fidelity, then, is presented as something built into the structure of the world from its beginning—Adam sets up the point, and Jesus scores. Jesus' resurrection, by extension, becomes a second creation of humankind.

Paul's argument that both Jew and Gentile are justified outside the bounds of Torah creates a number of problems for him, the first being moral accountability. If one is accepted by God "apart from the Torah," what motivation remains for righteous behavior? Paul has already claimed in 2:6 that God will repay people's *deeds,* and now he tries to explain the basis for Christian morality. Jesus' faithful death, says Paul, represented precisely his rejection of or "death" to sin; his resurrection is, correspondingly, a life lived exclusively "to God." The Christian participates symbolically in the messiah's death and resurrection through the initiatory rite of baptism. Initiation into the sect is represented as a form of death and rebirth. Christians, having "died," have thereby been freed from the body's enslavement to sin; through their symbolic resurrection they have been liberated to become "obedient from the heart."

Christians, through baptism, have *already* died and must therefore "act the part" of spiritual beings—demonstrating their freedom from this world by living morally pure lives. The Christian's obedience to God is an expression of his or her freedom from the power of sin. Paul never spells out what, exactly, Christian "obedience" looks like in practice. Is it adherence to the Torah? Or is obedience to God a strictly personal affair, an arrangement between oneself and the deity? Does "obedience" take different forms for Jews and for Gentiles? Paul does not address these questions, which seem to have gained in urgency in generations that followed. Instead, he turns to a related problem—the status of the Torah.

Paul returns to a problem that has been developing since the beginning of his argument: the model of Jesus—cursed under the Torah but blessed by God—and the model of an authoritative Torah are at odds; both cannot be normative. Paul takes up the unenviable task of defending the authority of the Torah even as he relativizes it. His strategy is to set up a distinction between the power of the Torah and the power of God. Once he argues that the two are different, it becomes easy for him to claim that the power of God surpasses that of the Torah (the walls of Eliezer's study house notwithstanding). The Torah, says Paul, is good, but despite its inherent goodness, it remains powerless to create goodness within the individual. In fact, says Paul, despite being "holy and just and good" (7:12) the Torah actually creates sin. It does so superficially by creating a category of prohibited actions. The absence of laws makes for a low crime rate. By creating prohibitions, the Torah also creates guilt when one does what is prohibited (cf. 3:20; 5:13). Paul points out this most obvious way in which the Torah creates sin, but his real interest lies elsewhere. For him sin represents a force active in the universe, and he believes that by creating standards for human obedience, the Torah actually creates an opportunity for sin to foster the urge to disobey. The commandment "You shall not covet," says Paul, "produced in me all kinds of covetousness" (7:8). This impulse, which we might just chalk up to a little rebelliousness, Paul conceives of as a spiritual battle: "The good that I would I do not, and that which I would not is what I do" (KJV 7:19). "The Torah," says Paul, "is spiritual. . . . And I delight in the Torah of God in my inmost self, but I see at work in my members another torah at war with the torah of my mind, making me captive to the torah of sin" (7:14, 22–23). This is a lot of torahs! Simply put, in a dualistic system in which the spiritual world (which includes the mind) is at war with the physical, the individual is torn between two natures. The Torah, as teaching, can express what is good, but it cannot empower the morally divided human being to accomplish it.

As he announced in his opening greetings (1:4), Paul finds the resolution for this tension in the "power" of the gospel. God, says Paul, has intervened to break the impasse created by humankind's divided impulses. Through baptism Christians share in the messiah's spirit of obedience. The bottom line for Paul is this: sin represents death, and the normal human condition is to tend toward both sin and death. The obedient death and subsequent resurrection of Jesus, however, represent the triumph of righteousness and life over both sin and death. The believer stands at an intermediate point, still subject to sin and death but also, by virtue of baptism, newly enabled to share in Jesus' new life. Through the messiah, God has accomplished something even the Torah was unable to effect, namely, the inner transformation of the individual. The believer's job is to cooperate as God completes the work of spiritual transformation.

Having finished explicating his thesis that the gospel represents "the power of God for salvation" to both Jew and Gentile, Paul turns in chapter 9 to a circumstance that causes him both emotional and intellectual discomfort: that God's decisive fulfillment of his promises to

The Jews as Problem

Romans 9–11 stands at the beginning of a long tradition in which the very existence of the Jews is perceived as problematic for Christianity. If Christian claims were true and Jesus represented the fulfillment of God's promises to Israel, then Israel should have been the first to embrace and follow the messiah. Israel's indifference to Christian claims contradicted both prophetic and popular expectations for the messianic age. The continued existence of Judaism thus created an implicit critique of Christianity's validity. Rather than defining their own movement as a failure, Christians soon came to see Jewish indifference to Christianity as a "rejection" of or "failure" to recognize the messiah; the continuation of a vital Jewish community equaled overt defiance of God's will. Paul's attempt to claim the continuing legitimacy of the Jewish people, however, has not been entirely ignored in Christian circles. On the contrary, his assertion in 11:29 that "the gifts and the calling of God are irrevocable" has formed the basis of several Christian bodies' affirmation that God's covenant with the Jews is still in effect.

Israel has met with resounding silence on the part of most Jews. Since he has no doubt that Jesus was the messiah, Paul sees only two options for explaining the Jewish community's decidedly cool response: either God has failed in his plan for creation or the Jews have failed to participate in God's plan. Not surprisingly, Paul is unwilling to implicate God: "It is not as if the word of God had failed." Paul therefore explains Jewish rejection of the Jesus group's claims as a spiritual failure on the Jews' part. "A hardening," he says, "has come upon part of Israel" (11:25).

Paul begins his consideration of non-Christian Jewry by expressing his anguish over their position and by affirming Jewish claims to the covenant and its promises. He then makes a rhetorical move that in later generations would have tragic consequences: he distinguishes be-tween "true Israelites," who accept Jesus as messiah, and the rest, "for not all Israelites truly belong to Israel" (9:6). In historical context Paul's assertion is unremarkable; Jewish sects regularly claimed to be the "true Israel" and condemned competing groups as idolaters or heretics (cf. Ps. Sol. 4:1–20; 1 Q.S. 8:6–8). Paul exercises the universal right of re-formers to claim that their reforms embody the true spirit of the tradi-tion. What is unprecedented in Paul's position, however, is his assertion that while many Jews are *not* part of the true Israel, many Gentiles *are*. Paul cites Torah to argue that birth is no guarantor of divine favor: Jacob the second-born son was chosen over Esau the heir; God told the prophet Isaiah that "only a remnant" of Israel would be saved (Isa. 10:22); and to Hosea he had announced that "those who were not my people I will call 'my people'" (Hos. 2:23). Earlier, Paul had made a case that in Jesus righteousness had been established "outside the Torah." Now he extends that principle, claiming, in effect, that membership in "Israel" is established outside the Torah as well.

Paul gives a pointed summary of his position: "Gentiles, who did not strive for righteousness, have attained it . . . through faith; but Israel, who did strive for the righteousness that is based on the Torah, did not succeed in fulfilling that Torah" (9:30–31). Paul is not arguing (as is often assumed) that only by "believing in Jesus" can a person be "saved." Rather, he is drawing a line between those willing to accept that God is working outside the boundaries of Torah and those who maintain the Torah as the immutable standard of righteousness. The goal, the *telos* of the Torah (not, as often misunderstood, "the end," or negation, of the Torah), says Paul, is Jesus the messiah (10:4). Paul once again assembles scriptural proof-texts, this time focusing on the "suffering servant" pas-sages of Isaiah 52–53, in which God's righteous servant is "numbered with transgressors." Paul is using scripture as evidence *against* scrip-ture's absolute authority. Scripture itself prophesies that "the righteous one" will be considered a transgressor.

Having identified Jews outside the Jesus group with Isaiah's "disobe-dient and contrary people" (10:21; Isa. 65:1–2), Paul then produces argu-ment upon argument to show that God has *not* rejected the Jews. First,

Root and Branch:
Paul's Metaphor of Jews and Gentiles

In Rom. 11:13–24, Paul compares the Gentile Christians to branches that have been grafted onto the ancient and holy tree that is Israel. In its original context Paul is warning Gentile Christians that although Israel may be rejecting the salvation God has offered through the messiah Jesus, it is not therefore to be despised. The Gentile Christians' are but a minor "branch" on the tree, a branch that lives and grows only by drawing its life from the trunk and root, that is, from Israel. Paul's metaphor continues to be widely used, especially among liberal Christians who wish to avoid supersessionism—the claim that Christianity has made Judaism obsolete. The metaphor, however, brings its own dangers. The image of Judaism and Christianity as root and branch is inherently developmental: Christianity "grew out of" Judaism. The metaphor of sequential development, in turn, lends itself to the view that Christianity is necessarily *more* developed, or more "highly" developed than the "earlier" religion. What began as Paul's observation that Gentile Christians were, so to speak, living off the vitality and rootedness of the Jewish community, has become an image of an "old" religion giving birth to the "new."

he argues, a remnant of Israel *has* been saved, namely the Jewish Christians (11:1–6). Second, the "hardening" of Israel's heart is simply a part of God's larger plan, in order to allow "salvation" to come to the Gentiles (11:11). God's acceptance of the Gentiles will soon make the Jews jealous and eager to be included. Finally, Paul castigates the Gentiles for their smugness; the Jews form the roots and trunk of the great tree into which Gentiles have been but newly grafted. Paul seems to be casting about for proof of what he already believes—that the Jews remain God's beloved people despite their general lack of interest in Jesus as messiah. At length Paul asserts that Israel's disbelief is, after all, a "mystery"—an unfathomable work of God—and that included in this mystery is the fact that, ultimately, "all Israel will be saved" (11:26). Presumably, Paul sees here the Jews' eventual acceptance of Jesus as messiah.

In chapter 12, having concluded the bulk of his theological considerations, Paul turns to more general concerns, exhorting the community to good behavior. He first emphasizes the community's unity as "one body" (12:4) despite differences among individual members (and, of course, between Jew and Gentile). He next advises respect for the ruling authorities, in effect encouraging the community to be "good citizens" of the Roman empire. Finally, Paul enjoins the congregation to "live honorably" because of the impending end of time (when, presumably, they will be judged for their deeds). In chapter 14 Paul turns from such general exhortations to address a question of more specific interest to this Jewish-Gentile community, namely kashrut or dietary laws. Some members of the community (called the "weak") avoid meat. The issue here is not concern over the method of killing the animal or handling the meat, but the fact that in Roman antiquity meat was ordinarily purchased at pagan temples (cf. 1 Cor. 8), where the animal had been slaughtered as an offering to a pagan god. These "weak" observe "certain days," apparently through fasting. Others (the "strong") despise such observance. It is unclear whether the division between "weak and strong" corresponds to that between Jew and Gentile. Are the Jews observant and therefore "weak," or is this an intra-Jewish debate over what constitutes proper observance for Jewish believers? In either case, Paul's response is simple and unequivocal: "Those who eat must not despise those who abstain, and those who abstain must not pass judgment on those who eat" (14:3). Paul's stand on ritual observance is remarkable, both in its own day and in ours. Then as now, Jewish sectarian divisions were often marked by what one would eat, with whom, and under what circumstances. And, then as now, those who kept stricter observance might feel justified in passing judgment on those whose observance was lax, while the less observant could smugly deride the superstition or hypocrisy of the strict. Though Paul

takes the position that "nothing is unclean in itself" (v. 14), he then declares that any food is "unclean for anyone who thinks it is unclean."
Going against one's conscience in this matter is wrong. The Jewish
Christian ought therefore to follow the dictates of conscience, but the
"strong" should defer to the conscience of the "weak," lest they alienate
those committed to observance. Regardless of their observance, which
is seen as a *personal* rather than a communal commitment, all members
of the community have a prior commitment to support and encourage
one another. The development of a new, Jewish-Gentile community,
then, has engendered a new approach to Jewish observance. Whereas
other Jewish sects advocated a single form of observance, which in turn
became one of the sect's defining characteristics, the messianists' mixture of Jews and unconverted Gentiles of necessity eliminated observance as a marker of group identity. For Jewish members, ritual
observance became a matter of individual conscience.

Paul concludes by asking the Roman Christians to "welcome one another," a surprising request coming from a stranger. He follows, however, with a concatenation of biblical citations (15:9–12) in which the
Gentiles are welcomed to share in God's blessings. If there is tension
between Jew and Gentile at Rome, Paul sides with the Gentiles. Scripture has explicitly included them in God's end-time plans; they have a
right to their place in the community. Paul hopes that he himself will
also be welcomed, and he reminds his readers of his hope that the congregation might "send him on" (read, "sponsor him") toward Spain.
Indeed, since the Gentiles have been so generously included in God's
spiritual blessings, they ought now to make themselves of service "in
material things" (15:27).

As it turned out, Paul did not live to undertake his westward mission. Only as a Roman prisoner would he be welcomed and supported
by the congregation at Rome.

The
Pastoral Epistles:
1 and 2 Timothy and Titus

THE THREE SO-CALLED pastoral epistles have been treated as a group since antiquity. In the modern period they are the most hotly disputed of the "disputed" Pauline epistles; many if not most interpreters consider them pseudonymous. The letters purport to contain Paul's instructions to Timothy and to Titus, pastoral assistants whom he has sent out to address problems in various churches. Whereas 2 Timothy centers on bolstering Timothy's self-confidence as a leader, 1 Timothy and Titus are largely concerned with the proper internal organization of local congregations. This concern with institutional structures is generally taken as evidence that the pastorals are second-century documents, written after the first flush of messianic excitement has passed and a sort of "apocalypse fatigue" has set in. Tired of waiting with bated breath for the end of time, Christians have settled down to create organizational structures for the long haul. While a second-century setting for all three letters is possible, it is by no means certain.

Many problems bedevil the question of the pastorals' "authenticity." At the most basic level, the pastorals, if authentic, would be the only existing correspondence between Paul and other missionaries. Paul would presumably write differently to co-workers than to troubled congregations, but we have no clearly authentic samples of such internal correspondence against which to measure the pastorals. The letters' diction is frequently considered "non-Pauline," but given the role of secretaries in composing letters in antiquity, any "author's" diction might vary from letter to letter, depending on the scribe. Two of the letters are addressed to Timothy, who served as coauthor of several of Paul's undisputed letters (e.g., 2 Corinthians, 1 Thessalonians, Philemon). It would come as no surprise that a letter written to Timothy would differ in style from a letter written, at least in part, by him. In practice, the same evidence can be made both to "prove" Pauline authorship and to "disprove" it.

Ideological biases frequently play a role in scholars' conclusions. It is difficult to avoid a gut feeling that an "authentic" letter is better than an "inauthentic" one, and the attribution of authenticity tends to be regarded as tacit validation of a letter's content. Religious conservatives are inclined to take the text at its word and assume Pauline authorship from the start. Liberals, on the other hand, have a strong motivation to label the letters, which emphasize hierarchy and prescribe silent subordination for women in the church, "inauthentic." Of the three letters, 2 Timothy has the closest affinity to Paul's undisputed letters, and will be treated here as a genuine Pauline epistle. First Timothy and Titus, which will be dealt with after 2 Timothy, are more likely to be pseudonymous.

SECOND TIMOTHY

PAUL WRITES THE LETTER called 2 Timothy from a prison in Rome. Paul's Roman imprisonment took place near the end of his life, probably in the early 60s. The location of Timothy, Paul's assistant in the field and the letter's recipient, is not mentioned. The letter follows the conventions of a paraenetic letter, or letter of exhortation. Timothy is evidently in need of reassurance, and Paul not only assures him that he really is "proficient, equipped for every good work," but also warns him to prepare to face persecution. Paul does not specify what sort of persecution he anticipates for Timothy but merely urges him to join him in "suffering for the gospel."

In light of the suffering ahead, Paul presents himself as Timothy's model. Having observed Paul's steadfastness in suffering, Timothy must "continue in what [he has] learned and firmly believed, knowing from whom [he] learned it." Nor is Paul Timothy's sole exemplar. Paul reminds him of the faith "that lived first in your grandmother Lois and your mother Eunice" (1:5). Timothy, it turns out, is a third-generation Christian. And, if the account of Acts is to be trusted, Timothy's maternal ancestors were Jewish Christians. Paul emphasizes Timothy's Jewish heritage along with his own as a powerful grounding "in the faith." If we assume that the letter is genuinely Pauline, 2 Timothy is unique in preserving Paul's discussion of Torah with another Jew. Speaking "in house," he draws no distinction between his ancestors' faith and his own. On the contrary, he asserts, "I worship with a clear conscience, *as my ancestors did*" (1:3). No divide between Judaism and Christianity disrupts Paul's sense of religious continuity. Timothy, for his part, has known since childhood "the sacred writings that are able to instruct you for salvation through faith in Christ Jesus" (3:15).

Paul's view of scripture is remarkable. On the one hand, he uses the Hebrew scriptures as a source of information about Jesus. On the other, he continues to employ and to recommend the Torah as a reliable, even authoritative guide. In striking contrast to his ambivalent portrayals of the Torah in gentile contexts (see Romans or Galatians), to Timothy Paul writes *entre nous,* reassuring him on the basis of his trustworthy grounding in Torah. No controversy about the relationship between observance and salvation enters the discussion, nor is Paul fretting over the relationship of gentile Christians to the Jewish people. Paul's is, of course, a sectarian perspective; he sees Jesus in the Torah, just as the Qumran sectarians saw their own Teacher of Righteousness there, and just as Rabbi Akiba would later see the rebel leader Bar Kochba. But the Torah remains a tree of life. "All scripture," as Paul says, "is inspired by God and is useful for teaching . . . and for training in righteousness" (3:16). "Scripture," for Paul and Timothy, means Torah, the legacy on which both rely.

Paul stresses Timothy's need for endurance in light of upcoming "end-time" tribulations. "In the last days," he says, people will display every possible unpleasantness: "lovers of themselves, lovers of money, boasters, arrogant, abusive, disobedient to their parents, ungrateful, unholy, inhuman, implacable, slanderers, profligates, brutes, haters of good, treacherous, reckless, swollen with conceit, lovers of pleasure rather than lovers of God" (3:1–4). The list is a fairly stereotypical Hellenistic vice list, and one can see why people in every age have been able to imagine their own days as the degenerate "last days." Paul wants Timothy to avoid panic when—not if—things go badly. Already Timothy must confront some whose destructive talk is spreading "like gangrene" through the community. These members claim that "the resurrection has already taken place," perhaps a position like that of the Corinthians who believed they had already transcended the mortal realm. Paul's primary concern, however, is not with the opponents, but with Timothy himself. His unwavering focus on Timothy's well-being and ability to endure in the face of both daily and cosmic crises, stems directly from the crisis Paul himself faces: his impending death. Paul's and Timothy's roles are about to diverge radically:

> As for you, always be sober, endure suffering, do the work of an evangelist, carry out your ministry fully. As for me, I am already being poured out as a libation, and the time of my departure has come. I have fought the good fight, I have finished the race, I have kept the faith. From now on there is reserved for me the crown of righteousness, which the Lord, the righteous judge, will give me on that day. (2 Tim. 4:5–8)

This may be the last guidance Paul will give his still-insecure protégé. Suddenly, the letter's encouraging tone takes on a more somber significance. "My child, be strong in the grace that is in Christ Jesus; and what you have heard from me, . . . entrust to faithful people who will be able to teach others as well." The legacy Timothy has received from Paul, from his maternal ancestors, and from the words of Torah, he must now carry on.

As it turns out, Paul's eloquent farewell is not his last word. Rather, his solicitous valediction is followed by a series of entirely pedestrian instructions regarding, not Timothy's, but Paul's welfare: "Do your best to come to me soon. . . . When you come, bring the cloak that I left with Carpus at Troas, also the books, and above all the parchments" (4:9, 13). Apparently, Paul is not *quite* at the point of being "poured out as a libation" but hopes to continue his work for some months. The shift in both tone and content is jarring and may even reflect a change in Paul's circumstances between the writing of the body of the letter and its rather brusque conclusion. Paul mentions a "first defense" that went badly but says that afterward he was "rescued from the lion's mouth." Perhaps Paul wrote the body of the letter when death seemed imminent but, in light of his improved prospects, added a coda with new instructions.

When read on its own, unclouded by concerns about either its authenticity or its relation to the other pastoral epistles, 2 Timothy creates a moving picture of the aging apostle's final words to his beloved student. Paul prepares Timothy both to continue his work ("do the work of an evangelist") and to meet the end of the world. Either form of preparation, or both, may be needed.

FIRST TIMOTHY

FIRST TIMOTHY IS A LETTER of instruction regarding "how one ought to behave in the household of God" (3:15). The Roman household was understood as a microcosm of the state, and the order of the state demanded order in both public and private venues. Instruction on household management was therefore one of the great set topics of Roman moralists. In Rome, as in most societies, household order was not understood as mere custom but was considered literally "natural," an extension of the natural order of the cosmos. The author of 1 Timothy assumes that Christians occupy at least three intersecting "households": their own, private households; the larger household (the *oikoumene*) of the empire; and the "household of God," the church. The church household is not identical to either of the other two, but neither is it independent of them. The ordering of the church will thus of necessity both affect and be affected by other forms of social order.

First Timothy purports to be Paul's instructions to his delegate Timothy, currently overseeing the church at Ephesus. The letter follows the conventions of the *mandata principis,* a letter sent by a ruler or commissioning officer, outlining the duties of a subordinate. Regardless of whether the letter is the work of Paul, it differs from the letters to the churches in that, rather than trying to *convince* its readers to behave (or stop behaving) in certain ways, it articulates organizational structures and policies. It is, in fact, exactly what it claims to be: a book of management tips for "the household of God."

After a brief greeting, the letter proceeds directly to business: Timothy is instructed to remain in Ephesus to prevent "certain people" from propagating deviant doctrines. The presence of maverick teachers (literally, those who teach otherwise, *heterodidaskalein*) seems to underlie at least some of the community's problems, and the author will return to them several times over the course of the letter. Here they are said to be concerned with "myths and endless genealogies," promoting "speculations," and wanting to be "teachers of the law" (1:4, 7). The author responds with a discussion of the law that, while not precisely matching any of Paul's varied appraisals of Torah, certainly reflects his nuanced way of thinking about it. "The law," he says, "is good." That is, it is good if used "legitimately," or appropriately. He then describes those to whom the law properly applies: it is "for the lawless and disobedient, for the godless and sinful, for the unholy and profane, for those who kill their father or mother, for murderers, fornicators, sodomites, slave traders, liars, perjurers" (1:9–10). The list of those who need the law is so exaggerated as to approach parody. Never mind people who don't "honor" their fathers and mothers; we're talking about people who *kill* them! These folks can fairly be said to need the law. But their behavior is also "contrary to the sound teaching that conforms to the glorious gospel of the blessed God." Here the author essentially identifies the behavioral norms of Torah and gospel; whatever deviates from one is also opposed to the other.

The author (it is hard at this point not to think of him as Paul) goes on to cite himself as an example. Despite having been "a blasphemer, a persecutor, and a man of violence," he has now received mercy as a sign that "Christ Jesus came into the world to save sinners—of whom I am the foremost" (1:15). The author's self-presentation strongly evokes Paul's statement in Galatians that precisely when he was most "zealous for the traditions of [his] ancestors," he was also opposing God by persecuting the church (Gal. 1:13–14). Although committed to the law, he used it "illegitimately," embodying the behaviors it was meant to counter.

The writer now turns from the specific problem of heterodox teachers to more general issues of church maintenance. First, prayers are to be made for "kings and all who are in high positions." The reasons are straightforward: "so that we may lead a quiet and peaceable life," and because this is "acceptable in the sight of God our savior" (2:2–3). The custom of offering prayers for foreign leaders (the Greek term would apply to anyone from a local client king to the emperor) goes back at least to postexilic times (see Ezra 6:9–10). Such prayers are not only permitted but enjoined, for the very practical reason that they enable the community to lead a "peaceable life." The empire was typically suspicious of voluntary associations, and a group whose founder had been executed for sedition would need to go out of its way to look innocuous. Conspicuous patriotism could only help.

A brief digression in 2:4–6 affirms the Christian message specifically in relation to the church's role in the gentile world. Asserting that God "desires everyone to be saved," the author declares that there is one God, and that Jesus is his one, human mediator, who became a "ransom" for all. The statement is highly compact. Beginning with a paraphrase of the *shema,* the affirmation of God's unity, the author then puts Jesus in Moses' role as the mediator between God and humanity. The move is surprising, but serves the purpose of changing God's election from the election of Israel to the salvation of "all." Like Moses, Jesus is not only a mediator but also a "redeemer." The word used is *antilytron,* a form of the word used in LXX for the Hebrew *goel,* "redeemer." Just as God is the "redeemer" of Israel, so Jesus is the redeemer of all. This brief affirmation anchors the author's discussion of "how to get along in the world." Like Jesus himself, the community must mediate between divine reality and the world in which they have been placed.

Following this all-encompassing declaration, the author returns to the nitty-gritty of how the community should comport itself in order to be perceived well by outsiders. He begins by ordering that men should "pray, lifting up holy hands without anger or argument." The posture is typical for prayer in both Hellenistic and Jewish traditions; the author's point is that arguments should be left behind during worship. He then declares that "the women should dress themselves modestly and decently in suitable clothing, not with their hair braided, or with gold, pearls, or expensive clothes" (2:9). The passage, not surprisingly, is infamous in liberal and moderate Christian circles. Men should pray properly; women should dress properly. However jarring in a modern context, the author's instructions are commonplaces of Hellenistic moral instruction: women should "adorn" themselves with virtue rather than with expensive clothing. Moreover, women should neither teach nor exercise authority over men. The instructions really amount to nothing more than a statement that both men and women should behave "appropriately" in the assembly. What is appropriate is defined both by what the author sees as decent and by Roman cultural values. Women are not to supervise men in "the household of God" any more than in their own households.

The author provides a rather convoluted biblical warrant for his position, concluding with one of the most difficult and confusing statements in the entire New Testament:

> I permit no woman to teach or to have authority over a man; she is to keep silent. For Adam was formed first, then Eve; and Adam was not deceived, but the woman was deceived and became a transgressor. Yet she will be saved through childbearing, provided they continue in faith and love and holiness, with modesty. (1 Tim. 2:12–15)

The argument runs as follows. Because Adam was formed first (Greek *protos*), he enjoys the preeminence of the firstborn. This is not stated in Genesis; rather, the author draws on cultural norms of primogeniture. Next, because the woman in Gen. 3:13 claims to have been deceived by the serpent, the author writes as if *only* the woman was deceived and *only* the woman transgressed. From this he extrapolates that all women are easily deceived and are liable, like Eve, to "teach" men to transgress. Again, this is not stated in Genesis, but the logic is clear. Now the author makes a statement as controversial as it is indecipherable: that "the woman" will be saved through childbearing. The text has been almost universally read as a claim that a woman's salvation is contingent upon her bearing children. This reading seems to be supported by 1 Tim. 5:14 and 4:3, in which young widows are ordered to marry and have children, and in which celibacy is condemned.

Was the author trying to shut down an early movement in which celibate women, freed from the constraints of the patriarchal Roman household, exercised leadership in the church? The scenario is not impossible, especially if one assigns the letter a late date. It is, however, equally possible that the reference to "salvation through childbirth" has simply been misunderstood. In Greek as in English, the word *save* (Greek *sozo*) can refer as easily to physical safety as to spiritual salvation (see, e.g., Acts 27:20, where the sailors despair of being "saved" from shipwreck). It is thus possible that the woman is "saved through childbearing" in the sense of being rescued from the dangers of childbirth. This reading, which does not at first glance relate to the question of female subordination, is consistent with the author's oblique use of the Adam and Eve story. In Gen. 3:16 the woman is given two punishments: subordination to her husband and greatly increased suffering in childbirth. In antiquity, whether the antiquity of Genesis or of the New Testament, the "suffering" of childbirth always entailed the possibility of death. Here the author has extended the *first* part of Eve's punishment to all women: they must be subordinate to their husbands. Yet, he says, the *second* part of the punishment can be avoided, at least for the pious woman: "She will be brought safely through childbirth" (my translation).

Having put men and women "in their places," the author takes up the question of church leadership, specifically, the proper qualifications for bishops and deacons. Historically, 1 Timothy's listing has influenced the development of offices in nearly all Christian bodies. One cannot, however, assume that the positions referred to in 1 Timothy bear any resemblance to the ecclesial offices as they developed in later periods. Bishops, for example, are not the exalted clerics of the modern or medieval church, but simply managers or supervisors (the Greek word *episcopos* referred to anyone in a supervisory role). The bishop must be neither quarrelsome nor a drunkard, and able to manage his own household well. The stipulation that he must be "the husband of one wife" is ambiguous; it could mean that he has only been married once, that he is faithful to his wife, or that he is monogamous. The intent, however, is clearly that in this, as in all things, he be "above reproach." These qualifications allow him to be an effective supervisor in the community, but they also contribute to his being "thought well of by outsiders." Deacons (male and female) are likewise to be persons of excellent character. Overall, the organization suggested in 1 Timothy seems to follow patterns known from both first-century synagogues and pagan voluntary organizations, religious and secular.

After his discussion of the proper qualities for church leaders, the author turns again to the "opponents." Here we are told that "they forbid marriage and demand abstinence from foods which God created to be received with thanksgiving" (4:3). The passage has given rise to a number of theories as to whether these false teachers are gnostics (in the second century), protognostics (in the first century), or even traveling teachers from Qumran. If they are the same false teachers mentioned in chapter 1, they desire to be Torah teachers, but their teaching includes extreme forms of asceticism as well as "myths and endless genealogies." Some early form of Jewish gnosticism is certainly possible, but so is an apocalyptic mysticism of the kind rebutted in Col. 2:8–23. In short, we don't know who they were. The author's primary objection is to their rejection of the physical world—sex and various foods. "Everything created by God is good" (4:4), says the author, provided it is received and used in the proper spirit.

Almost in passing, the author gives instructions regarding slaves, who are to "regard their masters as worthy of all honor, so that the name of God may not be blasphemed" (6:1). As in Colossians and Ephesians, the teaching on slavery is flatly conservative. In particular, Christian slaves with Christian masters must not show disrespect on the basis of their Christian "brotherhood." The conservative teaching is grounded in a specific anxiety: that rude or insubordinate behavior by slaves would bring the entire community into disrepute. As was the case with women and bishops, the community's behavior must be such that it will be perceived as decorous by outsiders. The practicality of it all may seem to go against the liberating spirit of Jesus, or even of Paul, the defender of Christian freedom. But, whether Paul or another, the author probably shared most of the values of his own culture. So, despite a theoretical belief that "God makes no distinctions," the idea of a woman exercising public authority or a slave claiming equality with his master was seen, by Paul and later church leaders alike, as both dishonorable and offensive to God.

The letter ends with admonitions that the rich in the community must take care lest they depend on their wealth rather than on God, and a reminder that "the love of money is a root of all kinds of evil" (6:10). The wealthy should "be generous," that is, act as patrons of the community. Timothy, for his part, should stay the course. First Timothy is a letter with little charm: no personal details, no emotional pleas or fierce condemnations. In contrast with 2 Timothy, it gives us no clear image of either the letter's author or its recipient. It is an elegantly reasoned memorandum; its goal, a community whose ethos and structure render it respectable without destroying its distinctive calling.

TITUS

Like 1 Timothy, Titus follows the form of the *mandata prin-*
cipis, a letter sent from a ruler or officer to a subordinate outlining
the latter's duties. It purports to be from Paul to Titus, whom Paul has
left temporarily on the island of Crete to clean up some problems. No
Pauline mission to Crete is known from Acts or from Paul's undisputed
letters, though the existence of such a mission is credible. As with
1 Timothy, it is possible, but not necessarily likely, that the letter was
written by Paul.

The author proceeds directly from the greeting to Titus's commission: "I left you behind in Crete for this reason, so that you should put
in order what remained to be done, and should appoint elders in every
town. . . . There are also many rebellious people. . . . Rebuke them
sharply, so that they may become sound in the faith" (1:5–13). The charge
to appoint elders seems to indicate that the Cretan congregation (or
perhaps congregations, since they are "in every town") is a new one,
only just establishing a coherent internal governance. Titus must deal
with two problematic groups: one, an opposing faction within the congregation; the other, *loyal* members of the congregation, whom the
letter portrays as little more than barbarians. The letter is short and to

the point; Titus must do remedial moral education with the one group while fending off the competing teachings of the other.

The author lists qualifications for both elders and "bishops," or supervisors. The qualifications show substantial overlap with those in 1 Timothy 3, but where differences appear, they suggest that the Cretan candidates are of a somewhat rougher cut than those at Ephesus. The head of the congregation (*episkopos;* bishop or supervisor), for example, must not be "violent" and must fully understand the gospel—qualities one might hope could be taken for granted. Like Titus himself, the supervisors must be prepared to counter the "many" who are insubordinate, "especially those of the circumcision" (1:10). "Those of the circumcision" are probably, as in Acts, Jewish believers who require circumcision for gentile converts. Crete was home to a large Jewish community in the first century; the presence of both Jewish messianists and Gentiles with an interest in Judaism is plausible. The opponents adhere to "Jewish myths and commandments" about purity and pursue "endless genealogies." The myths may be specifically called "Jewish" because Titus himself is a Gentile (Gal. 2:3); the reference to "genealogies" suggests mystical speculation of the kind found in the Dead Sea Scrolls or 1 Enoch, where arcane mystical "knowledge," including angelic genealogies, is developed. As in Galatia and Colossae, so also in Crete: gentile members of the congregation face pressure from those who seek to "improve" them through circumcision and mysticism.

The author writes off the opponents by quoting a saying attributed to the Cretan poet Epimenides (sixth century B.C.E.): "Cretans are always liars, vicious brutes, lazy gluttons" (1:12). The slur is directed at the circumcising opponents, but the bigoted view of Cretans seems to color the author's attitude toward loyal as well as "insubordinate" Cretan Christians. The old women, the author says, must be told not to be slanderers or enslaved to drink. The younger women must be *taught* to love husbands and children. Slaves are instructed not to pilfer. One gets an image of Titus dragging the whole congregation out of the gutter. The drunken, sharp-tongued old woman and the pilfering servant were negative stereotypes in Hellenistic literature, just as the loving wife and mother was a positive one, and the author portrays the Cretans as walking stereotypes of vice. We have no way to judge the fairness of his view. Regardless of his negative impressions, however, he is certain that God can transform the Cretan Christians. Believing in the Cretans' special need for moral education, the author stresses that God's gift "trains" us to live decent and righteous lives.

The apparently commonplace affirmation that God trains people to live decently is actually a dig at the opponents and an affirmation of uncircumcised gentile Christians. The circumcised opponents are portrayed as "detestable [literally, abominations], disobedient, unfit for any good work" (1:16). Jesus, however, has acted to "purify for himself a people . . . who are zealous for good deeds." "Unfit" for good deeds, the opponents are not the followers Jesus had in mind. The author's argument is essentially the same as that in Galatians and Philippians; Gentiles don't have to become Jews, because God has already made them into "chosen people" (cf. 1:1). Here, as in all of Paul's letters, the apparent rejection of the Jews applies only to Jewish messianists who insist on circumcising gentile converts. The status of Israel as a whole is not addressed.

The author concludes by instructing that the congregation be "reminded" to submit to the authority of secular rulers. Unlike 1 Timothy, which concerns "how to behave in the household of God" (the church), Titus focuses on the more secular themes of how to behave in one's own household and in the public *oikoumene* of the empire. Basics of law and order are at issue. But if the author is correct in his assessment of the community's moral development, they need basic instruction for practical as well as spiritual reasons. An abiding concern of early Christian communities was the perception of outsiders, since a sect whose members failed to uphold authority structures, whether in the household or in public, was liable to be outlawed. It was essential that opponents have "nothing evil to say" about their comportment. Despite its elegant theological dicta, Titus is all about survival. Mothers have to care for their children; grandmothers have to lay off the bottle; everyone has to show respect to the rulers. The rest will come in time.

ADDITIONAL LETTERS

THE LETTER TO THE HEBREWS

T HE SO-CALLED LETTER TO THE HEBREWS is a puzzle by any measure. Probably not a letter, it may not have been written to "Hebrews." The text combines the techniques of classical and midrashic rhetoric into such an elaborate maze of arcane argument that the book is almost indecipherable. A book more quoted than read, Hebrews's powerful images and beautiful language have made their way into standard Christian liturgies and hymns. Hebrews comprises a single extended argument to the effect that the movement centered on Jesus is at once continuous with and superior to the rest of Jewish experience. Jesus is the culmination of all that has gone before, but, as culmination, he is also substantially different from previous Jewish tradition. This rhythm of continuity and distinction appears already in the opening sentence: "Long ago God spoke to our ancestors in many and various ways by the prophets, but in these last days he has spoken to us by a son." Earlier, God spoke to the ancestors; now he speaks to us. To our ancestors he spoke through prophets; to us he speaks even more directly. Indeed, not only is Jesus "a son"; he has been "appointed heir of all things, through whom [God] also created the worlds."

The language describing Jesus is drawn from ancient and Hellenistic Jewish descriptions of divine Wisdom. Wisdom, in Proverbs 8 and

Wisd. of Sol. 9:9, is present at God's creation of the world. Just as Wisdom is "a pure emanation of the glory of the Almighty . . . a reflection of eternal light, a spotless mirror of the working of God" (Wisd. of Sol. 7:25–26), so Jesus is "the reflection of God's glory and the exact imprint of God's very being" (Heb. 1:3). Even as he portrays Jesus as a divine being, the author of Hebrews presents him in the form of Wisdom, a figure already known from Jewish tradition. This version of Christianity is not conceived of as un-Jewish or anti-Jewish. On the contrary, it is what our ancestors had and more: it is Judaism-plus.

The author of Hebrews is unnamed and unknown. For centuries the book was attributed to the apostle Paul, but that connection has been almost entirely discredited. The book's date of composition, its intended audience, and their location are also disputed. The title "To the Hebrews," which appears in manuscripts as early as about 200 C.E., was apparently added on the assumption that the work was a Pauline epistle addressed to a Jewish-Christian congregation. The work, however, does not follow widely accepted conventions of letter writing; it seems rather to be an encomium, a speech intended to move its hearers to hold fast to already shared values. Nothing in the work points conclusively to a Jewish audience. In fact, New Testament scholar Pamela Eisenbaum has argued that Hebrews represents the first thoroughgoing re-presentation of Jewish scripture and history as (gentile) *Christian* scripture and history. I find Eisenbaum's argument unconvincing and am inclined to consider the audience Jewish for a number of reasons.

First, the author of Hebrews begins with reference to how God spoke "to our ancestors" by the prophets. The intended reader is someone who knows without any explanation who "our ancestors" are and which "prophets" spoke to "us" of old. Our ancestors are not Romulus and Remus but Abraham and Sarah, and our prophets, Isaiah and Jeremiah. Elsewhere, the author depends heavily on his audience both knowing Jewish scripture and catching allusions to traditional Jewish interpretations. The entire book addresses the readers' relationship to Jewish tradition, a tradition presented as their rightful heritage. Even the metaphors assume the readers' Jewish identity. They are told that just as Jesus had to suffer crucifixion "*outside the city gate,*" so they too must "go to him outside the camp and bear the abuse he endured" (13:12–13). The image is drawn from Israel's wilderness wanderings, when the unclean were sent outside the camp. Hebrews's audience is currently *inside* the camp but must voluntarily put itself outside. Such imagery makes no sense if the text is addressed to Gentiles, who are already outside the camp. Hebrews addresses insiders who the author believes must choose between inclusion in the larger Jewish community and a new identity "outside the camp." Like the gospel of Matthew, Hebrews seems poised at a moment of realization that those who follow this way will pay the cost of becoming outsiders to their own tradition.

The date, place, and circumstances of Hebrews's composition are as disputed as its author and audience. Hebrews is quoted in 1 Clement, a Christian work usually dated to 95–100 C.E., making its composition by about 95 reasonably secure. Discussion of possible earlier dates centers on the status of the Jerusalem temple. Hebrews talks at length about rituals prescribed in Leviticus for the wilderness tabernacle. The problem is that the author speaks of the tabernacle service as something ongoing. The reference to the temple as "the tabernacle," the prototype of the temple built by Moses in the wilderness, would not be extraordinary during the period when the temple was still standing; temple and tabernacle were functionally interchangeable. The difficulties arise in trying to determine whether the author speaks of the temple/tabernacle service as ongoing because the temple is still standing, or whether, like Josephus (and Mishnah and Talmud), he continues to speak as if the temple still functioned even after it was destroyed by the Romans. The author's argument seems to depend on the continued existence of the Jerusalem temple. He makes an elaborate case that even though the temple service continues, it has been superseded; it is obsolete; it is, in fact, "passing away." Such an argument would have been absurd *after* the temple's destruction. Conversely, if the author had wished to discredit levitical ritual *after* the temple's destruction, he surely would have pointed to its fall as evidence of its transitory nature. The few facts available are most consistent with a Jewish (Christian) audience prior to 70 C.E.

The author writes a "word of exhortation" to the congregation, whom he perceives to be in spiritual danger, standing "on the verge of being cursed." We are told no details of the situation. The community has undergone some persecution and is facing more—apparently with decreased fortitude. The author urges them to remember "earlier days" in which they faithfully endured persecution, including the plundering of their possessions. He exhorts them again to "endure trials," chiding them for their weakness. After all, he observes, "you have not yet resisted to the point of shedding your blood" (12:4). The image of a Jewish-Christian community under persecution is tantalizingly suggestive. If, as is often thought, the community resided at Rome, then the persecutions could have been those under Nero in 64. Nero's persecution of Christians was, however, thoroughgoing and lethal, whereas this community has not suffered martyrdoms. We know that already in 49 C.E. Jews had been expelled from Rome following disturbances "over Chrestus," and it is possible that members of this community were expelled at that time, losing their possessions in the process. Having returned in 54, they are now wavering at the prospect of further and more serious persecution. Ultimately, the evidence available does not allow us to identify the audience or its exact situation with confidence.

After his initial warning that the community is about to fall under a curse, the author makes hardly any additional reference to their experiences. Almost in passing he acknowledges that although Jesus has already taken his throne in heaven, the results of his lordship are not yet in evidence on earth. Signs of divine triumph are conspicuously lacking. The author argues that Jesus' victory is unseen precisely because it is cosmic in scope and spiritual in nature. What is spiritual and invisible is superior to what is physical and visible. The author develops this contrast between things seen and things unseen by comparing the animal sacrifices performed in the temple with Jesus' superior offering of himself as a sacrifice. The similarity between the Romans' execution of Jesus and the levitical priests' job of performing temple sacrifices is not obvious, and it is worth considering why the author would connect the two in the first place. The answer may lie in a feeling of insufficiency on the part of Jewish Christians. Jews worshiped God through prayer and study at local synagogues, but the most important rituals were those performed in the Jerusalem temple. There offerings were intended to cleanse worshipers, altar, and land from the effects of sin. There the cosmic balance was maintained that allowed Israel to remain God's holy people.

Hebrews argues that Christians have a superior priest who has offered a superior sacrifice; therefore, the temple service is obsolete. In what situation, however, would someone feel the need to make such a case? The argument only makes sense in response to a situation in which the community is separating itself from the larger Jewish community, represented by the temple. Such separation might not indicate that the community saw itself as no longer Jewish—the Qumran sectarians, for example, had long ago disassociated themselves from the Jerusalem cult—but it would mark a radical break all the same. Hebrews's meticulous argument, however, suggests that some in the community are not comfortable with the break. These have "fallen away" in a manner that holds Jesus up to "contempt" (6:6). These need encouragement to take the step "outside the camp," instead of clinging to what is familiar and safe. In short, some in the Hebrews community are leaving the sect in favor of less controversial forms of Judaism. They are opting to stay "inside the camp" and they are doing so during a time of persecution. It is tempting to speculate that these "deserters" sought refuge from persecution by realigning themselves with Judaism, but it is difficult to pinpoint a time and place in which such a strategy would have been effective. In the absence of a secure date for Hebrews's composition, no reliable conclusions can be drawn.

Hebrews is addressed to Christian Jews who have come to doubt whether the "Christian" part was such a good idea after all. The author writes to persuade them that their Christian beliefs are really the same as their Jewish beliefs—only better—and that the reward for these beliefs, though still unseen, will justify their fidelity. The author rallies a string of scriptural quotations to prove that when God created Israel, he had something "better" in mind all along. The quotations are wideranging but center on verses 1 and 4 of Psalm 110, a psalm attributed to David:

The Lord says to my lord,
"Sit at my right hand
until I make your enemies your footstool.". . .
The Lord has sworn and will not change his mind,
"You are a priest forever,
according to the order of Melchizedek."

Of whom could David be speaking, whom he calls "my Lord," and who will sit at God's right hand? To whom has God promised both eternal kingship and eternal priesthood? Who but the one who, when he "had made purification for sins [like a priest], sat down at the right hand of the Majesty on high [like a king]" (Heb. 1:3). Jesus, according to the author, made sacrifice like a priest, is enthroned (by virtue of his resurrection) like a king, and is superior to the angels. "For to which of the angels did God ever say [as he does in Ps. 2], 'You are my son; today I have begotten you'?" (Heb. 1:5). "To which of the angels has he ever said [back to Ps. 110], 'Sit at my right hand until I make your enemies a footstool for your feet'?" (Heb. 1:13).

Having argued that Jesus is superior to the angels, the author sets about to prove that he is also superior to Moses. Moses was "faithful *in* all God's house" (Num. 12:7–8, LXX), whereas Jesus was faithful *over* God's house as a son. No contest. The son is greater than the servant. Besides, the people whom Moses led rebelled and failed to enter the promised land. Who wants a leader like Moses, or to be like the people he led? On the contrary, says the author, if you have read Psalm 95 lately, you surely noticed that it says, "Today, if you hear his voice, do not harden your hearts as in the rebellion." Now, since David wrote this psalm *after* the exodus, he clearly foresaw *another* time when the people would have an opportunity to respond faithfully to God and enter his promised rest. "Let us therefore make every effort to enter that rest," writes the author, "so that no one may fall through such disobedience as theirs" (4:11). Like true rabbinic exegesis, this almost fanciful mustering of "proof" tends to be convincing only to those who are already convinced.

Jesus, of course, is not only a son but also a priest, since God in the psalm clearly says to him, "You are a priest forever, according to the order of Melchizedek" (Ps. 110). What could be plainer? The entire central section of Hebrews, roughly chapters 5–10, will be spent unpacking the implications of God's designation of Jesus as a priest of the order of Melchizedek. To modern readers the entire enterprise seems far-fetched, since we have no reason to believe that God was addressing Jesus in the first place. The logic, however, is classically midrashic. Certain premises are taken for granted. Based on them, an author can then move freely throughout scripture, enlisting key quotations to support his point. Here the author's unspoken premise is that, having been raised from the dead, Jesus is now exalted in heaven. If that is the case, then it must have been Jesus whom David foresaw (in Ps. 110) seated at God's right hand. The figure seated at God's right hand is called a priest forever; therefore, Jesus is called a priest. The connections can now be made ad infinitum.

Hebrews's elaborate and lengthy discussion of Jesus' priesthood is in some ways peripheral to the author's concerns. The book is not about priesthood, Jesus' or anyone else's. The subject of priesthood, however, allows the author to argue several other points that are necessary to his goals. First and foremost, Jesus' otherwise unknown priesthood is used to prove Christianity's superiority over temple-based (or tabernacle-based) Judaism. Once this is proved to the author's satisfaction, he can argue for the general superiority of what is unseen (Jesus' sacrifice in heaven) over what is seen (temple sacrifices). He can also make a case that the utterly invisible rewards of belonging to a fringe-but-nonetheless-persecuted sect are superior to the rewards of belonging to the Jewish tradition *as expressed in the temple cult.* The author's goal is to define temple cult and Jesus cult in such a way that the Jesus cult seems infinitely more attractive—indeed, more worth suffering for—than temple-based Judaism. In so doing he hopes to reclaim a few disheartened followers.

The contrast between Jesus' priesthood and that of the temple priests depends loosely on the Platonic notion of a parallel between a spiritual world, or world of perfect forms, and the material world, inhabited by mere copies of the forms. The spiritual realities, are, of course, infinitely more real than the "real" ones. This dualism would have been familiar to any educated person in Greco-Roman antiquity. The author combines this Platonic model with ancient Israelite thought, which displayed a certain ambiguity as to whether God was in fact enthroned in the Jerusalem temple or "above the heavens." Some texts claim that the temple is God's throne, but in others it is his footstool, thus serving as the meeting place between heaven and earth.

Hebrews uses the contrast between an earthly and a heavenly temple to advantage. We all know, after all, who serves in the earthly temple; that would be the levitical priests. Jesus, however, made only one sacrifice—his own life.

> When Christ came as a high priest of the good things that have come, then through the greater and perfect tent (not made with hands, that is, not of this creation), he entered once for all into the Holy Place, not with the blood of goats and calves, but with his own blood, thus obtaining eternal redemption. (Heb. 9:11–12)

By virtue of his resurrection Jesus now inhabits the heavenly temple where, being immortal, he is, like Melchizedek, "a priest forever." Earthly priests serve in a sanctuary that is "a sketch and shadow of the heavenly one" (even Moses said he was giving the people a "pattern"), whereas Jesus serves in the true sanctuary. And, offering a superior sacrifice, Jesus becomes the mediator of a superior covenant. This, says the author, is the new covenant foreseen by Jeremiah:

> The days are surely coming, says the Lord,
> when I will establish a new covenant with the house of Israel
> and with the house of Judah;
> not like the covenant that I made with their ancestors. (Jer. 31:31–32)

"In speaking of 'a new covenant,' " says the Hebrews author, God has "made the first one obsolete. And what is obsolete and growing old will soon disappear" (8:13).

Jesus is identified in Hebrews as both a royal messiah (David's heir, seated at God's right hand) and a priestly messiah—an individual otherwise known to us only from the Dead Sea Scrolls community, which anticipated both a royal *and* a priestly messiah. Since making his sacrifice and sitting down at the right hand of God, Jesus "has been waiting 'until his enemies would be made a footstool for his feet' " (10:13). Jesus is *still waiting* for God's final conquest of evil. And if even Jesus has not seen the full results of his victory, then it is hardly surprising that we on earth have not seen it either. With this acknowledgment that Jesus' enemies have *not* been vanquished, the author turns to his real subject: encouraging his audience to persevere despite the lack of any tangible validation from God. He reminds them of their earlier suffering, when they endured the plundering of their possessions, "knowing that you yourselves possessed something better and more lasting." So now also, they must endure in order to "receive what was promised" (10:34, 36).

In chapter 11 the author undertakes a review of all of Israelite history, making the case that it has always been necessary for God's chosen ones to persevere *without* receiving what was promised: "Faith is the assurance of things *hoped for,* the conviction of things *unseen*" (11:1). The chapter is a rhetorical masterpiece, powerful and subtle in its reworking of familiar symbols. Like Stephen's speech in Acts 7, Hebrews 11 provides a Christian "roadmap" of ancient Israel, redefining Israelite history as a progression that culminates in the experience of the church. Like Stephen's speech, the Hebrews interpretation of the "Old Testament" is so deeply embedded in Christian consciousness as to seem the only possible reading of Israel's past.

Hebrews's account of Jewish history takes the form of a "heroes list" similar to those found in other Jewish literature of the period. Beginning with Abel, Enoch, and Noah, and culminating in the heroes of the Maccabean revolt, Hebrews 11 chronicles what the forebears achieved "by faith." As it turns out, it was "by faith" that Abel offered a more acceptable sacrifice than Cain's. By faith Moses was hidden as a baby. By faith Joseph "gave instructions about his burial." Even the walls of Jericho fell "by faith." Clearly, the author is using a rather unusual definition of faith. Faith, for this author, is the same quality he seeks to elicit in his audience—the willingness to act without reassurance as to the outcome. The heroes persevered in doubtful situations because they foresaw a better future. "Yet," says our author, "all these, though they were commended for their faith, did *not* receive what was promised" (11:39). All the heroes "died in faith without having received the promises, but from a distance they saw and greeted them" (11:13). A bittersweet conclusion at best! The history of the Jewish people, says the author, is a history of those who left their homeland, who crossed the Red Sea, who were dispossessed but not disheartened, who "looked forward to the city . . . whose architect and builder is God," that is, to a city that is invisible. Therefore, we are told:

> Since we are surrounded by so great a cloud of witnesses, let us also lay aside every weight and the sin that clings so closely, and let us run with perseverance the race that is set before us, looking to Jesus the pioneer and perfecter of our faith, who for the sake of the joy that was set before him endured the cross, disregarding its shame, and has taken his seat at the right hand of the throne of God. (Heb. 12:1–2)

All of Israelite and Jewish history has become a great relay race. Each generation has handed off its hope to the next, and now the ancestors—Abraham, Isaac, Jacob, and the rest—stand by cheering as the community prepares to run its course. Jesus, the "pioneer and perfecter" of faith, has already crossed the finish line and, seated at God's right hand, has become the guarantor of their reward.

Hebrews is a superb piece of motivational rhetoric. It becomes even more impressive if we assume that it was intended for Jews who had left or were tempted to leave the Jesus sect in favor of "safer" forms of Judaism. By the book's conclusion we are presented with fidelity to Jesus as the only legitimate Judaism available. "God spoke to our ancestors by the prophets, but *now* . . . God has spoken to us by a son." God has found a superior means of calling God's people. Before, human priests had to offer sacrifice again and again. Now an eternal priest has offered an eternal sacrifice. Before, we focused on an earthly temple. Now we prepare to enter the heavenly temple. What our ancestors hoped for, we possess—or we will, if we don't give up hope. Our suffering is not a stigma to be avoided, but proof that we continue the great race run by our ancestors.

How effective was Hebrews's argument with its original readers? Did *any* Jewish Christian, having decided to return to a less controversial interpretation of Judaism, find him- or herself saying, "Oh my gosh, all my Jewish ancestors are depending on me! I can't leave their great company now"? It is difficult, two thousand years removed, to picture Jews believing that only by "stepping outside the camp" and *leaving* traditional Judaism could they keep faith with their ancestors and with God. This, however, is precisely how some Jewish sectarians, among them the Qumran covenanters, the community called the *therapeutae*, as described by Philo, and the first members of the Jesus sect understood their Jewish identity. Regardless of whether Hebrews persuaded anyone to "step outside the camp" of traditional Judaism, its passionate call to endurance would have offered solace and courage to those who had already taken the step.

Hebrews accomplishes a great displacement of Jewish symbols and traditions. None mean what they have traditionally meant. Abraham becomes a man who desired, not the holy land, but "a better country, that is, a heavenly one" (11:16). Temple, covenant, Torah, and land all become mere way stations on the path toward a heavenly reality. Judaism is first devalued—it is, after all, merely the shadow of the things to come—and then reappropriated and revalued according to Christian categories. Such a translation of Judaism into exclusively spiritual terms was not unique to the Jesus sect—Philo remains the premier exemplar of "spiritualizing" Judaism—but within the world of Hebrews, biblical characters, institutions, and laws all point to a spiritual landscape occupied only by *Christian* Jews. Hebrews combines the Platonic allegorizing of Philo with the sectarian exclusiveness of Qumran. Moreover, the *displacement* of Jewish categories, the discounting of actual, tangibly Jewish persons, places, and rituals in favor of spiritualized, heavenly categories, turned out to be precisely the move the community would need. As Christianity became an increasingly gentile movement, a spiritualized Judaism served it best. The "new Israel," an Israel that included fewer and fewer actual Jews, became happy to affirm that the old covenant was "obsolete and growing old, [and would] soon disappear."

JAMES

THE LETTER OF JAMES provides one of the New Testament's best glimpses into the beliefs of a fully Jewish sect of Jesus-followers. The "Jewishness" of James has long been recognized, to the point that the book was nearly excluded from the Christian canon. Martin Luther did not consider James among the books that "show thee Christ," and in an important sense he was right. James says nothing about Jesus' life, death, resurrection, or relationship to God. Jesus' status as Lord and messiah is taken for granted, but it is by no means the primary subject of James's letter. Jesus fails even to show up as one of the author's moral exemplars; instead, Abraham, Rahab, Job, and Elijah demonstrate virtues to be pursued.

The letter is written by James to "the twelve tribes of the Dispersion" (diaspora). "James" is an English version of the Hebrew for "Jacob" (Greek *iacobos*), father of the twelve tribes of Israel. The letter can thus be read as a message from "Israel" to diaspora Jews—presumably diaspora Jewish Christians. Church tradition has long assumed that the author was James the brother of Jesus, but the book contains no clues allowing scholars to determine with certainty whether it was composed by Jesus' brother, whether it is an anonymous composition, or whether the book was written by some other, and otherwise unknown, James.

The attribution to one of Jesus' original followers, which ordinarily enhances a work's status, provides a more ambiguous pedigree in the case of James. In Galatians, Paul cites Jesus' brother James as the center of a movement that insisted on circumcision for gentile converts. The New Testament always portrays this traditionalist strand of the Jesus sect in a negative light, their only role being to "oppose" Paul's mission to the Gentiles. Because of the New Testament association between James and opposition to Pauline Christianity, readers have frequently seen James as the embodiment of a Jewish Christianity that was both legalistic and exclusivistic. By the end of the second century, when most Christian congregations had broken from the Jewish community, both Jewish believers who maintained their Jewish identity and Gentiles who attended synagogue or celebrated Jewish holidays came to be called "Judaizers" and were subjected to varying degrees of disapproval or sanction. James seemed the relic of a rejected Judaizing Christianity, and in some circles became little more than a foil to Paul—the corruption of Christian freedom into an essentially Jewish (and futile) pursuit of "salvation through works of the Law."

Only in very recent years, in the wake of efforts to reclaim the Jewishness of first Jesus and then Paul, have scholars begun to understand the letter of James not as "Judaizing," but as simply *Jewish*. That is, James was written within a Jewish messianic community whose Jewishness was not under negotiation. Concerns over the relationship between Jew and Gentile, with the attendant issues of circumcision and dietary restrictions that loom so large in Acts and in Paul's letters, are barely on the screen of this community. Whatever the James community's level of ritual observance, the messiah's arrival seems not to have been an event of great ritual significance. In fact, the author of James has other things on his mind. He is more worried about his readers' moral and spiritual lives than about doctrinal controversies.

James addresses the moral lives of his congregation by means of sayings—the sayings of Jesus and of the early rabbis, as well as sayings of his own. Repeatedly, James's advice—"Do not grumble against one another, that you may not be judged," "Ask God . . . and it will be given you," "Do not swear . . . but let your 'Yes' be yes and your 'No' be no"—mirrors Jesus' sayings as reported in Matthew and Luke. James was either directly dependent on the canonical gospels or was using the same or similar sources as theirs. The use of Jesus' sayings without any narrative framework suggests that the author may even have employed a "sayings source" such as Q. If James used a sayings source *rather* than a written gospel, then the epistle could actually predate the canonical gospels. Sometimes considered one of the latest New Testament writings, James may have been among the first.

James also employs rabbinic (or proto-rabbinic) sayings, particularly those in the Mishnaic *Pirke Aboth,* alongside those of Jesus. Both James and *Pirke Aboth* (published in about 200 C.E. but including much earlier material) include warnings on the perils of becoming a teacher, against judging others, and against uncontrolled speech and biased judgment; both contain repeated teachings about the importance of doing the law as opposed to merely studying it. A saying attributed to Simeon son of Gamaliel summarizes James's favorite themes: "All my days have I grown up among the Sages and I have found naught better for a man than silence; and not the expounding [of the law] is the chief thing but the doing [of it]" (*m. Pirke Aboth* 1.17).

The logic connecting James's sayings is extremely difficult to follow, so much so that many scholars consider the book no more than a loosely connected compendium of moral epithets. The disparate teachings are linked, however, by grammatical connectors such as *so* and *likewise,* suggesting that the author, at least, found them closely interrelated. A few clues help explicate James's structure. In 2:8 James instructs the reader to follow "the law of the kingdom" (NRSV, "the royal law"). This turns out to be Lev. 19:18, the instruction to love your neighbor as yourself. The theme of loving one's neighbor as oneself will run, albeit intermittently, throughout James. Lev. 19:18 was singled out by both Rabbi Hillel (*b. Shabb.* 31a) and Jesus (Matt. 7:12; Luke 10:27) as the law's summary and culmination. With literary links to the early rabbis as well as to Jesus, James is able to develop *both* rabbinic and early Christian traditions simultaneously. And why not? For an early Jewish sect member with ties to Pharisaic circles, Jesus would have represented another link in the chain of tradition. James drew on the wisdom of scripture, of the early rabbis, and of Jesus as sources for his teaching. If the messiah and the other sages agreed that love of neighbor led to the fulfillment of the whole Torah, what better grounding could exist for moral instruction?

Although James's moral exhortation centers on Lev. 19:18, the book is far from a unified argument. One difficulty stems from the fact that James includes the *context* of Lev. 19:18 — that is, the rest of Leviticus 19 — as part of its *content*. Like the rabbis, he does so without mentioning the other verses directly. Thus, the levitical prohibition against slander (19:16), the commandment to treat laborers fairly (19:13), and even the question of whether to swear oaths (19:12) are woven into his explication of what it means to "love one's neighbor" (see Johnson 1995). The connection between these laws and Lev. 19:18 is easy to miss. The issue of oaths, however, the least obviously connected with love of one's neighbor, plays an especially important role in the book, as it is vitally connected to James's other favorite topic, proper speech — specifically, the connection between speech (or beliefs) and action. If one combines the conviction that what one professes must be expressed through action with the principle of loving the neighbor (not an obvious combination, and not one that James makes explicitly), one gets roughly the range of issues addressed in the letter of James. A look at the first chapter, in which James touches on the topics he will later develop, illustrates how difficult it is to find unity in the letter, but also provides clues to a rudimentary coherence.

The letter opens abruptly with the exhortation "Whenever you face trials of any kind, consider it nothing but joy" (1:2). Already the interpretive difficulties begin. Who is experiencing trials, and of what kind? And why should trials be considered "joy"? We never learn who is suffering or how, but we do learn about the purpose of suffering: "the testing of your faith produces endurance . . . so that you may be mature and complete." Testing leads to maturity, presumably an occasion for joy. Without introduction, James next gives instruction to those lacking in wisdom: "Ask God, who gives to all generously and ungrudgingly, and it will be given you" (v. 5; cf. Matt. 7:7–11). He then moves on to the condition of rich and poor in the community. The believer who is lowly should "boast in being raised up, and the rich in being brought low." Most of us have never heard of anyone, rich or poor, boasting of "being brought low." In biblical tradition, God's reversal of the fortunes of rich and poor is specifically a reason for the rich *not* to boast. As Hannah counsels in 1 Samuel 2:

> Talk no more so very proudly, let not arrogance come from your mouth; for the Lord is a God of knowledge, and by him actions are weighed. The bows of the mighty are broken, but the feeble gird on strength. Those who were full have hired themselves out for bread, but those who were hungry are fat with spoil. (1 Sam. 2:3–5)

If the rich are to boast in being brought low, it can only be because, by willingly humbling themselves before God, they hope to escape the destruction so palpably awaiting them.

James immediately returns to the theme of testing (here the Greek *peirazo* is usually translated "tempt") and argues that we are not in fact tested (or tempted) by God, but by our own desires. For James, the indulgence of selfish desire is sin, leading to death. God, on the other hand, is the giver of "every perfect gift," including the creation of the community itself. This gift, however, must be "welcomed" if it is to be realized. An "implanted word that has the power to save" them, its growth must be cultivated. The specific forms of cultivation James enjoins are, first, the control of speech, and second, the translation of belief into action: "Be doers of the word, and not merely hearers" (1:22). "Religion," says James, "that is pure and undefiled before God, the Father, is this: to care for orphans and widows in their distress, and to keep oneself unstained by the world" (1:27). In the tradition of Amos and Isaiah, James assumes that moral "purity" in the form of social justice takes precedence over ritual.

All these topics—from boasting in lowliness to the control of one's speech and care for orphans—are compressed into a single, rather dizzying chapter. Most of the subjects raised are typical among both Greco-Roman and Jewish moralists. That endurance leads to maturity, that one should be "quick to listen, slow to speak," and that actions speak louder than words were clichés of moral discourse. The distinctive aspect of James's presentation is his conviction that God has "implanted" in the believers the power by which they may actually *fulfill* these moral bromides. James now begins to develop each of his teachings in light of Lev. 19:18. He starts with a scathing rhetorical question: "Do you with your acts of favoritism really believe in our glorious Lord Jesus Christ?" (2:1). "Acts of favoritism" (*prosopolempsia*) is a Greek approximation of the Hebrew *nasa panim* (lifting the face), a phrase denoting partiality in legal judgments. Partiality is severely condemned in Lev. 19:15 and elsewhere in Torah. James's question, impugning the readers' beliefs on the basis of their actions, recalls his injunction that right belief must show itself through right action. He supplies a hypothetical example:

> For if a person with gold rings and in fine clothes comes into your assembly [*synagoge*], and if a poor person in dirty clothes also comes in, and if you take notice of the one wearing the fine clothes and say, "Have a seat here, please," while to the one who is poor you say, "Stand there," or "Sit at my feet," have you not made distinctions among yourselves, and become judges with evil thoughts? (James 2:2–4)

The setting in the community assembly (the word *synagoge* could apply to either the assembly or the building) bluntly illustrates his point. The rich and poor individuals are both evidently members of the community, but their status difference is vividly demonstrated by their attire—radiant versus filthy. They receive treatment corresponding to, in fact replicating, their different statuses. The rich person is addressed deferentially and is seated "here," presumably in a place of honor. The poor person is told either to stand "there," at some remove, or to sit at the speaker's feet, in a position of subservience.

For most ancient readers the surprising aspect of this scene would not be the overt discrimination but the unexpected fellowship of the "dirt poor" and the rich as members of the same association. Given such an unusual arrangement, it would have been only natural to treat people, here as anywhere else, in accordance with their status. James, however, bluntly claims that such behavior, however socially acceptable, is literally criminal by the Torah's standards. Status- and wealth-based distinctions are not treated as matter-of-course social protocol but as a blatant example of "partiality in judgment." Acknowledgment of status differences was hardly optional in the rigidly hierarchical Roman world, but it was unquestionably contrary to the commandment to "love your neighbor as yourself." James seeks to impress this disjunction between social rules and "the royal law" upon his readers. "Friendship with the world," he says, "is enmity with God" (4:4).

James reminds his readers that the messianic age is an age of reversals: "Has not God chosen the poor in the world to be rich in faith and to be heirs of the kingdom that he has promised?" James echoes Jesus' promise, "Blessed are you who are poor, for yours is the kingdom of God" (Luke 6:20), just as Jesus echoed Hannah's, "He raises up the poor . . . to make them sit with princes and inherit a seat of honor" (1 Sam. 2:8). But you, says James, "have dishonored the poor." The irony is palpable. In an honor-based culture, honor ordinarily accrues only to someone whose position already entails honor. Thus, for example, men, particularly male heads of households, have honor, whereas those beneath them have only such honor as derives from association with the paterfamilias. A wayward daughter dishonors not herself but her father, in whose person the familial honor resides. For James to claim that his congregations have "dishonored the poor" is to utter nonsense. The poor have no honor to lose. But if God has already "raised up the poor," causing them to "inherit a seat of honor," then conformity to Roman norms equals the rejection of God's rule. James's identification of the rich as oppressors and the poor as the "deserving" poor is entirely consistent with biblical, especially prophetic, social analysis (see Amos 2:6–7; 8:4–8). Here, however, he adds his own observation that those in the middle (among whom he apparently includes his readers) often favor the rich and despise the poor despite the fact that, like the poor, they suffer the oppression of those with power and wealth.

James uses the community's practice of "partiality" as the spring-board for his discussion of "the law of the kingdom": "You shall love your neighbor as yourself" (2:8). James's discussion of the law is some-what confusing, as he says both that one is responsible for keeping "the whole law" and also that "mercy triumphs over judgment" for those judged by "the law of liberty" (apparently the same as "the law of the kingdom," Lev. 19:18). He then enjoins his followers to act like people who will be judged "by the law of liberty," that is, on the basis of Lev. 19:18, loving their neighbor. God's judgment will follow the princi-ple of Lev. 19:18: he will judge the merciless mercilessly, but for the mer-ciful, "mercy triumphs over judgment" (2:13). As Matthew's Jesus put it, the merciful will obtain mercy (Matt. 5:7).

Returning to the question of whether "belief" and partiality can co-exist, James points out the uselessness of faith without action. "If a brother or sister is naked and lacks daily food, and one of you says to them, 'Go in peace; keep warm and eat your fill,' and yet you do not supply their bodily needs, what is the good of that?" (2:15–16). The ex-ample—wishing someone well while allowing him or her to starve—is extreme, but the point is incontrovertible: profession of faith without corresponding action is meaningless. James now addresses the hypo-thetical objection that some people have faith while others have deeds—a variety of gifts like that described in 1 Cor. 12:28–31. This sec-tion of James is almost invariably discussed in comparison with Paul's teachings on faith and works in Romans and Galatians. Paul says that "a person is justified by faith apart from works prescribed by the law" (Rom. 3:28); James says that "a person is justified by works and not by faith alone" (2:24). Paul uses Abraham as the model of justification by faith; James says that Abraham was justified by *works*. This apparent op-position between the teachings of Paul and of James has, more than any other factor, accounted for James's marginalization, particularly by those for whom Paul stands at the heart of the gospel message. Setting Paul aside for the moment, what does James mean by "justification by works"?

James responds to the claim that some have faith while others have works with a challenge: "Show me your faith apart from your works, and I by my works will show you my faith" (2:18). The challenge is, of course, spurious. James's image of the well-wishing believer who watches a "brother" starve has already made his point: good works may express faith, but the lack of works exposes an empty faith. Belief is not, or ought not to be, a theoretical matter. "Even the demons," says James, "believe—and shudder" (2:19). The demons translate *their* belief into action; believing all too firmly in God's existence, they shudder to contemplate their doom. James now turns to Abraham, the premier exemplar of faith in the Jewish tradition, as proof that a person is justified by works. Rather than beginning, as Paul does, with the claim of Gen. 15:6 that Abraham's belief was counted as righteousness, James begins with the *akedah,* the binding of Isaac, then and now the crucial test and proof of Abraham's faithfulness to God's will. Abraham, says James, was justified by *works* when he put his son on the altar. His actions confirmed his belief in God's sovereignty. Abraham's actions *fulfilled* the statement that Abraham "believed God and it was reckoned to him as righteousness" (Gen. 15:6). First God *said* Abraham was righteousness, then Abraham went out and—by his works—proved it. Thus "a person is justified by works and not by faith alone" (2:24).

James's position, so often discredited as "works-righteousness," an attempt to buy God's favor by virtue of one's own merit, seems entirely reasonable on the face of it. God commands love of neighbor. Jesus both affirms that command and exemplifies it. Jews and pagans alike know that a belief that does not result in action is fraudulent. James does not dispute the effectiveness of faith; he simply notes that if faith does not result in works, it is hypocrisy. Paul, on the other hand, is not discussing the quality of his congregants' faith; responding to the notion that Gentiles can be saved only by a *specific* work, namely, circumcision, Paul condemns the proposition that God cannot find a person acceptable until he has been circumcised. (The implications of such a view for women were not even considered by ancient writers.) Paul counters that it is faith, that is, faithfulness to God's will, that justifies a person, not ritual status ("works of the law"). His position is virtually identical to James's: God "will repay according to each one's deeds" (Rom. 2:6). To those who patiently do good "he will give eternal life; while for those who are self-seeking and who obey not the truth but wickedness, there will be wrath and fury" (Rom. 2:7).

Paul's intuitively obvious principle, that God would reward good actions and punish bad ones, has been denied in many Christian circles. The conviction that Paul teaches "justification by faith" is so deeply entrenched that his position is commonly presented as "All your good deeds won't get you into heaven." Paul, however, agrees with James that faith, if it is genuine, must result in good deeds. Unlike Paul, James writes to Jewish congregations that are not embroiled in controversies over circumcision or, apparently, any other aspect of ritual observance. James is concerned with realizing "the law of the kingdom," the love of neighbor.

James follows up his proof that Abraham was justified by works with the example of Rahab, the prostitute who helped the Israelite spies escape safely from the land of Canaan. "Was not Rahab the prostitute also justified by works when she welcomed the messengers and sent them out by another road?" (2:25). The example is disconcerting; after Abraham, Rahab seems something of a comedown. It is true that before helping the spies she professes her faith in Israel's God (though James does not mention the fact), thus putting her faith into action. But Rahab seems an arbitrary choice among the many available in Israel's long history. Did James wish to give a female example? Or perhaps a gentile example? Any Christian leader would have been aware of the dispute over Gentiles in the sect. It was a painful social and halakic (legal) controversy that hit the Jesus movement early and hard. With the introduction of Rahab, James may be subtly weighing in on the inclusion of Gentiles. Even as our father Abraham was justified by a faith that was "completed" in his works, so also Rahab, a righteous Gentile, was "justified" by demonstrating her faith through her actions.

Having elaborated the implications of placing Lev. 19:18, the love of neighbor, at the center of the law, James now turns to the well-worn moral topic of proper speech, specifically, controlling the tongue. Control of one's speech may seem only loosely related to love of one's neighbor, but in both Lev. 19:16 and later Jewish tradition, the two are closely connected. In Jewish tradition, the damage done by slander, *lashon hara,* is taken so seriously as to be compared with murder. Chapter 3 opens with a concatenation of prosaic observations on the difficulty of controlling the tongue: the tongue is a rudder that steers a great ship; it is a small fire that can set the woods ablaze. In the midst of such platitudes, James returns to his underlying concern, the callous ease with which people abuse one another: "With [the tongue] we bless the Lord and Father, and with it we curse those who are made in the likeness of God" (3:9). James turns from the untamed tongue to untamed desires in general, portraying them in their worst possible light: "You want something and do not have it; so you commit murder." The claim seems almost ludicrous at first glance; how many of his readers have committed murder? If, however, one asks what emotions motivate murder, James's answer—unfulfilled desires, whether for power, property, affection, or respect—seems not far from the mark. It is not clear whether he believes that his community actually displays the various antisocial behaviors he describes, or if he simply wishes to warn them against the vices that follow from adopting the values of "the world" rather than of God.

Having chastised his congregation at length, James concludes by comforting them. They need only "be patient . . . until the coming of the Lord." The theme of patient endurance brings us full circle to the letter's opening exhortations to endure trials with joy. James sets forth the endurance of Job (*hypomonen;* traditionally translated the "patience" of Job), who, though not at all patient, was surely a model of endurance and its rewards. Elijah, whose prayers (as James tells it) held off the rain for three and a half years and then restored it, provides a model of persistent prayer. The community is enjoined to pray for one another, to confess their sins to one another, and to bring back "wanderers." James's final image is of a mutually devoted community who cares for and corrects one another with gentleness.

The epistle of James is a moral treatise, advanced by way of maxims and guided by the author's conviction that to love God means to love one's neighbor. The book's most impressive feature is the incisiveness with which its author lays bare human resistance to this simple principle and his insistence that no excuse is valid; this and no other is the law of the kingdom. A very Jewish book, James is practical in its moral instruction and attuned to what we would now call *tikkun olam,* the mending of a broken world. Perhaps it is no coincidence that one of the book's fiercest critics was also the author of the infamous "On the Jews and Their Lies." Martin Luther was correct that James does not "show thee Christ" in the same sense that Paul's letters do. Instead, it provides guidance for a community shaped by God's gifts of humility and mutual care. Perhaps more than any other New Testament book, James raises the question of what it means for an authoritative Christian text to be recognizably Jewish. James unambiguously substantiates the claim that not only Jesus himself but also his followers were and continued to be Jews. For this reason, the neglected epistle of James provides a rich resource for the ongoing conversation about Jewish and Christian identities, their necessary boundaries, and their shared truths.

FIRST PETER

FROM A JEWISH PERSPECTIVE, 1 Peter is one of the most disturbing books of the New Testament. The problem is not that its author
has bad things to say about the Jews. On the contrary, he says literally
not a word about them; the words *Jew* and *Israel* do not appear. Instead,
the author addresses a group of Gentiles and confers upon them the
traditional titles of Israel: chosen people, exiles of the diaspora, holy
nation, kingdom of priests, God's peculiar possession, children of Abraham and Sarah. First Peter seems almost to assume a world in which
Jews have simply ceased to exist. As Paul Achtemaier (1996) puts it,
"The language and hence the reality of Israel pass without remainder
into the language and hence the reality of the new people of God," that
is, *gentile* Christians. How and why the author of 1 Peter came so thoroughly to transfer the identity of Israel onto his gentile congregations is
a mystery that compels our exploration.

First Peter is traditionally attributed to Simon Peter, one of Jesus'
closest associates during his lifetime and later a leader in the Jerusalem
church. The attribution is considered pseudonymous by most scholars,
though the letter may have been produced by a "Petrine circle" in
Rome, where tradition says the apostle was martyred in the late 60s.
The letter is addressed from "Babylon" (a common Jewish cipher for

Rome) to five churches in northern Asia Minor. It has generally been considered a late composition, primarily on the basis of the "persecutions" reported in the letter. Recently, however, scholars have noted that the persecutions reported in 1 Peter are neither lethal nor state-sponsored; that is, they do not fit with what we would expect from a second-century document. Rather, the congregations face the ad hoc abuses that seem to have plagued gentile converts—slander and ostracism, perhaps beatings or imprisonment—in response to their withdrawal from pagan society. A reasonable estimate for the work's date would be 80–90 C.E., although earlier and later dates are possible.

As a circular letter, 1 Peter is necessarily general in scope. It concerns "sufferings" that seem common to all the congregations. The writer's central premise is that suffering tests the believers' faith but will result in their receiving honor and glory at the last judgment. Jesus, who also suffered before being raised from the dead and given honor and glory from God, provides both their model and their hope. Unjust suffering receives special mention because this most closely replicates the pattern of Jesus. Besides, "it is better to suffer for doing good, if suffering should be God's will, than to suffer for doing evil" (3:17). The letter contains little specific advice beyond instructing the readers to accept suffering and remain hopeful while demonstrating good morals and good citizenship.

The author assures readers that their current suffering is no cause for panic, as it forms part of a long-established divine plan. In fact, the biblical prophets themselves "made careful search and inquiry, inquiring about the person or time that the Spirit of Christ within them indicated when it testified in advance to the sufferings destined for Christ and the subsequent glory" (1:10–11). That is, by means of Christ's preexistent spirit, the prophets spoke about two things: Jesus' experiences and those of his followers. First Peter's claim that the prophets spoke by means of the "Spirit of Christ" assumes that the readers already believe that the messiah existed "before the foundation of the world." First Peter's perspective is similar to that of 1 Enoch, in which both the Son of Man (the messiah) and the divine plan have been present since before creation. The patriarch Enoch speaks "not for this generation

Jesus' Descent into Hell

The Apostles' Creed states that Jesus "descended into hell," a surprising statement for anyone who thought hell was reserved for sinners. The New Testament, however, reflects the ancient Israelite belief that Sheol (translated in the LXX as Hades) is the abode of all the dead, righteous or otherwise. Thus, in Rom. 10:7 Paul poses the rhetorical question "'Who will descend into the Abyss?' (that is, to bring Christ up from the dead)." In 1 Peter we get our only report on what Jesus *did* while in hell: he preached about himself to the dead. Because 1 Peter makes no mention of the result of Jesus' preaching, the Jesus sect was at liberty to decide. Already by the early second century, some taught that when he was raised from the dead, Jesus led the spirits of the righteous dead out of hell and into heaven (see, e.g., Ignatius, *Magn.* 9:2). This liberation of death's captives is known in Christian tradition as the "storming" or "harrowing" of hell.

but the distant one that is coming . . . about the elect ones and concerning them" (48:6–7). Each author places his own community at the center of Jewish messianic apocalyptic expectation; they are the generation foretold.

The author has a special concern with public displays of virtue. He sometimes suggests that attention to civic virtues may save the community from slander and its members from harm ("Who will harm you if you are eager to do what is good?"), but at other times he puts less faith in this approach: "Even if you do suffer for doing what is right, you are blessed" (3:14). Apparently conditions were too volatile to be controlled with any confidence. Civil authority, above all that of the emperor, was to be honored. The Christians' attitude toward civil authorities reveals much about the group's identity. "As servants of God," the author writes, "live as free people, yet do not use your freedom as a pretext for evil. Honor everyone" (2:16–17). As "slaves" (*douloi*) of God, the Christians have extraordinary freedom, presumably because their master is so exalted. Still, they must guard against a presumptuous and casual attitude. A Roman slave was expected to bring honor to the master; they must therefore behave honorably lest they dishonor God. The author's concern for honorable decorum, especially in the face of unjust suffering, extends particularly to those who might have the most opportunities to withstand injustice: literal slaves and wives. Household slaves are told that they have "God's approval" if they endure unjust pain from their masters; wives must continue to accept the authority of their husbands, including husbands who are unbelievers.

In addition to justifying suffering as sharing in the experience of Jesus or leading (like his) to a great reward, the author employs a second model of chosenness and endurance: Israel. Even though he is writing to a group of Gentiles, "Peter," traditionally known as "the apostle to the Jews," addresses his letter to "the chosen," "exiles" in the diaspora. He might as well have written "Dear Israel." Why? First, like all New Testament writers, this author would have believed in the community's right to claim inclusion in the Jewish people by virtue of God's promises to send "a light to the Gentiles" in the last days. The author of 1 Peter, however, emphasizes the community's pseudo-Israelite identity to respond to a specific problem: the profound social homelessness of pagan converts. First Peter is not addressed to urbane God-fearers, Gentiles who have found a place among the Jews while maintaining their pagan (non-Jewish) social contacts. Rather, the congregations of 1 Peter are people who were rescued from "the futile ways inherited from [their] ancestors" (1:18). These are recent gentile converts from paganism, paying the price for abandoning their society and religion.

Already in the first verse, the author acknowledges that the community's identity is, like Israel's, shaped by both "chosenness" and "exile"—inclusion and exclusion. The model of diaspora fits their situation well. Scattered across Asia Minor, these separate communities might have perceived themselves as having little in common. Here, however, they are defined as a single people; dispersion is simply one aspect of their shared identity. The communities are also called exiles, though their exile is not geographical; they live in their own lands. But like Jews throughout the Roman empire, the new converts experience a spiritual and social separation from those around them; they are no longer "at home" in the pagan world. The disjunction between the group's spiritual and earthly realities is experienced above all through social conflict. The readers find themselves misunderstood, harassed, and maligned by those around them. They don't belong. First Peter employs the peoplehood of Israel, a people whose identity transcends location because it is grounded in God, to replace the many lost identities of these beleaguered communities. The author assembles a great cascade of biblical epithets by which to identify these believers with the biblical people of God. "Sprinkled with blood," they await their "inheritance." They are the ones spoken of by the prophets, redeemed from Egypt and told to be holy, even as God is holy. Stripped of their former identities, they are provided a replacement patrimony.

These newly formed Israelites are called newborns, and as such are instructed to seek spiritual "milk" if in fact they have "tasted that the Lord is good" (2:3). The author is quoting Psalm 34, "O taste and see how gracious [*krestos*] the Lord is." The Greek *krestos,* delightful or delicious, allows a pun on Christ, *kristos.* They know that the Lord is Christ/*kristos.* A series of quotations relating to stones (an extended pun on the name Peter/Cephas, meaning "stone") allows the author to develop the image of the several communities as stones assembled into a single edifice. Jesus is the foundation stone but is also a "stumbling block" to those who "disobey the word," presumably those who malign and harass the community. The community, however, is "a chosen race, a royal priesthood, a holy nation, a people for his possession" (2:9, following NRSV note). Israel's titles, culled from Deut. 7:6, Exod. 19:6, and Isa. 43:20–21, now belong to this community of Gentiles. Curiously, the author follows up his many assertions that the community is Israel by acknowledging the opposite — the community has, in fact, no historical right to this identity: "Once you were not a people, but now you are God's people; once you had not received mercy, but now you have received mercy." The quotation derives from Hosea 1–2, where the prophet names his children "Not My People" and "Not Pitied" as a sign of God's rejection of Israel, but then promises that they will later be renamed "My People" and "Pitied." Here is the center of the author's claims: Gentiles who were "no people" and "without mercy" have, through God's mercy, become the people of God.

In addition to compensating for communal ties and heritage lost through affiliation with the Christian movement, 1 Peter's repeated naming of the community serves to direct the congregations' action: "I urge you as aliens and exiles to abstain from the desires of the flesh" (2:11). As "aliens and exiles," the community replicates the experience of Abraham as an "alien and sojourner" (Gen. 23:4). As *gerim,* sojourners, they must accept the social isolation that accompanies the outsider status of the people of God. Alienation is not to be resisted but embraced; they are called to be holy, and therefore separate. Their new lack of belonging is a *sign* of belonging to the "exiled" people of God. The community as a whole are called descendants of Abraham; the women, daughters of Sarah. Since ancient times, converts to Judaism, having no tribal or ancestral names within Israel, have been designated by the honorific "son [or daughter] of Abraham and Sarah." First Peter's entire community are such adopted members of the tribe. They even receive instructions on how to conduct themselves "among the Gentiles."

The sole dissonance in this otherwise harmonious schema, a dissonance repressed throughout the letter, lies in the existence of "another" Israel. First Peter is unique among the writings of the New Testament in mentioning no actual, living Jews. Paul constantly frets over God's relationship with the Jewish people; John and Matthew are furious with "the Jews"; Luke spends chapters explaining why it's all right that more Gentiles than Jews accept Jesus as messiah. Jews are a constant New Testament theme, if only because they are so very awkwardly "in the way" of the fledgling sect. But in 1 Peter the Jews simply disappear. Perhaps the author was so intent on providing a coherent identity for his readers that he simply didn't want to deal with the competing identity claims of non-Christian Jews. What he actually thought of the Jewish people, we cannot guess. As former pagans rather than God-fearers, his readers presumably had no loyalty to the Jewish people as such. Therefore, as Achtemaier puts it, not only the language but *the reality* of Israel seems to pass "without remainder" into the language and reality of Christianity. Certainly, the image of the church as the "new" Israel has found broad and continued acceptance in Christian circles.

One remaining question concerns the author's ethnic identity. Was 1 Peter's author a Jew himself, or a Gentile? If the letter was genuinely written by the apostle Peter, then the question is answered. But if, as is generally assumed, the letter is pseudonymous, the question remains open. Clearly, the author wanted to *appear* Jewish; hence the attribution to the ethnically Jewish "apostle to the Jews." But in light of the author's goal of claiming a Jewish identity for communities that are manifestly *not* Jewish, might he have provided himself a false Jewish identity as well? This question has no objective answer; one is left with a judgment call. Would a Jew or a Gentile be more likely to have produced such a work? I am inclined to see the author of 1 Peter as a Jew. First, the author's use of scripture, the almost playful linking of apparently unrelated passages, is essentially midrashic. Second, the free reworking of Jewish identity seems something a Jew would be more likely than a Gentile to undertake. *Modern* gentile Christians feel free to mix, match, and appropriate varied aspects of Israelite identity, but modern Christians have read 1 Peter; that is, they are heirs to a long tradition of understanding the church as "the new Israel." Gentile converts of the first century would presumably have been more aware of their status as "guests" in the household of Israel.

One additional factor favors identifying the author as a Jew: the way in which the Jewish experience of diaspora—an experience that would be lacking for a Gentile—undergirds the author's instructions on how to get along in a hostile world. Since the Babylonian exile, Jews had been negotiating the hazardous terrain of the social and ethnic outsider. The books of Daniel and Esther are essentially manuals on how to get along in someone else's empire. In the Roman world, Jews continued to face an uncertain legal and social status—sometimes protected, sometimes persecuted. Jewish diaspora communities were, in short, skilled in managing and appeasing non-Jewish neighbors and officials. Writing to those who are both chosen and exiles, the author of 1 Peter provides his communities with strategies for conducting themselves "among the Gentiles" (2:12). In this, he hands on wisdom accumulated through centuries of Jewish survival. The prospect that 1 Peter, a book appropriating Israel's identity "without remainder" for the church, was composed by a Jew, is painful. Ultimately, one has a choice between a gentile author who repressed Jewish claims to their own heritage and a Jewish author to whom it never occurred that Jewish identity could be compromised by the church.

SECOND PETER

S ECOND PETER HAS THE DISTINCTION of being an impassioned
defense of "traditional" Christianity composed sometime within
the first hundred years of the movement's existence. The letter has
never been among the most influential New Testament writings; it was
not included in the earliest canon lists, and scholars as late as the historian Eusebius (ca. 325) opposed its canonical status, probably because it
was already known to be pseudonymous. The letter purports to be the
work of the apostle Peter, conveying his "testament," or deathbed
advice. Testamentary literature, beginning with Jacob's blessing of the
twelve tribes in Genesis 49, was well known in Hellenistic Judaism, and
it was understood that the author pseudonymously appropriated the
authority of the dead patriarch in order to pass on teachings consistent
with the readers' and writer's heritage. In the case of 2 Peter, this presumption of pseudonymity is confirmed by the letter's heavy depend-
ence on the letter of Jude, by the community's concern over the death
of the "fathers" and the "delay" of Jesus' return, and by the reference in
3:15–16 to a collection of Paul's letters. No date for the work can be assigned with certainty, but sometime between 100 and 125 C.E. is most
likely. The author, who refers to himself using the Hebrew spelling
Simeon (rather than Simon) Peter, was almost certainly Jewish, but the

congregation includes at least some who "have just escaped from those who live in error," that is, from paganism. It is thus either a gentile or a mixed Jewish-gentile group. Their location is unknown.

The author ostensibly writes to remind his readers of what they already know, so that after his death they "may be able at any time to recall these things." In fact, the letter seems to have been occasioned by inroads being made by a group of what might be loosely called Christian Epicureans. Although ostensibly Christian (the author says they deny the Master [Jesus] who bought them), they subscribe to beliefs that correspond at least in outline to those held by the Epicureans. The best-known Epicurean tenet was the denial of divine providence. God did not concern himself with human affairs, whether to reward the good or to punish the wicked. No afterlife existed and no fixed moral order; each person was responsible for making sound choices in the here and now. This outlook was variously popularized, including among Jewish groups. Josephus, for example, reports that the Sadducees not only denied the resurrection (no afterlife) but also declared that all things were governed by Fate (no moral order). The rabbinic *Pirke Aboth* condemns those it calls *Apikoros* (possibly a form of "Epicurean"), who deny both the resurrection and the idea that God rewards and punishes. The Epicureans' denial of divine order and judgment laid them open to charges of moral license and corruption. What, after all, could the rejection of divine control (and, by extension, divinely ordained state control) mean but the grossest sort of libertinism? In 2 Peter, the opponents deny the *parousia,* the second coming of Jesus, along with its corollary, God's judgment of the world. The author condemns them on both moral and theological grounds; they are degenerate and, in a word, wrong. Not only will God judge the world, he will make a point of judging *them* for flouting his dominion as judge.

It is difficult today to imagine what it might mean to be a Christian while denying both the resurrection and God's activity in the world. But that, of course, is 2 Peter's point. We can no longer reconstruct what people who affirmed neither divine providence nor resurrection saw in the Jesus movement. Certainly, some of Jesus' early followers, like those who compiled his sayings, followed Jesus as a teacher. Could

2 Peter oppose a group that focused on Jesus' teachings and denied his resurrection? There is much room for speculation and little information to direct it, but the anonymous opponents provide at least a suggestion of the variety of uses to which the Jesus-traditions were put in the generations before "the New Testament" existed.

Second Peter so dramatically portrays the contest between author and opponents for the readers' loyalty that it is appropriate to speak of the letter as having a plot. From salutation to conclusion, the author struggles to establish ideological hegemony. Even his self-identification as "Simeon Peter, a *slave* (*doulos*) and emissary of Jesus Christ" (1:1; my translation) is not a gesture of self-abnegation but a claim of authority. He is both the well-recognized father of the church and a slave sent as the official emissary (*apostolos*) of the messiah. Writing to "those who have received a faith as precious as ours," the author both flatters and recruits the readers, telling them that their own faith is equal to that of Peter himself. Clearly, this is a heritage worth defending.

In 1:3–11 the author sets forth his premises. God has given the community "precious and very great promises" through which they can escape "the corruption" of the world, becoming instead "participants of the divine nature." They have the means for transformation from beings who are by nature "corruptible" into beings who share immortality with God. That said, they must now make use of the gift they have received. The readers must "make every effort" to support their faith through moral development and so "confirm" their calling.

This seemingly straightforward admonishment—you've been given the means, now use them—plays on specific expectations within the Hellenistic patronage system. As Jerome Neyrey has argued (1993), 2 Peter concerns itself throughout with matters of honor, particularly with countering the opponents' affront to God's honor. The author reminds his readers of their status as beneficiaries of a very substantial gift: God is their patron and they stand in his debt. As clients of a highly placed patron the readers are not expected to repay the debt in kind, but they are bound to repay it in loyalty and respect. Failure to acknowledge the gift, whether by word or by action, would constitute shameful behavior—shameful to the recipients and, above all, shameful to the patron. They must therefore use God's gift appropriately, not only for the sake of self-transformation but because it is God's due.

Having reminded the community of God's gift and their debt, the author sets about defending the worth of the gift he has been touting. "For we did not follow cleverly devised myths," says he, "when we made known to you the power and coming of our Lord Jesus Christ" (1:16). The transition is so abrupt that one is tempted to ask, Who ever suggested that you *did* teach us myths? Someone has evidently attacked the author's beliefs as nothing but "myths." Specifically, "the power and [second] coming" of Jesus Christ have been challenged as fabrications. "Peter" however, pulls himself up on his full apostolic authority. He, after all, was an eyewitness to the transfiguration, when God bestowed "honor and glory" upon Jesus, saying, "This is my Son, my Beloved. . . . So we have the prophetic message more fully confirmed." That is, Jesus' messiahship was not only foretold in the prophets, but confirmed by the *bat kol,* the divine voice testifying to Jesus' sonship.

The status of prophecy, or at least its interpretation, seems also to have been at issue. "No prophecy of scripture," says the author, "is a matter of one's own interpretation." Again, the denial that one can read into a prophecy whatever one wants suggests that the opponents have accused the author of doing precisely that. The charge is intriguing. Many texts interpreted by early Christians as messianic prophecies (e.g., Isa. 53) were not considered such by the other Jewish groups whose writings survive. Certainly, the messiah's resurrection and return as judge had not been expected on the basis of prophecy. The charge, then, that the interpretation of prophecy was a subjective undertaking (and that Christian expectation of Jesus' second coming was the result of biased interpretation) must have been common in Jewish circles.

The author is undaunted by such arguments. Rather, he assures his readers that just as false prophets arose in Israel, so "there will be false teachers among you." Their presence is to be expected; their destruction is assured. The author draws upon Jude for proof of the reality of God's judgment, citing almost the same biblical tales of judgment as Jude but substituting an account of Noah's flood for the wilderness wanderings. The substitution probably occurs because, first, the author of 2 Peter is not primarily interested, as Jude was, in God's response to rebellion. His focus is on the reality of God's judgment, which is far more impressive in the story of the universal flood than in the case of Israelites forced to wander in the wilderness. Second, in addition to exemplifying God's punishment of the wicked, the author wishes to demonstrate that the righteous will in fact escape destruction. Both Noah and Lot serve well as examples of God's rescuing of the righteous. Both figures, however, are expanded beyond their biblical portraits in ways consistent with postbiblical Jewish tradition. Noah is not only righteous but a "herald"—that is, he tries to convince his compatriots to repent—and Lot is "tormented in his righteous soul" by the immorality that surrounds him. The righteous ancestors sound a bit like the author himself.

The unrighteous, on the other hand, will be kept "under punishment" until the day of judgment, when they will presumably be punished some more. The opponents are headed for the very judgment they deny. After arguing on the basis of scriptural example that God does judge the world, the author turns to sheer invective against the opponents. They are accused of "depraved lust," adultery, licentiousness, and lawlessness, that is, the libertinism generally alleged against those who expect no divine retaliation. They are compared to beasts, acting on instinct and destined for slaughter. They follow the way of Balaam, whose own donkey (as reported in Numbers 22) knew better than he did. Finally, they are like the dog who eats its own vomit (see Prov. 26:11) or the pig who follows a good washing with a good wallow in the mud. The author's slander is so wide-ranging and stereotyped that it becomes impossible to reconstruct anything of the opponents' actual behavior.

The one promise the opponents apparently offer is "freedom," probably freedom from the very judgment 2 Peter is at pains to affirm. But freedom, in Roman society, was a legal status that involved very specific duties. The author lodges a charge against the freedom-loving opponents that they have denied "the Master who bought them." He portrays them as former slaves who refuse to acknowledge their indebtedness to the patron (Jesus) who purchased their manumission.

Such behavior was an outright violation of the usual legal terms of manumission; these obvious "slaves of corruption" are in no position to offer freedom to others. His invective spent, the author takes on the final argument against the second coming: that it hasn't happened yet. The "delay" of the *parousia* or second coming had become a pressing problem for Christians of the second and third generations. The Jesus of the gospels had said he would return within the lifetime of those around him. But they had died, and where was Jesus? Even Paul, in what may be the earliest New Testament document (1 Thessalonians), had to address worries over Jesus' "delay." The response of 2 Peter: God's perception of time has nothing to do with ours. Quoting Psalm 90, the author claims, "with the Lord . . . a thousand years are like one day" (3:8). If God delays, he does so out of mercy, "not wanting any to perish, but all to come to repentance" (see Sirach 18:9–11; Ezek. 18:32). When the judgment comes, however, it will be followed by "new heavens and a new earth, where righteousness is at home."

The author concludes with a curious note about the apostle Paul. He first enlists Paul's authority in support of his own ("so also our beloved brother Paul wrote to you"), then admits that some parts of Paul's letters are hard to understand (a comment universally considered an understatement) and suggests that "the ignorant and unstable" twist these difficult passages "to their own destruction." Is the author referring specifically to the exegesis of his opponents, perhaps matching their charge of biased interpretation with one of his own? And if so, which of Paul's teachings would be congenial to a pseudo-Epicurean outlook? The notion of freedom from God's condemnation as expressed in Romans 3 or Galatians 3 comes to mind, but the connection is by no means clear. The question of what Christian Epicureanism might look like remains without answer. In the end, we are left with only one side of the conversation—the side that would eventually become mainstream Christian belief.

JUDE

T HE LETTER OF JUDE purports to be a stopgap communication, and there is no reason to doubt this self-presentation. The author has abandoned a letter he had intended to write in order to fire off an urgent missive: "Beloved, while eagerly preparing to write to you about the salvation we share, I find it necessary to write and appeal to you to contend for the faith." The reason? "Certain intruders have stolen in among you, . . . who pervert the grace of our God into licentiousness and deny the only Master and our Lord, Jesus Christ" (vv. 3–4, NRSV alternate translation). Intruders are on the loose, and the faithful need warning. This brief letter tells its recipients almost nothing about what they *are* supposed to do; the crucial thing is that they *not* go astray with the newcomers.

The author is certainly a Jewish Christian, as are the recipients. Jude draws on both the Jewish Bible and later popular apocalyptic works, and does so in ways shaped by early Jewish interpretation. Cain, for example, is an epitome not of murder or violence (as would seem natural to modern readers) but, as he was to contemporary Jewish authors such as Philo and Josephus, of defiance and envy. The author could evidently depend on his audience to share these reading conventions. Jude's is a world in which the fallen angels of Enoch, the archangel Michael, wicked Balaam, envious Cain, and rebellious Korah are all lively and meaningful characters, each with a recognizable symbolic resonance. This is a world equally unfamiliar to modern Christians and modern Jews. And yet it is a vibrantly Jewish world. Jude is one of the few New Testament books that shows us Jewish messianists talking to one another, a fleeting glimpse of what Christianity might have been had it not spread so successfully in gentile circles.

The letter's recipients are not named. Its sender is "Jude, a servant of Jesus Christ and the brother of James." The designation "brother of James" immediately suggests that this Jude (Judas in Hebrew) is the Judas named in Mark 6:3 and Matt. 13:55 as one of Jesus' brothers. The identification, however, is not without its problems. Why, if the author is in fact the brother of Jesus, doesn't he just come out and say so? Modesty, the most popular scholarly answer, is hardly satisfying. After all, the author was not shy about naming his *other* illustrious brother. Was the author a half- or stepbrother of James, and thus not a blood relation of Jesus?

Debate about the letter's authorship has wreaked havoc with attempts to date the work. If it was written by Jesus' brother, it should be a relatively early composition. The author speaks, however, of "the predictions of the apostles of our Lord Jesus Christ" as if such predictions (and the apostles who spoke them) are definitely something of the past. It is likely that the book is either pseudonymous, as is generally assumed, or is the work of some other Jude, brother of some other James. Both names were extremely common; more than one of each is mentioned in the New Testament. Although we don't know the James to whom the author refers, we have no reason to think the original readers did not. In any case, the work was probably written after the death of Paul (68 C.E.?) and before the composition of 2 Peter (ca. 100–125 C.E.), which quotes Jude at length. The most likely dates of composition are between 70 and 100 C.E., making it contemporaneous with the composition of the gospels.

Jude's two charges against the opponents, that they twist God's grace into "licentiousness" and "deny the Master," are never defined in detail. The licentiousness may be sexual immorality, but the Greek (*aselgeia*) can refer to various other forms of vice. Denial of "the Master" is more fully developed in the letter as defiance of authority, both God's and that of God's representatives, presumably including the author himself. Affronts to authority were not taken lightly in the Roman world, and the author is at pains to demonstrate that the divine honor must and will be vindicated. The body of the letter (vv. 5–16) is devoted to a review of famous challenges to authority that did not go unanswered. The author sets forth three paradigmatic cases of biblical crime and punishment: the revolt of the Israelites who tried to return to Egypt after the exodus (Num. 14); the "angels" (Gen. 6:1–4) who mated with human women; and the inhabitants of Sodom, who tried to rape angels (Gen. 19). This combination of rebellions was something of a set piece in Jewish antiquity. Versions of the combination appear in Sirach, the Qumran scrolls, 3 Maccabees, and the pseudepigraphic *Testament of Naphtali* as examples of insurrection, retribution, or both. The triad of wilderness rebellion, angelic rebellion, and Sodomite affront to divine honor seems to have been the ancient Jewish version of "sex and drugs and rock 'n' roll"—things that get people into trouble.

The revolt in the wilderness is portrayed as a reminder that although the Lord "completely [NRSV, 'once for all'] saved a people out of the land of Egypt, [he] afterward destroyed those who did not believe" (v. 5). Salvation can be revoked for bad behavior. The description of "the angels" in verse 6 is somewhat more confusing, as it depends on a post-biblical embellishment of Gen. 6:1–4. In the original story the "sons of God" (*benei elohim*) mate with human women, producing a race of giants. In subsequent Jewish literature (Jude depends on 1 Enoch 6–10), the "sons of God" become rebellious angels who leave their appointed place, sleep with human women, and reveal various heavenly secrets to them. God is not pleased and throws them down into darkness, there to await judgment and eternal damnation. This is the origin of the tradition that Satan was a rebellious angel who had been cast out of heaven. The story of Sodom (v. 7), often taken by modern interpreters as a condemnation of homosexuality, was more accurately interpreted by ancient readers who were attuned to matters of status and honor. The men of Sodom attempt to rape guests (actually angels in

SATAN

The Hebrew Bible knows of no cosmic opponent to God—no devil or Satan. The New Testament, by contrast, presumes a cosmic adversary so well known as to need no introduction. The devil thus "appears" in the period after the writing of the Hebrew Bible and before the writing of the New Testament. In the Hebrew Bible the root *satan* means "challenge" or "accuse," and both human and divine beings may be "satans," that is, as opponents. Even when the root is applied to a divine agent, it generally appears with the definite article attached ("the *satan*"), not as a proper name. In Job 1-2, for example, "the *satan*" seems to be the title of a heavenly functionary, someone whose job consists in testing the loyalty of God's human subjects. In the postexilic period, however, probably under the influence of Zoroastrian thought, Jewish texts increasingly reflect a cosmic dualism—a heavenly battle between good (God) and evil (the devil). In Jewish texts of the turn of the era, the cosmic opponent appears under several names (Mastema, Asmodeus, Beliar), among them Satan, a name also widely used in rabbinic literature.

disguise) who are under the protection of an Israelite householder. As Jude puts it, the men "went after other flesh," that is, the flesh of the angels. The male householder, his divine guests, and God (whose representatives have been attacked) have all been profoundly dishonored by the men's assault. Their death, says Jude, serves as an example of what awaits the insolent "intruders" in his own community.

Jude's opponents, it turns out, are guilty of the big trifecta of rebellion against God. Like the Sodomites they "defile the flesh"; like the rebellious angels they "reject authority"; like those who maligned both Moses and God in the wilderness they "slander the glorious ones." Despite their egregious crimes, the community is merely to shun them, leaving their punishment in God's hands. Jude provides a model for his congregation in the archangel Michael, who in ancient traditions such as *The Assumption of Moses* rebukes but does not punish the devil for dishonoring Moses. Like Michael, the community can count on God to repay offenses against his servants.

The opponents, it seems, will not last long. They "go the way of Cain, and abandon themselves to Balaam's error for the sake of gain, and perish in Korah's rebellion" (v. 11). The letter begins to sound like a Bible trivia quiz. Cain represents envy and insolence toward God. The seer Balaam is a more ambiguous character. In Numbers 22 he accepts money to curse Israel (but only after receiving God's permission to do so) and is then opposed by both an angel and his own talking donkey. (The story is definitely worth a read.) In Numbers 31 he is killed by the Israelites in response to a claim that he had incited Israel to idolatry. Later Jewish tradition portrays Balaam as a type of those who wish to destroy Israel. Korah, the last member of the evil triad, was swallowed alive by the ground (Num. 16) after challenging the authority of Moses and Aaron. Opposition to God, God's messengers, and God's people will not go unpunished.

The opponents eat freely at the community's "love feasts . . . shepherding only themselves" (Neyrey 1993). The image is drawn from Ezek. 34:2, in which corrupt leaders or "shepherds" eat the sheep instead of tending them. They are called "wandering stars," a label reflecting the notion that the planets are angels who have abandoned their appointed places (1 Enoch 21; 80:6). Like the Israelites in the wilderness, they are habitual "grumblers" against authority. One gets the impression that these people are probably no more than a group of insolent freeloaders. But not for long. Jude invokes the words of Enoch, that "the Lord is coming with ten thousand of his holy ones, to execute judgment on all" and avenge himself for "all the harsh things that ungodly sinners have spoken against him." These scoffers, says Jude, are simply another part of the end-time scenario foreseen by the apostles (probably a reference to 2 Tim. 3:1). For their own part, the community should go about their business, rescuing whomever they can from the camp of the opponents.

The letter of Jude is little known and seldom read in modern Christian contexts. Except for its admonition to steer clear of those who rashly challenge authority, it contains no ethical teachings. It does, however, preserve the distinctively sectarian voice of a Jew whose symbolic world resembles that of the Dead Sea Scrolls more than it does most New Testament texts. What, one wonders, would Jude have had in common with the urbane and hellenized author of Luke? Jude might well derive from the same Torah-observant circles that Luke portrays as impeding the spread of the gospel to the Gentiles. In one sense Jude seems neither Jewish nor Christian, but a reminder of the distance that both traditions have traveled.

The Writings

of the

Johannine Communities

THE GOSPEL ACCORDING to John, 1, 2, and 3 John, and Revelation make up what is known as the Johannine literature. The name is somewhat misleading since only Revelation, the one document not named "John," actually names John as its author. Nor does Revelation claim to have been written by *the* John, Jesus' disciple to whom church tradition ascribes the composition of all five Johannine documents. The gospel is attributed to John because of its claim that "the beloved disciple," known in tradition as John, is "the disciple who is testifying to these things and has written them down." The brief collection of writings known as 1, 2, and 3 John is so named because it shares similar themes and vocabulary with the fourth gospel.

The connection among the five writings is thus considerably less certain than the "Johannine" label suggests. The five do share a family resemblance, however, beginning with their starkly dualistic language: everyone and everything belongs either to the light or to the darkness, to life or to death, to good or evil, the Spirit or "the world." The gospel and the three Johannine letters view Jesus as a preexistent being, and their communities are bound by the commandment to love one another. Revelation shares with John's gospel the language of Jesus as Word of God and Lamb of God, and imagery of his death as an atoning sacrifice. All the Johannine literature reflects a community deeply scarred by a schism. "Those who went out" are vilified while those who remain are exhorted to loyalty and endurance. Both the gospel and Revelation allude to conflict with local synagogues. If we consider the five books as the product of a single community (perhaps a group of churches loyal to a single founder), then the probable location of the Johannine community is Asia Minor, the site of the seven churches to which Revelation is addressed. Based on the evidence of the fourth gospel, the community, which includes ethnic Jews and Samaritans as well as Gentiles, seems to have originated in Palestine and then moved elsewhere. Scholarly consensus tends to place the composition of the various Johannine documents between 95 and 110 C.E.

THE GOSPEL ACCORDING TO JOHN

THE GOSPEL OF JOHN concludes with the observation that if *all* the things Jesus did were to be written down, "I suppose that the world itself could not contain the books that would be written" (21:25). The claim could be applied to the fourth gospel itself, a work that continues to generate a seemingly endless proliferation of commentary. Unrelentingly obscure, the gospel has nonetheless been pivotal in forming Christian consciousness. If Christians perceive their early history according to Luke's version, they perceive their spiritual identity according to John's. In addition to its unparalleled importance in shaping Christian self-consciousness, the gospel of John has the dubious distinction of being the most painful gospel for Jewish readers. Where Matthew's Jesus excoriates the Pharisees, John's Jesus names the Jews children of the devil.

The origins and setting of the gospel are far from clear. The author's intimate acquaintance with the customs and geography of Palestine suggests an early date and a location at least connected with the Jewish homeland—possibly Galilee or southern Syria. Samaritans appear among Jesus' followers in this gospel, and may have formed part of the author's community. Such evidence of firsthand knowledge of places and events is consistent with the tradition that the gospel originated with Jesus' disciple John. The matter is not quite so simple, however, and several factors argue for a later composition and a location outside Palestine. First, the author translates several common Hebrew/Aramaic terms (words like *rabbi* and *messiah*) for the reader. This suggests either a partly gentile audience or an audience of highly hellenized Jews. Second, the gospel claims that Jesus' followers will be "put out" of synagogues, suggesting a far more serious rift with the local Jewish community than the synoptic gospels' prediction that the disciples will be beaten *in* synagogues. John's gospel seems to reflect a further step toward the eventual separation of Jesus' followers from the rest of the Jewish world. John is not obviously dependent on the synoptics (the plot differs dramatically in some places), but the texts are occasionally close enough that some material must at least derive from a common source. Densely symbolic, John's gospel presupposes that the reader has an additional, more straightforward source of information, since elliptical references to key figures and events (for example, "John [the Baptist] had not yet been thrown into prison"; 3:24) presume a reader already familiar with some other gospel account.

One clue in particular points toward a possible solution regarding the gospel's date and authorship: the narrator addresses confusion caused by the death of someone called the beloved disciple. In chapter 21 the risen Jesus explains to Peter that some had misunderstood him (Jesus) to say that the beloved disciple would not die before he returned. Jesus denies that he said any such thing. Indeed, the author then claims that it was the beloved disciple who wrote the narrative. The gospel thus claims the beloved disciple as its author but reflects a period after his death. Scholars speculate that the gospel may contain elements deriving from the original disciple, John, but that it reached its current form after his death, perhaps after the community had relocated to Asia Minor.

The gospel's social setting continues to be extremely controversial, largely because of its wholesale condemnation of the Jews. The most widely accepted scenario for the gospel's setting is that proposed by J. L. Martyn. Martyn reads John as a response to the expulsion of Christians from the synagogue (by which he means a sort of excommunication from the Jewish people) around 85 C.E. According to this scenario, after the destruction of the temple in 70, an increasingly intolerant Pharisaic/rabbinic leadership quickly came into conflict with Jesus' followers. The struggle eventuated in the composition of the *birkat ha-minim,* the "blessing" of (or against) the heretics. According to this perspective the gospel of John directly reflects the trauma of expulsion from the synagogue; it records the first and extremely bitter reaction of the Christian community following an unwanted parting of the ways.

The primary strength of the "expulsion trauma" reading is that it explains the intense rancor of John's gospel. Unfortunately, the hypothesis depends on dubious assumptions, such as the rapid rise of rabbinic (Pharisaic) authority after 70 C.E. and its spread throughout the Jewish world. Recent research has debunked the notion of a far-reaching Pharisaic takeover in the first century; the development and spread of rabbinic hegemony seem to have taken centuries rather than decades. It is now doubtful that the "blessing" was composed specifically with Christians in mind or that it effected universal exclusion from the Jewish community. The Johannine group had clearly been rejected by some other Jewish group; beyond this, little can be known. Certainly, attempts to see in John evidence of the definitive break between Judaism and Christianity are overreading. Whatever break underlies the gospel of John, it was more likely a local skirmish in a growing conflict than its decisive conclusion.

The fact that John's gospel continues to generate controversy is anything but coincidental. Consummately sectarian literature, John was written to be obscure, arcane, even offensive. Composed for insiders, it was equally written *against* outsiders. Its cryptic language has been identified (Malina and Rohrbaugh 1992) as an "anti-language," the kind of code developed by isolated subgroups (including modern gangs) to consolidate group identity, and to consolidate it specifically in opposition to the larger society's values and norms. Crucial to such anti-language is that it make no sense to the rest of the world. The obscurity of anti-language is thus not simply a means of privileging insiders; linguistic obscurity—undermining publicly shared language—undermines the status of the larger culture itself. "Our" language makes no sense to "them" because they themselves make no sense. So John's Jesus is for-ever telling his opponents unhelpful things such as "Because I tell the truth, you do not believe me" and "Where I am you cannot come." And his opponents are forever demonstrating their profound inability to ap-prehend him: "Where does he mean to go that we will not find him? Does he intend to go to the diaspora?" John's Jesus always hides as much as he reveals. What he does reveal is deliberately shocking: "Unless you eat the flesh of the Son of Man and drink his blood, you have no life in you." Long centuries of Christian theology have domesticated John's off-putting images, blunting their original shock value, but the gospel is designed both to reveal and to conceal a great mystery, assuring insiders that they and they alone may "eat this bread and live forever."

At some levels, though, John's gospel is a model of clarity. His narra-tive world is categorically divided into two kinds of people governed by two powers: the light and the darkness. These powers are represented by those who accept Jesus and those who reject him, and who are cor-respondingly children of good or of evil, of truth or of lies, of God or of Satan. While it is true that nearly all of those whom John portrays "coming to the light" are Jewish (John's is the only gospel that appar-ently includes no gentile converts), "the Jews" in John's gospel are firmly on the side of darkness, evil, and the devil. Jesus himself, uniquely in John's gospel, is depicted as "the man from heaven" whose home is not in "the world" but with the Father in heaven. Sent by the Father, Jesus descends to earth (John includes no narrative of Jesus' human birth), where he reveals the Father before ascending (by his death and resur-rection) back to heaven. Because Jesus' coming represents the full and definitive disclosure of God to the world, Jesus' descent is also the world's judgment. Having received in Jesus a complete revelation of God ("The Father and I are one"), the world is itself revealed as either accepting or rejecting God's presence. Those who accept Jesus' revela-tion (namely, the members of John's community) are thereby empow-ered to become "children of God," further manifestations of God's presence in the world and sharers in God's eternal life. The fate of those who reject Jesus is not made entirely clear. In one verse (5:29) Jesus refers in passing to a "resurrection of condemnation," apparently some form of eternal punishment. For the most part, however, he simply says that those who reject him will "die"; that is, they will fail to share in God's gift of new life, both in this world and the next.

John's gospel is commonly divided into four parts: the prologue (1:1–18), the book of signs (1:19–12:50), the book of glory (13:1–20:31), and the epilogue (21:1–25). The prologue provides an overview of the plot in strictly symbolic terms; the book of signs recounts Jesus' earthly ministry, focusing on miracles (signs) that indicate his true identity; the book of glory relates his "glorification," by which John means his death and resurrection. The epilogue, apparently a later addition to the book, ties up loose ends regarding the apostle Peter and "the beloved disciple." The book is further structured by events and sayings that occur in clusters of seven, the biblical symbol of completeness. Thus, Jesus performs seven signs, he employs seven metaphors in the form "I am . . . ," and seven times he simply announces "I am." Jesus' encounters also follow a highly stylized form in which he addresses his interlocutors by means of a metaphor. He announces, for example, that he is "the bread of life"—and they take the metaphor literally, wondering whether he is selling baked goods on the side. The solemnity of John's presentation is balanced by a constant and often comic irony, in which the representatives of this world simply do not and cannot "get it."

The opening verse of John's gospel, which echoes the beginning of the book of Genesis, is one of the most famous lines in Western literature: "In the beginning was the Word, and the Word was with God, and the Word was God." John's prologue, remarkably, makes only passing mention of Jesus (1:17). The prologue concerns the *"logos,"* the divine Word. Although much has been made of a possible Stoic background to this divine *logos,* the term was widely used in Jewish literature of the period to identify God's personified Word or Wisdom. Already in Proverbs, Wisdom is God's assistant in the creation; in the first-century Wisdom of Solomon it is "a pure emanation of the glory of the Almighty;. . . a reflection of eternal light, a spotless mirror of the working of God" (7:25–26). According to Philo, "God's First-born [is] the Word. . . . And many names are his, for he is called 'the Beginning,' and the Name of God, and His Word, and the Man after his image" (*Conf.*

Ling. 146–147). In affirming that the Word "was in the beginning with God," John is not importing Greek categories into Jewish thought but contributing to a surprisingly rich stream of Jewish reflection on the preexistent divine Word.

The second-century B.C.E. author ben Sira describes the divine Word or Wisdom's search for a home in the world it helped to create: "I dwelt in the highest heavens, and my throne was in a pillar of cloud. . . . Over waves of the sea, over all the earth, and over every people and nation I have held sway. Among all these I sought a resting place; in whose territory should I abide? Then the Creator of all things gave me a command, and my Creator chose the place for my tent. He said, 'Make your dwelling in Jacob, and in Israel receive your inheritance' " (Sirach 24:4–8). In John, God's Word finds a less warm welcome: "He was in the world, and the world came into being through him; yet the world did not know him. He came to what was his own, and his own people did not accept him" (1:10–11). As in ben Sira's poem, Wisdom's proper home was with Israel. Here, however, "his own people" did not accept him. The divine Word was forced to look elsewhere to find those "who received him, who believed in his name." John's plot is the story of the divine Word's search for a home in this world.

John gives the New Testament's clearest statement of what would later become the doctrine of Jesus' incarnation: "The Word became flesh and lived among us, and we have seen his glory, the glory as of a father's only son" (1:14). To anyone brought up in contemporary Christian circles, the phrase is a truism: Jesus was God's Word made flesh. In its original context, however, such a claim would have been scandalous. The dualistic thought that sought to articulate the nature of the divine *logos* did not broach the possibility of that *logos* becoming flesh. Spirit could be entrapped in matter (the emperor Marcus Aurelius quotes his teacher, Epictetus, as saying, "You are a little corpse carrying around a soul"), but it did not dwell there by choice, let alone "become" flesh. And yet the gospel that, in contrast to the synoptics, depicts Jesus as the "man from heaven" who is one with the Father, is also the one that insists upon his material reality. This paradox of Jesus' incarnation may provide clues about the community in which it was written. The community that produced 1 John had suffered a painful rift with believers who denied "that Jesus Christ had come in the flesh." The gospel of John's "doubting Thomas," who refuses to believe in the resurrection until he touches Jesus' bloody side, provides a paradigm of those who wrongly deny Jesus' physical resurrection. The doubter's designation as "Thomas" is significant. By the second century, Jesus' sayings had been developed into the Gospel of Thomas, a gospel that would be widely used in gnostic Christianity, a Christianity that not only denied Jesus' incarnation but in some forms held that the world itself was the creation of an evil being, and not of God. Taken together, John's doubting-Thomas episode, 1 John's repudiation of those who "deny that Jesus came in the flesh," and the image of the Word made flesh seem calculated to counter a growing emphasis on Jesus' spiritual nature and a corresponding denial of his humanity. In comparison with the gnostics, John revels in the physical world.

One phrase in John's prologue deserves special attention. "No one," says John, "has ever seen God. It is God the only Son, who is close to the Father's heart, who has made him known" (1:18). John's primary claim is straightforward enough: since human beings cannot see God, we "see" God only by means of the "Word made flesh," that is, Jesus. The expression "God the only Son," however, has caused scandal and confusion from earliest times. Some manuscripts do not contain the phrase, instead reading, "It is the only Son" who has made God known. The idea of the Word as God's only or *unique* Son is consonant with Philo's designation of the Word as "God's First-born." The notion that the Son *is* God is far more provocative; indeed, it looks so much like later formulations of the Trinity and so unlike anything else in the New Testament that many scholars believe the phrase must have been altered to make the gospel conform to later church doctrine. Elsewhere in John's gospel Jesus *prays* to the Father, *goes* to the Father, *obeys* the Father, and is *close* to the Father's heart. Jesus is not, in John's gospel, God. Nearly, but not exactly. In such niceties, centuries of christological controversies had their genesis.

John interrupts his introduction of "the light" with a mention of John the Baptist. All we learn about John, though, is that he was *not* the light. He "came to testify to the light." As the narrative proper gets under way in 1:19, we begin again with John. His message? "I am not the Messiah." Elijah, maybe? "I am not." The prophet? "No." The author takes great pains to emphasize that John the Baptist played no role in God's revelation through Jesus. In this gospel only, John does not baptize Jesus; he merely acclaims him as "the Lamb of God, who takes away the sin of the world." Jesus also takes away some of John's disciples. In light of Jesus' manifest superiority, however, John does not object. This unique rendition of John the Baptist seems to represent some conflict between the Johannine community and a group that followed John the Baptist as its founder. The author seeks to demonstrate that John in no way competed with the messiah, and that he always considered Jesus his superior.

As John begins his description of Jesus' ministry, he continues to emphasize Jesus' unique, even celestial, identity. Jesus' calling of his disciples differs from that in the synoptic gospels, not least in the inclusion of Nathanael, who appears nowhere in the synoptics but is hailed in John as "an Israelite in whom there is no deceit." Nathanael, upon seeing a decidedly minor-league demonstration of Jesus' power, acclaims him at once as "son of God" and "king of Israel." Jesus responds that Nathanael will see "heaven opened and the angels of God ascending and descending upon the Son of Man" (1:51). The image is borrowed from Genesis 28, in which Jacob ("Israel") sees angels ascending and descending at Bethel, the "gate of heaven," the point where heaven and earth are joined. As Son of Man, the one who himself "came down from heaven," Jesus is the true point of access to heaven, "the gate," as he will later say.

After calling his disciples, Jesus attends a wedding where he transforms water into wine. For the "insider" reader, the wine is a transparent symbol of the Christian Eucharist or Last Supper. This, says John, was the first of Jesus' "signs." Jesus goes next to Jerusalem, where he is approached by "a Pharisee named Nicodemus, a leader of the Jews." The encounter between Jesus and Nicodemus is typical of Jesus' conversations in John. Usually hinging on a pun, which in turn represents some symbol of the community's identity, the conversations run on in either maddening or (depending on one's perspective) highly amusing circles. Jesus greets Nicodemus with a puzzle: "No one can see the kingdom of God without being born again" (3:3). The truth of Jesus' statement hinges on the double meaning of the Greek *anothen*, which can mean either "again" or "from above." Jesus means the word in both ways, since the way to be born "again" is to be born, as he himself was, "from above." Unacquainted with the phenomenon of the "born-again" Christian, Nicodemus hears only the biological conundrum: "Can one enter a second time into the mother's womb?" Jesus responds that one must be born "of water and Spirit," probably an insider reference to Christian baptism. Nicodemus, however, "a teacher of Israel," fails to comprehend the new life shared by the Johannine community.

In chapter 4 Jesus has another elliptical conversation, this time with a Samaritan woman; what the "teacher of Israel" missed, the marginalized Samaritan will understand. Returning from Jerusalem to Galilee, Jesus passes through Samaria, where he rests at a site known as Jacob's well. Jacob's well was revered as the location where the patriarch met his future wife Rachel, and where Jacob's own mother, Rebecca, was asked to marry Jacob's father. When an unaccompanied woman meets Jesus at Jacob's well, the audience is primed for a little romance, a dimension that undoubtedly added a comedic layer for the book's first readers. The woman, however, is a Samaritan, and so "unclean" from a Jewish perspective. Jesus (like Jacob before him) asks the unknown woman for water. She is startled and questions his willingness even to consider such sharing with a Samaritan.

Now the punning begins. Jesus informs the woman that if she had known who he was, she would have asked *him,* and "he would have given [her] living water." The phrase "living water" ordinarily refers to spring water (fresher and easier to retrieve than well water), but in John's insider language it designates God's spirit. The woman (taking the bait) observes that Jesus *can't* give her water, as he doesn't even have a bucket. Jesus drops his pretense and explains: "Everyone who drinks of this water will be thirsty again, but those who drink of the water that I will give them will never be thirsty. The water that I will give will become in them a spring of water gushing up to eternal life" (4:13–14). The woman responds that it would be really nice not to have to come and draw water all the time. One can almost picture Jesus rolling his eyes. The vignette is a comic diversion, but it reinforces the reader's insider reality as well as the outsiders' ignorance. Eventually the woman realizes that Jesus is the messiah (a figure awaited in Samaritan as well as in Jewish traditions) and goes off to tell her neighbors. Jesus stays two days with the Samaritans, "many" of whom believe in him. This unique mention of Samaritan followers is generally taken as evidence that the Johannine community included Samaritan members.

Jesus next performs two healings in rapid succession (his second and third signs). The second, which takes place on a sabbath, provides the first occasion for conflict between Jesus and "the Jews." The identity of "the Jews" in John's gospel is vexed. Some suggest that the term refers to Jewish "officials" of various kinds, thus creating the kind of division seen in Luke's gospel between bad rulers and innocent people. This definition, however, cannot be applied consistently. For example, the word sometimes refers simply to Judeans (since *ioudaioi* means "Judeans" as well as "Jews") as opposed to Galileans. Occasionally, as when the bereaved Mary and Martha are comforted by "the Jews," it means the neighbors who, like Mary and Martha, also happen to be Jewish (and, for that matter, Judeans). Such neutral uses seem natural and unconscious on the author's part. In most instances, however, the word *Jews* may as well be translated "bad guys." Jesus repeatedly makes statements about "the Jews" as those who don't, won't, and can't accept him as son of God because they "hate the light."

In chapter 6 Jesus miraculously feeds more than five thousand people with five loaves of bread and two fish, and the people proclaim him the messiah. By the next day the people are ready for another miracle—how about something like the manna, the "bread from heaven" that Moses gave the people in the wilderness? Ironically, the people's "grumbling" exactly replicates the relationship between Moses and the people in the wilderness in Exodus, where people fed miraculously one day were discontented by the next. Jesus engages them in a typically elliptical dialogue built on his announcement, "I am the bread that came down from heaven." As they have already said, the people *want* miraculous bread. Jesus, however, responds with increasingly bizarre and off-putting claims about himself: "The bread that I will give for the life of the world is my flesh. . . . Very truly, I tell you, unless you eat the flesh of the Son of Man and drink his blood, you have no life in you" (6:51–53). This is anti-language par excellence. Insiders know perfectly well that Jesus is describing the Eucharist, the ritual in which bread and wine represent the body and blood of Christ. Jesus (the spiritual nourishment) came down from heaven and they have partaken of his sustenance. But the author chooses to present Jesus' offer in the most objectionable terms possible—as cannibalism. Outsiders cannot help but be offended by Jesus' claim that they must eat his flesh. To insiders, the claim that Jesus has made eternal life available to those who love him lies at the very heart of John's gospel. That others take offense merely proves that outsiders are "of the world" and blind to the things of God.

In 6:60–71 John makes the surprising statement that some of Jesus' disciples found this teaching "difficult" and "turned back" in response to it. This is the only suggestion in the gospels that some of Jesus' followers, disagreeing with his teaching, stopped following him. As with so many gospel descriptions of Jesus' followers, however, it may say more about the author's generation than about the first disciples. Remarkably, not only John's gospel but also the Johannine letters and Revelation contain explicit mention of a schism that has traumatized the group: "They went out from us, but they did not belong to us; for if they had belonged to us, they would have remained with us" (1 John 2:19). This defection of community members may underlie much of the rancor in John's gospel.

The mounting conflict between Jesus and "the Jews" continues during his visit to Jerusalem for Sukkoth (the festival of Booths, commemorating Israel's wilderness wanderings). Earlier, during Passover, the festival of Unleavened Bread, Jesus had proclaimed himself the "bread of life." At Sukkoth, a holiday celebrated both by pouring water on the temple altar and by the illumination of giant torches (*m. Sukkah* 4.9, 5.2–4), Jesus declares himself to be "living water" and "the light of the world." John is systematically identifying Jesus with each of God's major self-revelations to Israel. During the festival, Jesus first engages in yet another ironic dialogue, this time with the Pharisees, and then addresses someone John calls "the Jews who had believed in him" (8:31). In a viciously escalating argument, Jesus challenges their loyalty to him and to God, finally denying their descent from Abraham. The Jews counter that they are indeed children of Abraham and of God. Jesus, *the* son of God, responds that since they do not love him they cannot be children of God; instead, they are children of the devil, the father of lies and a murderer "from the beginning." John's words drop like a stone into the text and into the world, sending out their ripples across the centuries.

It is noteworthy that Jesus' harshest condemnation is directed, not against Jews in general, but against "the Jews who had believed in him." Who are these Jews, and why do they provoke even more venomous treatment than Jesus' avowed enemies? First, whatever it might have meant for these Jews to have "believed" in Jesus, they have clearly changed their minds and abandoned the community of Jesus' followers. The fact that these defectors are "Jews," however, is confusing since (with the possible exception of a few Samaritans) *all* of Jesus' followers were Jews. Their designation as "Jews" makes sense only in the later context of the book's author, by whose day the community had become mixed, consisting of Jews, Gentiles, and Samaritans. The Jews who believed in Jesus, then, are none other than early members of the movement, perhaps those described in chapter 6 who "drew back" when Jesus' teachings (or the community's teachings about Jesus) went beyond what they could validate. If the Jews who believed in Jesus represent former members of John's own community, then the origin of his invective becomes clear. These Jews are not simply Jews but "those who went out from us," who chose the other side in the conflict of light with darkness.

Jesus' argument with the former believers culminates in a statement calculated to make most Jews' participation in the movement impossible. After rejecting the Jews' status as children of Abraham, he announces, "Before Abraham was, I am" (8:58). Jesus is making two claims, the first being that he existed before Abraham. Here John invokes the language of the preexistent Word that dominated his prologue. But Jesus goes even farther than the claim to preexistence. His jarring "I am" (in Greek, *ego eimi*) quotes God's self-identification at the burning bush in Exodus 3 ("I am what I am"). Jesus' former followers understand him fully. This is blasphemy, and "the Jews," obeying the commandment, pick up rocks with which to stone him. Ironically, the scene does not seem to reflect a break between John's community and the Jews as such, but between the Johannine group and more traditionally Jewish *Christians* who were put off by the community's growing elevation of Jesus to divine status. The Johannine book of Revelation will similarly denounce a competing Jewish-Christian group, denying that they are Jews at all and calling them a "synagogue of Satan."

In chapter 11 Jesus performs his last and greatest sign, the raising of a man from the dead. Mary and Martha, friends of Jesus, send word that their brother, Lazarus, is ill. Jesus intentionally delays going to them in order that Lazarus's illness may "lead to God's glory." That is, he waits for Lazarus to die, creating the occasion for a greater miracle. When Jesus arrives Martha confronts him with the truth: "If you had been here, my brother would not have died." Jesus, however, rejects the role of healer and instead announces, "I am the resurrection." Proceeding to the tomb, he calls Lazarus, who has now been dead for four days, to come forth. "The dead man came out, his hands and feet bound with strips of cloth, and his face wrapped in a cloth. Jesus said to them, 'Unbind him, and let him go' " (11:44). Although Lazarus is, technically speaking, resuscitated and not resurrected (since he comes back to the same mortal life he so recently left), the miracle embodies John's claim: the resurrection is effective *now*. Jesus has power to give new life in this world, and not only after one's death.

John reports that again in the wake of Jesus' greatest miracle "many of the Jews" believed in him. The "chief priests and the Pharisees" become concerned for the very credible reason that a widespread messianic movement would bring about reprisals from Rome. "If we let him go on like this, everyone will believe in him, and the Romans will come and destroy both our holy place and our nation" (11:48). From the post-70 C.E. perspective of John's readers, the leaders' fears had already been realized. Caiaphas, the chief priest, offers the obvious solution: "It is better for you to have one man die for the people than to have the whole nation destroyed." Get rid of Jesus and avert the wrath of Rome. The priests and Pharisees order that he be arrested, but Jesus rides into Jerusalem, announcing that the hour has come for him to be "glorified." Glory, in John's gospel, is part of Jesus' nature as the divine Word, but it has been masked by his "descent" into the world. Now he prepares to reascend to the Father, to be "lifted up," first on the cross and then by his resurrection.

All of chapters 13–17 describe Jesus' farewell meal with his disciples. The meal is apparently not, as in the synoptics, a Passover seder. In order to portray Jesus as the "Lamb of God," John shifts the action so that Jesus is killed at the hour when the Passover lambs were slaughtered. Passover thus begins on Friday night in John's gospel but on Thursday night in the synoptics. After Judas leaves the supper to betray him, Jesus delivers first a speech and then an extended prayer for the future of his disciples. His message is straightforward: just as "the world" hated Jesus, so also will it hate his followers; they, for their part, must above all love one another. Jesus' metaphor of the vine captures the dynamics of the Johannine ideal. Jesus is the vine, God the grower. The disciples are branches, sustained by "abiding" in him. Finally, Jesus announces that after he has returned to the Father, he will send them the "Paraclete" (*paracletos;* NRSV, "Advocate"). The Paraclete, a comforter or counselor, is the equivalent of the Holy Spirit or, in Jewish terms, the Shechinah, the active presence of God. In later Christian doctrine it constitutes the "third person" of the Trinity. Although the Paraclete's role is analogous to that of the Holy Spirit in Acts, only in John is the Paraclete explicitly named as Jesus' representative, who will continue the work and presence of Jesus after his death.

John's version of Jesus' arrest and trial closely follows that in the synoptic gospels. Jesus is arrested and taken first to Annas, a former high priest, and then to the high priest Caiaphas. Jesus gives elliptical and rather rude answers to the priests' questions and is then taken before Pilate. John adds the ironic detail that Jesus' Jewish accusers, those who would soon claim to have "no king but Caesar," refused to enter the

Roman headquarters, lest they defile themselves on the eve of Passover. Pilate questions Jesus on the charge of sedition: "Are you the King of the Jews?" As he has done throughout John's gospel, Jesus gives a cryptic answer: "My kingdom is not from this world." As in the synoptics, Pilate finds no wrong in Jesus (an astonishing claim, given Jesus' refusal to deny that he has pretensions of kingship) but has him flogged and mocked. Even more than the synoptic authors, John seems intent on depicting Pilate as a hapless weakling. The Jews had Pilate trapped: "If you release this man, you are no friend of the emperor" (19:12). The Jews are right, of course; no prefect could allow a known seditionist to go free. It is, however, highly unlikely that Pilate needed reminding of this basic fact of imperial power.

Unlike Mark's Jesus, who dies abandoned and in agony, John's Jesus dies in full control of his destiny, proclaiming that "it is finished" and handing over (*paredoken*) his spirit. Pilate has agreed to complete this particular day of crucifixions early, so that the criminals will not be left hanging when Passover begins at sundown (a schedule unique to John). However unlikely such a gesture might be (showing respect for the locals was not exactly the point of crucifixion), it allows John to complete his portrayal of Jesus' symbolic end. The soldiers set about breaking the legs of the crucified criminals so as to hasten their deaths. When they get to Jesus they find that he is already dead. Like a kosher Passover lamb, "none of his bones shall be broken" (19:36; see Exod. 12:46). In order to certify, however, that Jesus is truly dead, a soldier pierces his side with a spear, and "at once, blood and water came out." Here we have Johannine symbolism at its richest and most obscure. Blood would be expected from such a wound, but water requires an explanation. John provides one, at least for the insider. This, says John, fulfilled the scripture "They will look on the one whom they have pierced" (Zech. 12:10). Well, yes, they pierced him. But why the water? As is often the case in midrashic explanations, the text quoted gives only a hint of the author's meaning. In this case the full text of the passage cited is crucial: "And I will pour out a spirit of compassion and supplication on the house of David and the inhabitants of Jerusalem, so that, when they look on the one whom they have pierced, they shall mourn for him, as one mourns for an only child. . . . On that day a fountain shall be opened for the house of David and the inhabitants of Jerusalem, to cleanse them from sin and impurity" (Zech. 12:10, 13:1). The water that flows from Jesus' side is the eschatological fountain foretold by Zechariah, purifying the people Israel. This is the "spring of water, gushing up to eternal life" that Jesus promised his followers (4:14, 7:38). Having now "gone to the Father," Jesus has become a source of life for the world.

John's account of Jesus' resurrection differs significantly from the accounts found in the synoptics. In John's version, Mary Magdalene comes alone to the tomb and sees only that the stone covering the entrance has been moved. She runs to get Peter and "the other disciple, the one whom Jesus loved." The two disciples race to the tomb, enter, and see the empty cloths lying where the body had been. They then leave Mary alone again, and she now encounters a man whom she assumes to be "the gardener." The gardener turns out to be Jesus himself. Jesus now issues the famously baffling command "Do not hold on to me, because I have not yet ascended to the Father" (20:17). If nothing else, the command suggests a rather surprising physical intimacy between Jesus and Mary. Respectable single women were not expected to "hold" respectable single men in Jewish antiquity. Jesus, however, does not warn Mary out of propriety, but because he has "not yet ascended to the Father." Jesus seems not fully of one world or the other. Mary tells the disciples of her encounter, and that evening they too see Jesus, who, like God creating Adam, breathes on them, saying, "Receive the Holy Spirit." With the giving of the Spirit, Jesus' promise to send the Paraclete has been fulfilled. Jesus gives an even more dramatic demonstration of his reality fully a week later, when the incredulous Thomas is told to put his hand in Jesus' wounded side. This was probably the final scene in an early version of John's gospel, as it concludes with a benediction and a note that the book has been written "so that you may continue to believe that Jesus is the Messiah, the Son of God, and that through believing you may have life in his name" (20:31, following NRSV translation note).

But the gospel as we have it does not end there. Two pieces of unfinished business seem to have resulted in the addition of a coda. First, John provides an occasion for Peter to redeem his three denials of Jesus during his trial. Three times Jesus asks Peter if Peter loves him, three times Peter affirms that he does, and three times Jesus assigns Peter to care for the community. Jesus then foretells Peter's martyrdom. Peter now sees the disciple whom Jesus loved and asks simply, "What about him?" What about the disciple generally considered the founder of the Johannine community? Jesus responds, "If it is my will that he remain until I come, what is that to you?" The author quickly (and uncharacteristically) interprets Jesus' words for the reader: "So the rumor spread in the community that this disciple would not die." That seems a perfectly reasonable interpretation of Jesus' words, and the narrator's insistence that "Jesus did not say to him that he would not die" strongly implies that the beloved disciple has in fact died, and that his death has taken the community by surprise. The author seeks to reassure them, if only on a technicality: Jesus never actually *said* the disciple wouldn't die. With this somewhat surprising piece of information, the author again concludes the work, this time with the baffling announcement, "This is the disciple who is testifying to these things and has written them, and we know that his testimony is true" (21:24). The narrator first tells us that the beloved disciple is dead and then claims that he himself is that disciple! Both may be true, of course, in the sense that the narrator claims that although the beloved disciple has now died, the narrative originated in his reliable testimony.

John's gospel, a gospel built upon opposites, has held and continues to hold opposite meanings for those it eternally divides into "the children of light" and "the children of the devil." As Adele Reinhartz has pointed out (Reinhartz 2001), every Jewish reader continues to come to the text as its designated "Other," an embodiment of darkness, death, rejection, hatred—everything John assigns to those who are from "below." Most contemporary Christians *don't* think of Jews as "children of their father, the devil," but it is vital to see that this gospel gives its readers permission to think of Jews in exactly these terms. Perhaps the greatest irony of all is the likelihood that the Jews whom John condemns most viciously were other Jewish *Christians,* Jews who had "believed in Jesus" but were not willing to affirm the Johannine community's views of him. In the Johannine world of absolute light and darkness, there was no middle ground.

FIRST, SECOND, AND THIRD JOHN

T HE JOHANNINE LETTERS are not all letters and not obviously "Johannine," as they make no mention of John. They are, however, closely linked to the gospel attributed to John by virtue of shared vocabulary and imagery. The readers are "children of light" and of God, who "abide" in God, bound by the commandment that they "love one another." As in John's gospel, so here also the world is deeply divided between those who are "of God" and those of "this world." No scholarly consensus exists as to the letters' setting. Their occasion, however, is certain: they were written in response to a schism in the church. But did this schism occur as the tensions reflected in John's gospel deepened in succeeding generations, or did it form the *background* of the gospel, contributing to its defensive and embattled tone? Either reading makes sense. It is not even certain that all three letters were written in response to the same crisis or by the same author.

For our purposes we will assume that the letters were, if not all by one author, then at least intended to circulate as a "packet." As Luke Johnson points out (Johnson 1999), it is hard to imagine why 2 and 3 John would have been preserved at all had they not from the outset formed part of a larger and more coherent message. Their current order in the Christian canon reflects their length, and possibly their perceived importance. Third John presents itself as a "cover letter," introducing Demetrius, the author's delegate, as well as something the author has written "to the church." The "something" for the church is probably either 2 or 1 John (or possibly both). Because 3 and 2 John provide the most details about the letters' occasion (and little more), they will be discussed briefly first, before the lengthier and more difficult 1 John.

In both form and content 3 John bears the marks of a "personal" letter. Its author identifies himself as "the elder" and addresses "the beloved Gaius," apparently the author's protégé who is the leader of a house church. Identifying himself as elder and Gaius as his child, the author makes an unmistakable claim of authority. This claim is not incidental, since it turns out that the elder's authority has been challenged. After urging Gaius to welcome and support certain "brothers," presumably the delegation bearing the letter, the elder broaches the larger problem: "Diotrephes, who likes to put himself first, does not acknowledge our authority." Diotrephes seems to be known to Gaius and is probably the leader of another congregation in the same region as Gaius's. Diotrephes has refused to "welcome the brothers," to the point of expelling others who wished to welcome them. Travel in Roman antiquity was expensive and dangerous, and inns often doubled as brothels. If missionaries were to spread the group's message, and if communication among far-flung congregations was to be maintained, hospitality, including funding for the next leg of the journey, was imperative. By refusing to "welcome" brothers, Diotrephes has effectively declared the elder's delegates to be renegades, outside the circle of Christian hospitality. Small wonder that "the elder" should draw himself up on his full authority (the exact nature of which is unknown to us) in writing to a congregational leader who knows Diotrephes. The elder hopes to visit Gaius in person, at which time he will counter the "false rumors" his rival has spread. In the meantime he sends his warm recommendation of Demetrius, presumably the head of the elder's delegation, as well as "something written to the church."

Second John closely mirrors the language of 3 John. Both are addressed from "the elder" to a recipient "whom I love in [the] truth," and both close with the hope that the author can soon come and talk "face to face" instead of with "paper and ink." It is tempting to see in 2 John the message for the church mentioned in 3 John. Although we will assume this to be the case, it is important to realize how very tenuous such a reconstruction really is. Written to an unnamed church and urging, "Let us love one another," the letter could just as easily represent the elder's plea to *Diotrephes's* church rather than Gaius's, urging them not to follow "the deceiver and the antichrist" (that is, Diotrephes) who wishes to lead them astray. In either case, 2 John gives a brief sample of the elder's own teaching as well as his polemical depiction of his opponents.

The elder writes to "the elect lady and her children," that is, to an honored church and its members. After an initial greeting he comments that he was "overjoyed" to find that "some" of the lady's children are "walking in the truth." No sooner does one wonder what the *others* are doing than the elder alludes to them: "Many deceivers have gone out into the world, those who do not confess that Jesus Christ has come in the flesh. . . . Be on your guard, so that you do not lose what we have worked for" (2 John 1:7–8). The lady is in danger of being seduced. She is therefore instructed not to "receive into the house or welcome" anyone who does not conform to "the teaching of Christ." The instruction seems ironic in light of the elder's own complaint that Diotrephes has refused to welcome *his* workers. On both sides, however (and, of course, we cannot guess who shunned whom first), the refusal of hospitality is a palpable method of denying a common purpose: "To welcome is to participate in the evil deeds of such a person."

Who are these deceivers, and what exactly are they teaching? This is the most difficult question posed by the Johannine epistles, and one that can be answered only in part. In 2 John we learn that the opponents have "gone out into the world"; indeed, they may soon be knocking at the elect lady's door, expecting to receive hospitality as Christian coworkers. We do not know what they teach, except that they "do not confess that Jesus Christ has come in the flesh," a fact that makes them not only deceivers but "antichrists" (1:7). The latter term need not have the full, diabolic implications it later accrued. Appearing in the New

Testament only in 1 and 2 John, the word literally means "against the messiah." Rather than labeling the opponents as the *opposite* of Christ, the elder may merely be claiming that they deny Jesus' messianic status.

The denial that Jesus the messiah had come "in the flesh" has given rise to centuries of speculation over how, if not "in the flesh," the opponents believed Jesus *had* come. The opponents may have been gnostics or at least docetists, affirming Jesus' divinity but denying his humanity. Speculation over Jesus' divine and/or human nature was certainly in the air by the end of the first century, and it is possible that the elder weighs in on this question. Other solutions, however, are equally possible. For example, like "the Jews" of John's gospel, the opponents may object to the absoluteness with which the Johannine community identifies Jesus as God's son. The elder assures his readers that "whoever abides in the teaching has both the Father and the Son." Do the dissenters lack one or the other? The antichrist is defined as "the one who denies the Father *and* the Son." "No one," says the author, "who denies the Son has the Father; everyone who confesses the Son has the Father also." The status of the son is clearly at issue, along with the interconnection between belief in the son and belief in God. We find ourselves deep in the symbolic world of the fourth gospel, but no clear delineation of the opposing claims presents itself.

In 2 John the elder sketches the opponents' claims, asks the elect lady to reject their overtures, and instead urges, "Let us love one another." He closes by noting that although he has "much" to write to her, he hopes instead to communicate with her face-to-face. We know nothing more of the relationship between the elder and the "lady." We do, however, have a far more extensive composition, written within the Johannine circle, in which the problem of "antichrists" is addressed at length, and in which a community receives ardent direction on how to love one another in a time of crisis. First John may or may not be a third document by the elder who wrote 3 and 2 John, but it was written by someone who shared the elder's beliefs and addressed a congregation facing the same problems the "elect lady" faced.

First John is a work of comfort and exhortation for a beleaguered community, its tone at once tender and ominous. The readers are "little children" who are first comforted in their fears, then warned that their opponents are "children of the devil" and "murderers." By and large, the situation seems to resemble that reflected in 2 John, but with one key addition. As in 2 John, the reader is warned about "antichrists," but whereas in 2 John these deniers "went out" into the world, we now learn that they went out "*from us*" (2:19). The antichrists are not only a hostile and dangerous force; they are also our own. The community defined by mutual love and interdependence has undergone a schism so painful that the deserters are accused of a murderous hatred. The trauma of the community's divorce does much to explain both the author's intensity and his oscillation between solace and rage. Even as he explains and warns of how evil the offenders are, he must attempt to heal and nurture his confused and injured "children."

The teacher's pain and anger permeate the letter, but not to the exclusion of a tender concern for those who remain. How, after our communal disaster, can we have confidence that we are doing the right thing? "God is love, and those who abide in love abide in God." Over and over again, the teacher reassures the community that they *do* know God, they *have* been freed from sin, they *are* God's children. "Little children, let us love, not in word or speech, but in truth and action. And by this we will know that we are from the truth and will reassure our hearts before him whenever our hearts condemn us (3:18–20)." The community stands in deep need of such reassurance. They know that they are from the truth, and yet their hearts may condemn them. God, however, is "greater than [their] hearts"; abiding in God, they are also born of God. Ultimately, they will "be like him."

First John can be read with an emphasis on either the healing rebirth God offers the downcast community or the author's literal demonizing of "those who went out from us." The solace and the rage are equally real. First John vividly manifests the pain and consolation inherent in a sectarian worldview. "The reason the world does not know us is that it did not know [God]." The author tells us little of substance about the opponents. They deny "that Jesus is the Christ" and fail to confess that "Jesus Christ has come in the flesh." The theological controversy, however, is not the author's primary concern. The opponents have "gone out from us"; this in itself proves that they "were not of us." They are and, it turns out, always were "other." "They are from the world. . . . We are from God. Whoever knows God listens to us, and whoever is not from God does not listen to us" (4:5–6). Like the Jews of John's gospel, these are children of the devil, and as such were bound from the beginning to hate us. The teacher's rhetoric cauterizes the community's regrets. They are other; they were always other; by their very nature they hate the truth and they hate us. Vilification of these former brothers and sisters as "children of the devil" raises the strong possibility that "those who went out" from the community are the same group as John's "Jews who had believed" in Jesus. If so, then the Johannine community, often considered an example of "post-Jewish," gentile Christianity, would seem instead to be a community that, at least until its recent past, included a substantial Jewish component. What's more, these Jewish defectors have left specifically over debates concerning the relationship between Jesus and God. The Johannine community has reached the boundaries of what its Jewish members can affirm; it is poised to become "Christianity."

REVELATION

APOCALYPTIC LITERATURE BEGINS with the premise of cosmic dualism, the existence of good and evil as active forces. Good and evil are at war, and though the battle takes place primarily in a heavenly venue, both sides have agents who fight it out on earth. As the devil tells Jesus in Luke's gospel, all the kingdoms of the world have been given over to him, "and I give [them] to anyone I please" (4:6). Evil has nearly blotted out the good, but just as things seem to be at their absolute worst, God will intervene to vanquish evil and establish unchallenged rulership of heaven and earth. All of this is already known in heaven; indeed, it is proceeding according to a predetermined plan. Human beings, however, require a special revelation, an *apocalypsis* or "unveiling," in order to understand and respond properly to the events of the last days.

The book called Revelation is an apocalypse. As such it belongs to a literary genre with roots deep in biblical tradition, in prophets such as Ezekiel, Joel, and Zechariah, who saw and recorded visions of God's final triumph over evil. The book of Daniel, written during the Seleucid persecutions of the second century B.C.E., is probably the first fully developed apocalypse. In Daniel, a figure from the past (Daniel lived in the sixth century B.C.E.) is granted dreams of the future, which are interpreted by an angelic guide. The seer's dreams "foretell" events leading up to the second century (the reader's present day), thereby validating the reliability of his visions. When the seer reaches the reader's present, the action slows and events unfold in detail. The present age, it turns out, is the climax of history, and it is imperative that the faithful understand the heavenly significance of their own experience. They, the righteous, are about to undergo severe trials at the hands of those who oppose God's rule. They must stand firm, however, as the end is near, when their enemies will be punished and they will be rewarded for their fidelity.

Apocalyptic literature typically reveals its secrets through the use of symbolic numbers, fantastic beasts, and bizarre cosmic phenomena that are as cryptic as the events they purport to reveal. Hence the need for a heavenly interpreter. For generations, scholars believed that the use of obscure symbols to express a "countercultural" message indicated that apocalyptic literature was the product of oppressed groups. It was a code language by means of which an underground association could communicate safely. More recently, crosscultural analysis has concluded that one does not need to be oppressed to participate in an apocalyptic group; one need only *feel* oppressed. Apocalyptic thought and writing are as often the product of an elite group as of an impoverished or marginal group. The key experience is one of alienation. The apocalyptic solution—that this world has become so corrupted that only God's violent disruption of the universe can set it straight—may appeal to any group that experiences the world as dominated by forces hostile to the truth. Beneath its dazzling numerology and grotesque beasts, apocalyptic literature is a word of hope—of certainty, really—for a group that finds itself outflanked and outraged by "the powers that be." "Here," as Revelation puts it, "is a call for the endurance and faith of the saints."

The book of Revelation purports to be the work of a seer named John, writing from the Aegean island of Patmos to a group of seven churches in western Asia Minor (the Roman province of Asia). The tidiest church traditions identify the author as John son of Zebedee, Jesus' disciple, who in turn is considered the author of the Gospel According to John, as well as the Johannine letters. It is unlikely that Revelation was written either by Jesus' disciple John or by the author of the other "Johannine" writings (the prose styles differ dramatically), but the book shares the distinctive symbols of the gospel and the letters.

The historical circumstances of Revelation's composition have proved extremely elusive (ironically so, in light of the book's detailed if veiled discussion of political matters), although a date in the 90s is generally assumed. The book purports to be "the revelation of Jesus Christ, which God gave him to show his servants what must soon take place." God has sent this revelation by means of an angel to "his servant John." John begins by describing his vision of "one like the Son of Man," who dictates letters for John to deliver to seven churches. From the outset, John's imagery is almost too dense to follow. John sees:

> seven golden lampstands, and in the midst of the lampstands . . . one like the Son of Man, clothed with a long robe and with a golden sash across his chest. His head and his hair were white as white wool, white as snow; his eyes were like a flame of fire, his feet were like burnished bronze, . . . and his voice was like the sound of many waters. In his right hand he held seven stars, and from his mouth came a sharp, two-edged sword, and his face was like the sun shining with full force. When I saw him, I fell at his feet as though dead. (Rev. 1:12–17)

Here already we come up against the most difficult aspect of interpreting John's visions, namely, which parts to interpret and why. The vision has an extensive biblical pedigree. From Daniel we might recognize the Son of Man as God's agent at the end of time (with white hair recalling Daniel's "ancient of days"). From Ezekiel we know that a voice "like the sound of many waters" belongs to God, and we have a model of a prophet falling on his face in the presence of such a vision. The robe and sash are royal garb—and if we happen to be familiar with the apocalyptic 1 Enoch, we know that it depicts the Son of Man wearing precisely this raiment. But what else? Ought we to connect the bronze feet with the bronze feet in Daniel's vision? Or with the bronze legs of

Ezekiel's cherubim? Or neither? Ought we to recognize the "sword of his mouth"? Isaiah uses the phrase, but what does it really mean? Just how much are we expected to get? How much do we *have* to get, in order to "get it"?

The first and most important answer is that the reader is not expected to get it all. John must inform us, for example, that the seven lampstands are the seven churches and the stars their angelic patrons. The vision is not intended to be fully comprehended, but to dazzle, to confound the senses. Confusion is built into the text as a means of demonstrating that these matters surpass mortal understanding. If the point is simply to bedazzle, though, why bother to interpret at all? John's narrative presumes that the reader is able to track the overall significance of the vision. Apocalyptic texts typically depend on images drawn from traditional texts, allowing the author to draw on the authority of the tradition. The text only "works" for readers who recognize its key symbols. But we are not intended to decode it all. This necessarily limited level of comprehension is frustrating to the reader who seeks full understanding. But this frustration, the off-balancing of the reader, forms part of the singular language of apocalyptic literature, which unveils a reality that is inherently "other"; we are not to master the vision but to obey it.

In chapters 2 and 3 John relays to each of the seven churches a message from "him who holds the seven stars in his right hand, who walks among the seven golden lampstands," Jesus. The churches are located in the cities of Ephesus, Smyrna, Pergamum, Thyatira, Sardis, Philadelphia, and Laodicea, all in western Asia Minor. Most of the churches are commended for their endurance, but they are also warned, especially against succumbing to false teaching. Churches that have not denied their faith in the face of persecution receive special commendation. In the city of Pergamum, "where Satan's throne is," a believer named Antipas has been martyred. Pergamum was famous for temples to Zeus, to the late emperor Augustus, and to the goddess Roma, any of which might have qualified as "Satan's throne" from John's perspective. Little is known about state-sponsored persecution of Christians in first-century Asia Minor, but it is likely that Antipas was killed for refusing to worship one of these embodiments of imperial authority. As late as the early second century, Pliny, the governor of Bythinia in northern Asia Minor, still needed to ask the emperor Trajan (97–117) whether Christians ought to be killed outright or only if they refused to recant and worship the local gods. Pliny's question indicates that no imperial policy was yet in place. Revelation reflects a similar situation in which lethal persecution occurred, but on a sporadic rather than a systematic basis.

As dangerous as persecution, in John's opinion, are competing Christian groups. Three groups—the Nicolaitans, those who follow the way of Balaam, and the followers of the prophet Jezebel—are condemned for bad doctrine and degenerate behavior. The "Balaam followers" (presumably not their self-designation, as Balaam was a notorious enemy of Israel) are particularly intriguing because John faults them for their violation of Jewish purity regulations: they advocate eating food sacrificed to idols. John's fierce condemnation of those who eat food sacrificed to idols deviates from Paul's cautious permission to do so in 1 Corinthians. Paul had been involved in many congregations of Asia Minor, particularly that at Ephesus. Ought we to see in Revelation an anti-Pauline strain of Christianity? Probably not. Paul, after all, wrote that although the idols themselves had no power, the good of the community ought to govern each person's choice. In John's congregations mounting persecution would have created the need for tighter boundaries. No community could sustain the threat of martyrdom for its purists while allowing others to pass social scrutiny by participating in the gods' feasts. Even the "liberal" Paul would have agreed that community welfare demanded unity in the face of persecution.

John writes to churches trapped between "false" Christian teachers on the one hand and persecution (most likely sporadic) on the other. In addition to these perils, at least two of the churches, at Smyrna and Philadelphia, have been "slandered" by a group who "say they are Jews and are not, but are a synagogue of Satan" (2:9). The crucial thing to notice about John's accusation is his attitude toward Jewishness. Often taken as a slam against Jews in general, John's comment reveals that, on the contrary, he holds high standards for how Jews should behave. Just as some of his opponents "claim to be apostles but are not" (2:2), so these "claim to be Jews" but, by his standards, are not. Who were these "false Jews"? The traditional interpretation holds that the Jews of Asia Minor were turning in members of John's communities to the Roman authorities. That scenario is possible, but not necessarily likely. We have no evidence either of Jews who would be interested in informing on Christians or of Romans who would be interested in hearing about them. We do know that the Jewish communities of both Smyrna and Sardis were large and prosperous, and included members who held prominent leadership positions in the two cities; at least some urban Jews of Asia Minor were highly assimilated into Roman culture. It is hard to imagine that such Jews would care much what a Jewish sectarian group did or did not believe. Nor had Christian practice been outlawed by Rome—though the group would certainly have seemed suspicious. In short, the image of a dominant Jewish community handing Christians over to Roman authority owes more to the gospel accounts of Jesus' crucifixion than it owes to what we know of Asia Minor at the turn of the second century.

But if John's "false Jews" are not the hostile chief priests and Pharisees of the gospels, who are they? With the exception of the Roman empire itself, all other opponents in John's letters to the seven churches are members of competing Christian groups. Could "those who say they are Jews but are not" be other *Jewish* Christians? Certainly, the author of Revelation was himself a Jew, and he envisions a specifically Jewish future for the community. He is, for example, profoundly concerned that the group maintain its ritual purity. His new Jerusalem will come equipped with a gate for each of the twelve tribes, and he has foreseen the exact number of each tribe to be saved. (Interpreters from the second century to the nineteenth actually impugned Revelation as being "more Jewish than Christian.") John is not, in his own imagination, a "Christian" as opposed to a Jew, but a Jew who affirms Jesus as messiah. It is therefore entirely plausible that, like the Qumran author who called other Jews "a synagogue of Belial" (1QH 2.22), John calls another Jewish messianist group "a synagogue of Satan." John's hostility toward another Jewish messianist group becomes even more suggestive in light of Revelation's connection with the other Johannine writings. Both John's gospel and 1 John express anger toward Jews who have left the messianist community, Jews the gospel calls "children of the devil." Is John engaging in similar name-calling in response to a similar schism? The possibilities are tantalizing, but the data remain too thin for certainty.

As soon as John delivers the letters to the churches, he sees a door open in heaven and ascends to learn "what must take place after this." In heaven the terrain becomes more fantastic. John sees someone who looks "like jasper and carnelian" upon a throne, with twenty-four elders enthroned about him. Four living creatures, composites of those seen by Ezekiel (chap. 1) and by Isaiah (chap. 6), sing "Holy, holy, holy." The figure upon the throne holds a scroll sealed with seven seals, which "no one in heaven or on earth or under the earth" can open. A lamb "standing as if it had been slaughtered" (that is, Jesus, the "lamb of God") appears and opens the first four seals. The four horsemen of the apocalypse, four riders who release war, famine, and plagues upon the earth, are released. At the opening of the fifth seal, John sees "the souls of those who had been slaughtered for the word of God" beneath the altar in heaven, calling on God to avenge their deaths. The identity of these martyrs is not clear; they could be individuals known personally to John's communities or Christians killed in other times or places — for example, those killed by Nero in 64. The martyrs are told that they must wait for vengeance until the "complete" number of their brothers have been killed.

At the opening of the sixth seal, the sun and moon are darkened, the stars fall, and an earthquake occurs. The destruction seems to have reached a climax, but in fact Revelation's visions will return over and over again to the brink of oblivion, only to move on to new manifestations of God's wrath. The opening of the climactic seventh seal is delayed while God sends angels to mark the foreheads of those who will be spared the coming disaster (a reference both to Ezek. 9:4–6 and to the Exodus narrative). Twelve thousand from each tribe of Israel are chosen, 144,000 in all. In addition, "a great multitude that no one could count" is chosen "from every nation, from all tribes and

Bathed in the Blood of the Lamb

Those who have already died are repeatedly referred to in Revelation as having "washed their robes and made them white in the blood of the Lamb." The imagery is startling, but the logic is consistent with ancient Israelite beliefs about ritual purity. Purity, in the biblical world, was not equivalent to either moral uprightness or physical cleanliness. Although purity was a physical condition, it was simply that condition deemed appropriate for contact with the realm of the holy. Sometimes purity entailed washing (as in Lev. 15:21), but at other times it required the sprinkling of blood or the use of herbs (Lev. 14:49–52). Blood in particular served as, in Jacob Milgrom's phrase, "ritual detergent." Human sin was understood to contaminate the altar in the temple. To cleanse the altar, the blood of sacrificed animals was poured onto it, restoring it to ritual, if not hygienic, purity. If Jesus, "the Lamb," had been sacrificed for the forgiveness of sins, then those who had been "washed in his blood" were pure.

peoples and languages" (7:9). Both Jews and Gentiles are designated for salvation. Finally, in 8:1, the seventh seal is opened. In place of destruction there is silence while seven angels appear with seven trumpets. Sevens, threes, and fours—biblical symbols of holiness and completeness—appear in endless combination. The first four trumpets are blown, each creating cosmic disasters. After the fifth trumpet an army of locusts with human faces (based on those seen by the prophet Joel) rises from a bottomless pit. The sixth trumpet releases a plague that kills a third of humankind.

At the blowing of the seventh trumpet, God's heavenly temple opens and an entirely new set of visions begins. Now we see a woman, pregnant and clothed with the sun, wearing a crown of twelve stars (= Israel). A red dragon appears, waiting to swallow up her child. Her child is born, a male who will "rule all the nations with a rod of iron" (see Ps. 2:9). He (Jesus) is taken up to God's throne, while the woman, like a second Hagar, flees into the wilderness. Only then does a war break out in heaven, "Michael and his angels" against "the dragon [Satan] and his angels." The scenario is built on that of 1 Enoch 6–10, in which rebellious angels are thrown down from heaven. Here Satan and his angels are ejected from heaven and thrown, not into a fiery pit, but onto the earth, thereby increasing its misery.

Satan (the dragon) gives his authority to a beast from the sea. A sort of deputy beast now shows up and forces everyone to worship the first beast. The identity of the first beast is one of the most intriguing questions in Revelation. The beast has seven heads, one of which has been healed after an apparently mortal injury. The mortally-wounded-yet-living beast is a clear foil to Jesus, the Lamb that was slain and yet lives. And, just as the righteous were previously marked with the name of God, the beast requires everyone to be marked with "the number of the beast" (13:18). The number of the beast (presumably reached by gematria, a calculation based on the numerical value attached to the letters of his name) is in some manuscripts the infamous 666; in others it is 616. These numeric options correspond to the value of the Greek (*Neron Caesar* = 666) and Latin (*Nero Caesar* = 616) for "Caesar Nero." Remarkably, the emperor responsible for the first persecution of Christians was widely rumored either not to have died or to have come back from the dead. The beast, Nero, is the "Terminator" of Revelation, the embodiment of evil that refuses to die.

Just as things look their bleakest, we see the Lamb with the 144,000 righteous standing on Mount Zion while an angel proclaims (in advance, as it turns out), "Fallen, fallen is Babylon the great." The Son of Man appears on a cloud and is assigned to reap the earth, throwing the harvest into "the great winepress of the wrath of God" (14:19). The grapes of wrath are trodden and a river of blood flows out onto the earth. We see yet another set of seven angels; these carry bowls containing seven plagues. The plagues, mirroring the plagues of the exodus (boils, blood, darkness, frogs), are poured onto the earth, which once again suffers unimaginable devastation. The Great Whore of Babylon

ARMAGEDDON

According to Rev. 16:16, the Last Battle will take place at Armageddon (NRSV, Harmagedon). Revelation specifies that the word is Hebrew, in which case it would seem to be a corruption of *har megiddo,* the mountain or hill of Megiddo. Situated on a pass above the Jezreel Valley, Megiddo is a strategically important locale, and has been the site of significant battles since ancient times. It is not, however, on a mountain, nor does the site have any prior religious significance. For this reason, two alternative possibilities have been proposed. First, the "mountain of Megiddo" could be the mountain near Megiddo, namely, the far more dramatic Mount Carmel, where the prophet Elijah defeated the prophets of the god Baal (1 Kings 18). Second, the word *Armageddon* has been construed as a corruption of the Hebrew for "mountain of assembly," that is, Mount Zion or the Temple Mount in Jerusalem. Both sites have their supporters; both have been places of assembly for those hoping to have a front-row seat at the end of the world.

enters. Babylon is a cipher for Rome in much Jewish literature following the First Revolt. Here she is drunk on the blood of the saints, seated on the beast whose seven heads represent the seven hills of Rome. (Both beast and woman represent Rome, but this is precisely the kind of problem one is supposed to ignore in apocalyptic literature.) The Word of God (the Lamb) appears on a white horse to fight the beast. The beast and his deputy are captured and thrown into a lake of fire. An angel grabs Satan, throwing him also into the lake of fire.

Now the martyrs are brought back to life and, together with Jesus, rule the earth for a thousand years. The author informs us that this is the "first" resurrection; the rest of the dead will not be raised until the end of the thousand years. This vision of a "preliminary" divine triumph (a scheme that also appears in 4 Ezra) has given birth to various forms of "millennialist" Christianity, each with its own version of how, when, and where the saints will rule. Surprisingly, after the thousand years of peace, Satan will be released from prison. This, of course, is not something in the reader's near future, since we are all pretty sure that the thousand years of peace have not yet occurred. The question of *why* Satan should be released is not addressed, although Revelation's plot parallels that of Ezekiel 38–39, where, after Israel has returned from Babylonian exile and is living in peace, a final enemy attempts to destroy the people of God. Ezekiel's ultimate enemy, Gog of the land of Magog, appears in Revelation as *two* nations, Gog and Magog, who join Satan for the last battle. The engagement is brief; fire from heaven consumes the armies almost before they get started. Again the devil is thrown into the lake of fire (this time for good, it seems), the dead are raised and judged, and death and Hades are destroyed. The conflict has ended.

No reader will live to see the conflict's denouement, which (no matter when one reads) lies more than a thousand years in the future. On the other hand, readers have for centuries sought to find in their own days signs that the end was near. This tantalizing near-clarity is the genius of Revelation's "call for the endurance of the saints" in time of trial. The apocalypse concludes with a vision of a new heaven and a new earth. The new Jerusalem descends from heaven, adorned like a bride, "the wife of the Lamb." (Revelation's female figures are notoriously stereotyped, consisting exclusively of the good mother, Jezebel, the bad prostitute, and the good wife.) Like the Hebrew Bible's prophecies of the end time, the vision is both distinctly Israelite and universal: the city has one gate for each of the twelve tribes of Israel, but "the *nations* will walk by its light, and the kings of the earth will bring their glory into it." Like Ezekiel before him, John receives a tour of the city, with its twelve "pearly gates" and streets paved with gold. As in Ezekiel 47, a revivifying stream flows from the center of the city, with miraculous trees along its bank. City and Garden have been joined into an earthly paradise, a new Eden. The vision ends with Jesus' promise, "Surely, I am coming soon" (22:20).

It is easy to become swept up in Revelation's dazzling panorama of end-time battles, plagues, and triumphs and to forget the rather less glamorous conditions under which John is writing. John's primary purpose, however, is not to reveal events that will occur after more than a thousand years but to issue a "call for the endurance of the saints" in the present moment. Ultimately, the kind of paradise John needs determines the kind he envisions. John describes a city paved with gold and inhabited by saints but adds a peculiar and telling comment: "Outside," he says, "are the dogs and sorcerers and fornicators and murderers and idolaters, and everyone who loves and practices falsehood" (22:15). Even at the end of time the enemies have not disappeared but remain snarling outside the city gates. The heavenly vision is thus a haunted one. John sees the future Jerusalem, but his urgent and overriding desire is for his followers to find haven in the present storm. Having the "dogs" safely outside the gates would be enough.

John's vision of a still-divided heaven provides an apt ending to the bittersweet story of the first Christians' struggle to articulate their identity. John calls his enemies "those who say they are Jews, but are not," but he was himself open to the same charge. The community, a mixed group of Jews and Gentiles, refused to live as Gentiles but had lost the protections extended by the empire to Jews. In the eyes of Rome and of the larger Jewish community, it was *they* who said they were Jews but were not. Fearful of Rome, of other Jews, and even of other Jewish Christians whom they defined as enemies, the faithful longed for the city where no unclean thing would enter. They had taken God's side in a cosmic war; their hope now was to be safe within a heavenly fortress.

EPILOGUE:
THE IMAGE OF THE JEW
IN CHRISTIAN SCRIPTURE

THE NEW TESTAMENT is a book written by Jews but not read by Jews. This seemingly trivial point is crucial to understanding its meaning for modern readers. Regardless of its origins, the New Testament is no longer a Jewish book. Technically, it never was one, since the collection of twenty-seven writings into a single canon was undertaken long after Jews and Christians had parted company. Leo Baeck's bold claim that the New Testament is a Jewish book might more accurately be restated as: The New Testament is a collection of books, each of them originally Jewish. The New Testament's journey from a set of Jewish books to a sacred collection used exclusively by non-Jews has fundamentally changed—and distorted—its authors' portrayal of Jews. In order to discuss the New Testament image of the Jew, one must first distinguish between the ways in which the ancient Jewish writers saw and depicted Jews and the ways in which modern, non-Jewish readers perceive the Jews portrayed in the text. One might hope that a sensitive reader could come close to hearing what the authors intended to say, but in the case of the New Testament the barriers to an ideal reading are very high indeed. First, the texts are nearly two thousand years old and from a culture whose norms, customs, and idioms are only partially understood today. Second, what the New Testament authors said about Jews, they said about members of their own group—other Jews. For a modern Christian, Jews are most definitely not members of the same group, but always the Other. Finally, and perhaps most important, whereas the New Testament authors originally wrote words of guidance for beleaguered congregations, today those writings are scripture; most Christians do not read them as merely the advice of ancient teachers. Because of the New Testament's status as scripture, what it says about Jews matters more today—and it matters differently—than it did in the first century C.E. To sketch the image of the Jew in the New Testament, then, we must begin by summarizing what the New Testament authors wrote about other Jews, before turning to a consideration of how those ancient images function today.

Paul, the earliest of the New Testament authors, had already come to see that the continued existence of the Jews as Jews posed an implicit challenge to claims that the messiah had come. Ideally, all the Jews should have become what we today would call Christians. Paul therefore posited that, just as Pharaoh's heart had been hardened at the exodus, so now a "part" of Israel (that is, the larger part) had become hardened, temporarily preventing them from accepting God's work in Jesus (Rom. 11:25). Paul's image of a hard-hearted segment of Israel was further developed by the author of Luke-Acts, who carefully identifies Jesus, his family, and his followers as "faithful Israel" before introducing the category of "failed Israel," defined as any Jew who does not follow Jesus. Hoping to validate the sect's Jewish legitimacy while explaining why most Jews show no interest in joining, Luke posits that "faithful" Jews did join; only those Jews who were essentially hostile to God "rejected God's purpose for themselves" (Luke 7:30). Like any other sect members, the New Testament authors divided the world into "us" and "them." But because the sect was originally Jewish, that us–them division was expressed as a division among Jews: in effect, between good Jews and bad Jews.

In addition to the clearly visible "good Jew–bad Jew" division, a second, less obvious division had a tremendous impact on the New Testament authors and their communities: a rift between two groups of Jewish Christians. Here again, Luke-Acts provides the clearest picture of the division, but it is a separation that can be seen to affect most books of the New Testament. As Luke tells it, when non-Jews began to join the sect, "believers who belonged to the sect of the Pharisees" insisted that non-Jewish converts be "circumcised and ordered to keep the law of Moses" (Acts 15:5). As a Jewish sect, they would accept non-Jews in the biblically prescribed way. Some, however, saw it differently. According to Luke, a vision convinced Peter that God had personally accepted gentile converts without circumcision. Luke suggests that the entire sect agreed on the point, but other New Testament books reveal that a schism developed over the issue of gentile conversion.

Paul's letters, for example, are filled with invective against sect members who "persecute" gentile congregations by urging them to become circumcised (Gal. 4:29). Most or all of the New Testament books were written by "liberal" sect members, those who did not require that converts be circumcised; for these authors, "the circumcisers" form a persistent, and persistently vilified, opposition. Although circumcision provides the most vivid example of division among Jewish members of the sect, debates over dietary restrictions and, eventually, about Jesus' relationship with God caused additional ruptures pitting Jew against Jew within the sect. By the end of the first century, the author of John's gospel could label Jewish Christians who rejected Jesus' divine origins "children of [their] father the devil" (John 8:44). The New Testament thus portrays not two but three kinds of Jews: Jews who accept Jesus as messiah, Jews who "reject" Jesus, and Jews who accept Jesus as messiah but do so on terms different from those of the New Testament authors. Of the three kinds of Jews, it is the dissenting Jewish Christians who come in for some of the worst invective: it is the competing Jewish followers of Jesus, rather than Jews as a whole, who constitute a synagogue of Satan (Rev. 2:9).

The New Testament division of the Jews into those who do not follow Jesus, those who follow Jesus but in the wrong way, and those who agree with the New Testament authors, came to look very different when the texts became "Christian" texts read by non-Jewish Christian readers. To begin with, the "good Jews" of the New Testament, people like Mary and Paul, came to seem less and less Jewish. After all, they were the leaders and role models of the church. As the terms *Christian* and *Jew* came to describe groups perceived as polar opposites, it began to seem like nonsense that the heroes of the New Testament were Jews. They were the first Christians—the Jews had *opposed* Jesus, not followed him.

Luke's narrative scheme in which Israel had become divided into faithful and failed came increasingly to be read as a narrative in which Christians, or just good people in general, had followed Jesus, while the Jews had, by definition, "failed." To compound matters, as Christians began to be born into the movement (rather than converting, as in the first generation), and as the movement came to include fewer and fewer ethnic Jews, Jews as a whole became strangers to the group. The "failed" Jews of the New Testament had been the authors' parents, sisters, and children—not inherently "other." As Christianity became a gentile religion, Jews became outsiders, and as such seemed all the more hostile.

The third group of New Testament Jews, traditionally observant members of the Jesus sect, came to be largely forgotten. Luke's report that the Judean Christians who wished to circumcise converts had immediately been corrected by God seemed to cover the situation. Certainly, it was easier to believe that observant Jewish Christians had been deviants from the outset than to imagine a fully Jewish Christianity. Paul's vehement condemnation of Jewish traditionalists ("I wish those who unsettle you would castrate themselves!") suggested that these "opponents" had opposed not only Paul but the Christian message itself. The disappearance of observant Jewish Christians—not their historical disappearance, but their disappearance from the Christian imagination—was a decisive turn in the Christian understanding of its own Jewish texts. If Christians could no longer imagine a fully Jewish Christianity—a sect that non-Jews joined only through conversion to Judaism—then they could no longer understand the New Testament's invective against Jewish-Christian opponents. At that point the "children of the devil" were no longer understood to be Jewish Christians who happened to disagree with John; they were the Jewish people as a whole.

At the end of the day, the church's move from an ethnically Jewish to an ethnically gentile body, and the concomitant forgetting of its original Jewish identity, created a text with virtually no positive images of Jews. As it is read today, the New Testament is almost unremittingly hostile to the Jews. Its heroes, people like Paul and Timothy, are, of course, Jews, but they are no longer perceived as *Jewish,* that is, as practitioners of Judaism. With Luke's "faithful Israel" regarded by Jews and Christians alike as Christians, and with both "failed Israel" (known to modern people as "the Jews") and the traditional Jews within the Jesus movement equally under condemnation, this "collection of originally Jewish books" has moved far from its origins.

What, then, can be recovered by looking behind the reluctant parting, to learn from the second and third generation of Jesus' Jewish followers? Certainly, the New Testament is a place where both Jew and Christian may attempt to "know the heart of the stranger." Read as a collection of Jewish texts, the New Testament becomes equally unfamiliar territory to Christian and Jew alike. One of the most remarkable characteristics of the New Testament turns out to be the passion with which its authors fought to affirm the legitimacy of their Jewish identity. This defense of the group's Jewishness came, however, at a cost: much of the New Testament's "self-defense" takes the form of attacks against other sorts of Jews, portrayed as at best misguided, at worst demonic. The texts retain, however, not only traces of a primordial conflict but also traces of a primordial love. Difficult as it is to affirm today, the New Testament authors wrote out of a deeply grounded love of the heritage entrusted to them, the tree of life that was and is Judaism. The task of taking the New Testament authors seriously as Jews is demanding, often even threatening, for Jews and Christians alike. A new Jewish understanding of Christian scripture will not—and should not—undo the parting of Jew and Christian. But it seems right that we should at least pause to appreciate how reluctant that parting really was, and perhaps one day to transform it into a parting of friends.

ACKNOWLEDGMENTS

THE PARTICIPANTS IN MY adult education classes at Temple Bet Aviv in Columbia, MD, were the first to suggest this project, and they own this book as no one else does. I hope it comes close to justifying their trust in me. The initial opportunity to teach at Bet Aviv was provided by Marc Lee Raphael. Marc has spent countless hours helping me think through the issues touched upon in this book, and I am deeply in his debt. Throughout the process of writing I have been sustained, energized, and taught by the questions and enthusiasm of the members of adult education classes at Temple Anshe Emeth in New Brunswick, NJ, HAZAK of Reston, VA, Temple Beth El of Williamsburg, VA, and especially by the members of the Adult Education Committee and the Outreach Committee of my own congregation, Temple Rodef Shalom, Falls Church, VA.

Luke Timothy Johnson has, as always, been as faithful in his criticism as in his encouragement; I am profoundly grateful for both. Many of this book's best insights I owe to him. Michael Daise's thoughtful responses to the manuscript likewise saved me from several missteps. The staff of the Bishop Payne Library at Virginia Theological Seminary have been cheerful and generous in their help. The College of William and Mary kindly provided a research leave in 2002–03, during which I conducted the bulk of the research for the project. Damian G. Stephen stepped in at a crucial moment to help prepare the manuscript. Alice R. Falk answered questions from Apocrypha to Zechariah. I am deeply indebted to Anne Connolly, my editor at HarperSanFrancisco, upon whose superb judgment and efficiency I was able to rely with utmost confidence throughout the publication process. Most of all, I thank Rob and Aaron Goler for their patience, and for having faith in me when I lacked faith in myself.

SUGGESTED FURTHER READING

ANCIENT SOURCES

This list provides readily available translations of the ancient texts cited in this book. Many of these texts can be found online at: www.earlyjewishwritings .com.

Charlesworth, J., ed. *The Old Testament Pseudepigrapha*. 2 vols. Garden City, NY: Doubleday, 1983–85. (Includes: 1 Enoch, Jubilees, The Letter of Aristeas, 4 Maccabees, The Martyrdom of Isaiah, The Psalms of Solomon, The Testament of Job, The Testament of Naphtali).

Danby, H., trans. *The Mishnah*. London: Oxford Univ. Press, 1933. (Includes: Pirke Aboth, Sukkah, Sanhedrin).

Ehrman, B. D. *The New Testament and Other Early Christian Writings: A Reader*. Oxford: Oxford Univ. Press, 1988. (Includes: The Coptic Gospel of Thomas, The Didache, The Gospel of the Ebionites, The Gospel of the Nazareans, The Gospel of Peter, Ignatius's Letter to the Ephesians, Ignatius's Letter to the Magnesians, The Infancy Gospel of Thomas, The Letter of Barnabas, The *Shepherd* of Hermas).

Epstein, I., ed. *The Babylonian Talmud*. London: Soncino Press, 1935. (Includes: Baba Metzia, Sanhedrin, Shabbat).

Goldin, Judah, trans. *The Fathers according to Rabbi Nathan [Aboth de Rab. Nathan]*. New Haven: Yale Univ. Press, 1967.

Havener, I. *Q: The Sayings of Jesus.* Collegeville, MN: Liturgical Press, 1990.

Stern, M., ed. *Greek and Latin Authors on Jews and Judaism.* 3 vols. Jerusalem: Israel Academy of Sciences and Humanities, 1974–84. (Includes: Pliny, Suetonius).

Vermes, G. *The Complete Dead Sea Scrolls in English.* 4th ed. New York: Penguin, 1995.

Whiston, W., trans. *Josephus: The Complete Works.* Nashville: Thomas Nelson, 1998.

Yonge, C. D., and D. M. Scholer, trans. *The Works of Philo.* Unabridged updated ed. Peabody, MA: Hendrickson, 1993.

GENERAL INTRODUCTIONS TO THE NEW TESTAMENT

Ehrman, B. D. *The New Testament: A Historical Introduction to the Early Christian Writings.* Oxford: Oxford Univ. Press, 2000.

Johnson, L. T. *The Writings of the New Testament: An Interpretation.* Minneapolis: Fortress Press, 1999.

White, L. M. *From Jesus to Christianity.* San Francisco: HarperSanFrancisco, 2004.

BOOKS AND WRITERS OF THE NEW TESTAMENT

The following selection includes one or two nontechnical introductions to each New Testament book, plus those works to which *The Reluctant Parting* is especially indebted.

Gospels

Farmer, W. R., ed. *Anti-Judaism and the Gospels.* Harrisburg, PA: Trinity Press International, 1999.

Malina, B. J., and R. L. Rohrbach. *Social-Science Commentary on the Synoptic Gospels.* Minneapolis: Fortress Press, 1992.

Vermes, G. *The Changing Faces of Jesus.* London: Allen Lane, 2000.

Matthew

Harrington, D. J. *The Gospel of Matthew.* Sacra Pagina series. Collegeville, MN: Liturgical Press, 1991.

Levine, A.-J. *The Social and Ethnic Dimensions of Matthean Social History: "Go Nowhere Among the Gentiles."* Ceredigion, Wales: Edwin Mellen Press, 1988.

Overman, J. A. *Matthew's Gospel and Formative Judaism: The Social World of the Matthean Community.* Minneapolis: Fortress Press, 1990.

Saldarini, A. J. *Matthew's Christian-Jewish Community.* Chicago: Univ. of Chicago Press, 1994.

Mark

Hooker, M. D. *The Gospel According to St. Mark.* Peabody, MA: Hendrickson, 1991.

Marcus, J. *Mark 1–8.* Anchor Bible. New York: Doubleday, 2000.

Perkins, P. "Mark." In *The New Interpreter's Bible,* vol. 8, edited by L. E. Keck, 509–733. Nashville: Abingdon Press, 1995.

Luke-Acts

Johnson, L. T. *The Gospel of Luke.* Sacra Pagina series. Collegeville, MN: Liturgical Press, 1991.

———. *The Acts of the Apostles.* Sacra Pagina series. Collegeville, MN: Liturgical Press, 1998.

Sanders, J. T. *The Jews in Luke-Acts.* London: SCM Press, 1987.

Tyson, J. B., ed. *Luke-Acts and the Jewish People: Eight Critical Perspectives.* Minneapolis: Augsburg Press, 1988.

John

Bieringer, R., D. Pollefeyt, and F. Vandecasteele-Vanneuville, eds. *Anti-Judaism and the Fourth Gospel.* Louisville, KY: Westminster John Knox Press, 2001.

Cook, M. J. "The Gospel of John and the Jews." *Review and Expositer* 84.2 (1987): 259–71.

Kimelman, R. "*Birkat Ha-Minim* and the Lack of Evidence for an Anti-Christian Jewish Prayer in Late Antiquity." In *Jewish-Christian Self-Definition,* vol. 2, edited by E. P. Sanders, 226–44, 391–403. Minneapolis: Fortress Press, 1981.

O'Day, G. R. "The Gospel of John." In *The New Interpreter's Bible,* vol. 9, edited by L. E. Keck, 493–865. Nashville: Abingdon Press, 1995.

Reinhartz, A. *Befriending the Beloved Disciple: A Jewish Reading of the Gospel of John.* New York: Continuum, 2001.

Paul

Barclay, J. M. G. "Paul Among Diaspora Jews." *Journal for the Study of the New Testament* 60 (1995): 89–120.

Boyarin, D. *A Radical Jew: Paul and the Politics of Identity.* Berkeley and Los Angeles: Univ. of California Press, 1994.

Gager, J. *Reinventing Paul.* Oxford: Oxford Univ. Press, 2000.

Sanders, E. P. *Paul and Palestinian Judaism: A Comparison of Patterns of Religion.* Philadelphia: Fortress Press, 1977.

Segal, A. *Paul the Convert: The Apostolate and Apostasy of Saul the Pharisee.* New Haven: Yale Univ. Press, 1990.

Romans

Johnson, L. T. *Reading Romans: A Literary and Theological Commentary.* New York: Crossroad, 1997.

Nanos, M. D. *The Mystery of Romans: The Jewish Context of Paul's Letter.* Minneapolis: Fortress Press, 1996.

Stendahl, K. *Paul Among Jews and Gentiles, and Other Essays.* Philadelphia: Fortress Press, 1976.

Stowers, S. K. *A Re-reading of Romans: Justice, Jews, and Gentiles.* New Haven: Yale Univ. Press, 1994.

First and Second Corinthians

Barrett, C. K. *A Commentary on the First Epistle to the Corinthians.* Peabody, MA: Hendrickson, 1993 [1968].

——. *A Commentary on the Second Epistle to the Corinthians.* Peabody, MA: Hendrickson, 1993 [1973].

Hays, R. B. *1 Corinthians: Interpretation.* Louisville, KY: Westminster John Knox Press, 1997.

Martin, D. B. *The Corinthian Body.* New Haven: Yale Univ. Press, 1983.

Colossians

Dunn, J. D. G. *The Epistles to the Colossians and to Philemon.* Grand Rapids, MI: Eerdmans, 1996.

MacDonald, M. Y. *Colossians and Ephesians.* Sacra Pagina series. Collegeville, MN: Liturgical Press, 2000.

Ephesians

Lincoln, A. T. *Ephesians.* Word Biblical Commentary. Dallas: Word Books, 1990.

Perkins, P. *Ephesians.* Abingdon New Testament Commentaries. Nashville: Abingdon Press, 1997.

First and Second Thessalonians

Bruce, F. F. *1 and 2 Thessalonians.* Word Biblical Commentary. Dallas: Word Books, 1982.

Donfried, K. P. "2 Thessalonians and the Church of Thessalonica." In *Origins and Method: Towards a New Understanding of Judaism and Christianity,* edited by B. H. McLean, 128–44. Sheffield, England: Sheffield Academic Press, 1993.

Galatians

Hays, R. B. *The Faith of Jesus Christ: The Narrative Substructure of Galatians 3:1–4:11.* Grand Rapids, MI: Eerdmans, 2002.

Nanos, M. D. *The Irony of Galatians: Paul's Letter in First-Century Context.* Minneapolis: Fortress Press, 2002.

Perkins, P. *Abraham's Divided Children: Galatians and the Politics of Faith.* Valley Forge, PA: Trinity Press International, 2001.

Philippians

Hooker, M. D. "Philippians." In *The New Interpreter's Bible,* vol. 11, edited by L. E. Keck, 467–549. Nashville: Abingdon Press, 2000.

Osiek, C. *Philippians, Philemon.* Abingdon New Testament Commentaries. Nashville: Abingdon Press, 2000.

Tellbe, M. *Paul Between Synagogue and State: Christians, Jews, and Civic Authorities in 1 Thessalonians, Romans, and Philippians.* Stockholm: Almquist & Wiksell, 2001.

Philemon

Barclay, J. M. G. "Paul, Philemon and the Dilemma of Christian Slave-Ownership." *New Testament Studies* 37 (1991): 161–86.

Petersen, N. R. *Rediscovering Paul: Philemon and the Sociology of Paul's Narrative World.* Philadelphia: Fortress Press, 1985.

First and Second Timothy, Titus

Bassler, J. *1 Timothy, 2 Timothy, Titus.* Abingdon New Testament Commentaries. Nashville: Abingdon Press, 1996.

Johnson, L. T. *Letters to Paul's Delegates: 1 Timothy, 2 Timothy, Titus.* Valley Forge, PA: Trinity Press International, 1996.

James

Johnson, L. T. *The Letter of James.* Anchor Bible. New York: Doubleday, 1995.

Sleeper, C. F. *James*. Abingdon New Testament Commentaries. Nashville: Abingdon Press, 1998.

Revelation

Aune, D. *Revelation 1–5*. Word Biblical Commentary. Dallas: Word, 1997.

———. *Revelation 6–16*. Word Biblical Commentary. Dallas: Word, 1998.

———. *Revelation 17–22*. Word Biblical Commentary. Dallas: Word, 1998.

Frankfurter, D. "Jews or Not? Reconstructing the 'Other' in Rev. 2:9 and 3:9." *Harvard Theological Review* 94.4 (2001): 403–25.

Malina, B. J., and J. J. Pilch. *Social-Science Commentary to the Book of Revelation*. Minneapolis: Fortress Press, 2000.

Rowland, C. C. "The Book of Revelation." In *The New Interpreter's Bible,* vol. 12, edited by L. E. Keck, 503–736. Nashville: Abingdon Press, 1998.

First Peter

Achtemaier, P. J. *1 Peter: A Commentary on First Peter*. Minneapolis: Fortress Press, 1996.

Craddock, F. B. *First and Second Peter and Jude*. Interpretation. Louisville, KY: Westminster John Knox Press, 1995.

Second Peter, Jude

Kraftchick, S. J. *Jude, 2 Peter*. Abingdon New Testament Commentaries. Nashville: Abingdon Press, 2002.

Neyrey, J. H. *2 Peter, Jude*. Anchor Bible. New York: Doubleday, 1993.

First, Second, and Third John

Black, C. C. "The First, Second, and Third Letters of John." In *The New Interpreter's Bible,* vol. 12, edited by L. E. Keck, 363–469. Nashville: Abingdon Press, 1998.

Rensberger, D. *1 John, 2 John, and 3 John*. Abingdon New Testament Commentary. Nashville: Abingdon Press, 1997.

Hebrews

Anderson, H. "The Jewish Antecedents of the Christology of Hebrews." In *The Messiah: Developments in Earliest Judaism and Christianity,* edited by J. H. Charlesworth, 512-35. Minneapolis: Fortress Press, 1992.

Eisenbaum, P. M. *The Jewish Heroes of Christian History: Hebrews 11 in Literary Context*. Atlanta: Scholars Press, 1997.

Pfitzner, V. C. *Hebrews.* Abingdon New Testament Commentaries. Nashville: Abingdon Press, 1997.

FURTHER READINGS ON FORMATIVE JUDAISM AND CHRISTIAN ORIGINS

Ben-Chorin, Schalom. *The Nazarene Through Jewish Eyes.* Translated by J. S. Klein and M. Reinhart. Macon: Univ. of Georgia Press, 2001.

Borgen, P. " 'Yes,' 'No,' 'How Far?': The Participation of Jews and Christians in Pagan Cults." In *Paul in His Hellenistic Context,* edited by T. Engberg-Pedersen, 30–59. Minneapolis: Fortress Press, 1994.

Bruteau, B., ed. *Jesus Through Jewish Eyes: Rabbis and Scholars Engage an Ancient Brother in a New Conversation.* Maryknoll, NY: Orbis, 2001.

Cohen, S. J. D. *The Beginnings of Jewishness.* Berkeley and Los Angeles: Univ. of California Press, 1998.

———. *From the Maccabees to the Mishnah.* Philadelphia: Westminster John Knox Press, 1987.

Collins, J. *The Apocalyptic Imagination: An Introduction to Jewish Apocalyptic Literature.* 2d ed. Grand Rapids, MI: Eerdmans, 1998.

Flusser, D. *Judaism and the Origins of Christianity.* Jerusalem: Magnes Press, 1988.

Fredriksen, P. *Jesus of Nazareth, King of the Jews.* New York: Knopf, 1999.

Gamble, H. Y. "Canon, New Testament." In *The Anchor Bible Dictionary,* vol. 1, edited by D. N. Freedman, 852–61. New York: Doubleday, 1992.

Goodman, M. "The Emergence of Christianity." In *A World History of Christianity,* edited by A. Hastings, 7–24. Grand Rapids, MI: Eerdmans, 1999.

———. ed. *Jews in a Graeco-Roman World.* Oxford: Clarendon Press, 1998.

Grabbe, L. L. *Judaism from Cyrus to Hadrian.* 2 vols. Minneapolis: Fortress Press, 1992.

Hayes, J. H., and S. Mandell. *The Jewish People in Classical Antiquity: From Alexander to Bar Kochba.* Louisville, KY: Westminster John Knox Press, 1998.

Horbury, W. *Messianism Among Jews and Christians.* London: T. & T. Clark, 2003.

Horsley, R., and J. Hanson. *Bandits, Prophets, and Messiahs: Popular Movements at the Time of Jesus.* Minneapolis: Fortress Press, 1993.

Johnson, L. T. "The New Testament's Anti-Jewish Slander and the Conventions of Ancient Polemic." *Journal of Biblical Literature* 108 (1989): 419–41.

Levine, L. I. *The Ancient Synagogue: The First Thousand Years.* New Haven: Yale Univ. Press, 2000.

Lieu, J., ed. *The Jews Among Pagans and Christians in the Roman Empire.* Oxford: Routledge, 1992.

Price, S. R. F. *Rituals and Power: The Roman Imperial Cult in Asia Minor.* Cambridge: Cambridge Univ. Press, 1984.

Sanders, E. P. *Judaism: Practice and Belief, 63 B.C.E.–66 C.E.* Philadelphia: Trinity Press International, 1992.

Sandmel, S. *Anti-Semitism in the New Testament?* Philadelphia: Fortress Press, 1978.

Segal, A. *Rebecca's Children: Judaism and Christianity in the Roman World.* Cambridge: Harvard Univ. Press, 1986.

Vermes, G. *Jesus in His Jewish Context.* Minneapolis: Fortress Press, 2003.

——. *Jesus the Jew: A Historian's Reading of the Gospels.* New York: Macmillan, 1973.

INDEX